The Klei..

The Klein Revolution

Mark Lisac

NeWest Press
Edmonton

First Edition

Canadian Cataloguing in Publication Data

Lisac, Mark, 1947–

    The Klein Revolution

    Includes bibliographical references.
    ISBN 0-920897-83-5

    1. Alberta – Politics and government – 1971 - 2. Klein, Ralph.
1. Title.
FC 3675.2.L57 1995   971.23'03   C95-910076-8
F1O78.2.L57 1995

Editor for the Press: Satya Das
Editorial Coordinator: Eva Radford
Cover and book design: John Luckhurst / GDL
Cover photograph: Mark Lisac

NeWest Press gratefully acknowledges the financial assistance of The Canada Council; The Alberta Foundation for the Arts, a beneficiary of the Lottery Fund of the Government of Alberta; and The NeWest Institute for Western Canadian Studies.

Excerpts from *The Autobiography of Lincoln Steffens*, copyright 1931 by Harcourt Brace & Company and renewed 1959 by Peter Steffens, reprinted by permission of Harcourt Brace & Company.

Thanks to Alfred A. Knopf Canada for permission to use quotations from Vaclav Havel's *Summer Meditations*, copyright 1992 by Vaclav Havel and published in 1992 by Alfred A. Knopf Canada.

Printed and bound in Canada by Hignell Printing Ltd.

NeWest Publishers Limited
Suite 310, 10359 - 82 Avenue
Edmonton, Alberta T6E 1Z9

To My Family

Acknowledgements

Many hands had a direct or indirect part in the making of this book. I am indebted to the board of NeWest Press for their faith in the work and to a number of staff at NeWest for their detailed work on it, including Eva Radford, Liz Grieve, Wendy Dawson, Jennifer Keane, and Kathy McLean. Colleague Satya Das began the project by asking if I were interested in writing a book on the Klein government. The *Edmonton Journal* cooperated in a number of ways which made publication easier, with particular thanks owed to editor Murdoch Davis, photo editor Steve Makris, and librarian Pat Garneau and her dedicated staff. Library staff at the *Calgary Herald* offered friendly help with research into Klein's earlier days which began as material for a *Journal* column and ultimately became useful for this book. The staff in the *Journal*'s newsroom are all due thanks for the constant inspiration of their talent and energy and for the cheerful company. This is especially true of staff I have worked with at the Alberta legislature and depended upon in many ways. Ultimately, I also owe a debt to former colleagues at the Canadian Press.

Thanks are due to various students of Alberta politics whose earlier work provided a foundation to build upon; to the unfailingly helpful and friendly staff at the Alberta legislature library who make daily work at the legislature much easier than it would otherwise be; and, of course, to Lincoln Steffens.

For comments on early drafts and for steady friendship my gratitude goes to Brian, Richard, and Sandy, and particularly to Ellen. This book was written without help from any government grant. That meant it was written during hours I could have spent with my wife and children. For their patience and tolerance and encouragement, a large part of whatever credit may be due this effort goes to Ellen, Maren, and Matt. Any criticism was earned by me alone and will be happily accepted, in recognition of all the times I have freely offered advice to Ralph Klein and to many others in positions of public responsibility.

Contents

1

Ralph

Who is Ralph Klein? I'm still not sure. Maybe just a hired hand or maybe a master political manipulator. I watched him for five years and had a suspicion he could be either when he had to be—but mostly a good-hearted and sentimental realist, someone who would drag other people into a lifeboat but would not likely give up his own seat, the one near the tiller.

Yeah, I knew him a little. Others had known him longer and better but I saw him around.

By the fall of 1994 we didn't have much contact any more. He was spending more and more time out of Edmonton. Not that premiers of Alberta had ever had much contact with newspaper columnists anyway.

By then I had seen him laugh, joke, stall for time, sneer and, I think, cry. His moods were plain. It was tougher to figure out whether he knew where his government was going and how fast. He spent ten days down east that fall. He got rave reviews from the guys on Bay Street and in the Ottawa Rotary Club and from Jean Charest's crowd in Sherbrooke. Other people seemed to pay little attention. Ralph Klein, the populist of the pinstripes. The idea would have seemed ludicrous a few years earlier. By 1994 he had largely disappeared into a cocoon of expectations and stereotypes that other people had spun around him.

I first saw him on television. Most Albertans first saw him on television. He exuded fallibility, common sense, cunning. When he ran for the legislature in 1989, the early campaign pictures were comical. He winced as the distracted drivers of three different cars he was waving at on an icy street slid into accidents. Things seemed to happen around him.

I went to Calgary during that election, stood on street corners talking to people and heard his name again and again. I came home convinced he would save four or five Calgary seats for the Progressive Conservatives, which he pretty much did.

He was only an image for me all through the eighties. He still seemed remote when he came to the legislature to become environment minister in 1989. We finally met during the 1990 Conservative convention in Calgary, on a night of portents.

I was with some other reporters: Brian Laghi and Richard Helm from the *Edmonton Journal*, Ashley Geddes from the *Calgary Herald*, Miro Cernetig from the *Globe and Mail*. We ended up at Frank's Restaurant late after a day's work. Frank's was a warm, small place of red tablecloths and Mediterranean murals, one of Klein's favourite haunts, located across the street from his legendary watering hole at the St. Louis Hotel. We walked in about midnight. He was at a back table with his wife, Colleen.

He knew some of our group and invited us to sit down. I sat across the table from him. Someone made introductions and ordered a round of flaming Sambucas.

Colleen began confiding her apprehension about her husband's switch to provincial politics. She knew it was a different and far bigger arena than any he had fought in before. Everything seemed uncertain.

Sambuca is a flammable Italian liqueur. A waitress brought out the glasses, each a lake of blue fire. She handed them around. Cernetig's glass tipped. A rivulet of flame ran down his thumb, off his wrist, into a bright, flickering pool on the carpet. The hand escaped serious damage. Helm called it "the immolation of Miro Cernetig." Klein just looked on as if watching something very far away. Unusual things always happened around him.

He was sitting quietly. Perhaps he was thinking of his debut performance the next morning at the Conservatives' traditional breakfast—a ritual display of submission the party put on each year. Cabinet ministers and other members of the legislature served pancakes to more than a thousand delegates, then put on skits. Klein was rumoured to have a part in which he would put on a garbage bag and appear as Mr. Environment or Mr. Green. It seemed as much like an initiation rite as anything. Despite his occasional clowning, the image did not seem to fit. But I really knew nothing about him, although I had seen him in the legislature and had written about his difficulties with the developing Alberta pulp industry.

The conversation drifted to the other end of the table. He looked there. He looked down at his glass. Finally he looked up across the table at me and spoke, in a slow, grumpy, alcohol-raked voice.

He said, "I know you. You're an asshole."

There are moments when time hangs still. This was one. Something happened in the waiting silence. I looked at him and for the first time he seemed to resolve from local myth into real person.

He had an exceptionally thick face, not broad but thick, to go with his thick body. His ears stuck out just slightly and his hair was always combed so as to look a bit rumpled. He had an ample forehead. Thick slabs of jowl hung down from his cheekbones and curved together to form a huge neck, which made it easy to believe he was the son of a onetime wrestler. A round dinner bun of a chin was set into the massive curve of jowl-neck. Above the chin his face was creased by a wide, thin mouth habitually turned up into a secret smile. Some called it a smirk but Klein never acted superior to anyone. His nose came down stubborn straight and finished mildly bulbous. Deep amid all these dominating features lay an unprepossessing set of grey-blue eyes. They were always watchful. I never saw them when they were not alert. They took in everything around, reaching out like radar or, in friendlier moods, like a handshake.

His eyes were watching now—apparently irritated by something written months before, perhaps touched with humour, probably questioning what kind of person he had in front of him. There was no telling everything going on in them.

Anyone else would have received a reply in kind. With Klein there was too much held in reserve, too much private self behind the watching to know what he meant to say and why. Whatever the motivation, for a newspaper columnist it was a compliment. I grinned and lifted my glass to him. His mouth creased up into the V-shaped smile. The smile could have meant many things. Was it complicity? Was it satisfaction at having told off an irritant? All I knew was that no other politician could have said something like that and still seem friendly.

We left after a while; Klein stayed. The next morning he missed the skits. Someone said he had slept in. Sleeping in was his habit but he could have arranged it on this day to avoid his performance. He always carried a hint of shyness around him. He preferred to do his acting on a stage of his choosing and with his own script. Delegates still gathered around him. They were more eager to see and hear him than to meet most of the other cabinet ministers who thought they knew all about running the province.

Four years later, most of those other cabinet ministers were gone. Klein had emerged as one of the few survivors from that crowd. He was leading a government intent on turning the province upside down.

The government was supposed to be balancing the budget and getting control of an overall debt which had topped $30 billion. It was supposed to be bringing remote politicians back into touch with the voters. It did begin these tasks. But the debt and the commitment to openness started to look like a cover story. There were too many other things going on: a massive privatization which began to creep into health and education; the start of tax shifts certain to benefit the wealthy and large corporations at the expense of lower-income workers and small business; expansions of power in a government that claimed to be making itself smaller; a diminishing of the role of the legislature; a general devaluation and withering of political debate; a fracturing of the population into mutually distrustful splinters.

You could not write these other effects off as accidents. They fit together too well. They matched too well with developments in the United States during the Reagan era.

Some people were looking at Alberta by this time and liking what they saw. Toronto business leaders were enthusiastic and said so when Klein spoke to them in September 1994. Ontario Conservative Leader Mike Harris was incorporating Klein government ideas into what he called a common-sense revolution. Charest, interim leader of the federal Conservatives after their election disaster in 1993, said Klein was setting the agenda for the whole country. I heard the talk but, looking out from Edmonton, it was tough to get a clear sense of how much effect Klein and his government were having elsewhere. It was tough enough sorting out what was happening inside the province.

The government was forcing broad, deep-seated changes. I wrote that these changes amounted to a revolution. You have to allow for journalistic hyperbole, of course—the enthusiasm of watching history take shape in front of your eyes. But big changes were happening and some involved a turning around of long established orders. In those terms it was a revolution. It was a revolution led by many of the same people who had been running the province for years. Large parts of it began before Klein became premier. As for Klein himself, how much he was aware of all the events in his government, how much he directed them . . . who knew? I never did figure out where he left off and his revolution began.

Was he like anyone else you've ever met or heard of?

Sometimes he reminded me a lot of the guy in F. Scott Fitzgerald's book, *The Great Gatsby*. Jay Gatsby had started out without many advantages and ended up in a fast, rich crowd where it was never really clear who was in control. You could think about Ralph Klein in those terms, although it is possible to sentimentalize too much.

The details of his youth were blurry. He really did start with few advantages by the usual standard of Canadian politicians. I knew enough to say that. His father Phil was a road builder and sometime wrestler who grappled in the ring as Logger Felix or The Mask. He passed his build and his personality on to his son. After Klein became premier, old Phil, built like a cannonball, joined a Progressive Conservative constituency association in west Edmonton. I saw him at a meeting once. He had a natural geniality. He didn't really mean to work the crowd but by the time he finished greeting people and shaking hands he had done so, better than most elected politicians could ever hope to.

Klein's parents split up when he was about eight. He grew up living with his mother's parents in Calgary in the 1950s, although he also spent a couple of years with his dad in Rocky Mountain House. He left school just after he finished Grade 10, or sometime early in Grade 11. One of his staff told me he was turning into a handful and his grandparents told him to shape up or ship out. His younger brother Lynn told me that he, Lynn, was actually the one always in trouble, causing endless embarrassment for his grandparents and for Ralph. Ralph was busy with sports and a throng of friends. Ralph was the guy everyone wanted at their parties. But Lynn remembered more than good times: "I love my brother. In my early days he was there for me. He was truly his brother's keeper."

Ralph kicked around for a while and joined the Royal Canadian Air Force. He was stationed at Portage La Prairie for a couple of years. Then he came back to Calgary and signed up at Calgary Business College, a private vocational school. It was one of the few places in those days where dropouts could complete their education. He finished the courses and became one of the teachers. Within three years he became the college principal, a feat never really explained.

In his early twenties, he moved to a public relations job with the Red Cross and then with the United Way of Calgary. He did well. He switched in the seventies to a reporting job at CFCN television—an oddity because the usual progression at the time was from reporting to public affairs. At CFCN he became a popular city hall reporter, famous for his ability to find out the inner workings of city council and of the city itself.

He had a growing family all this time. He married Hilda May Hepner in 1961. He would have been eighteen or just barely nineteen. They had two children and divorced in 1972. That year he married Colleen. She had two children of her own and together they had one more.

He was covering city hall when he decided to run for mayor. From then on he never acted alone. He had an alter ego, a man behind the scenes who thought the way Klein thought and handled the details. The other self was Rod Love, a quick-witted, self-assured former political science student and restaurant waiter. Love became Klein's executive assistant. He wrote the speeches, he talked to the people who phoned. He studied politics. He joined his career to Klein's and Klein depended on him. They went through a lot together, including nearly being killed when a half-ton truck broadsided their car on a Calgary street in 1981. A decade and a half later Love was still with him, and if a Klein speech had a particularly funny shot at a political opponent in it that was Love's handiwork.

You know what's most interesting about thinking of Klein as someone who grew up without advantages? The whole province was the same.

Alberta was rich but it was not securely rich. Older Albertans knew poverty first-hand from the days of the Depression and the Dust Bowl. A fear of poverty seemed to live on like some kind of folk memory. It was not just memory either. Alberta lived through wilder economic swings than any other province, and money was always somewhere near the core of Alberta politics.

You could create graphs showing the rise and fall of income and of Conservative party support in Alberta during the 1970s and 1980s. They would show a boom starting in 1974, the year after the Arab oil embargo—and a crash in 1987, the year after world oil prices collapsed. There was grief and turbulence in the early 1980s, too, but the essential curve stretched over the longer period. Through the 1960s and early 1970s Albertans had per-person income about the Canadian average. The numbers dipped in the early 1970s during a period of low grain prices, drew back even in 1974 and kept soaring up. At the peak, in 1981, personal income in Alberta was running more than 10 percent above the Canadian average. In 1986, oil fell off a thirteen-year price plateau. Natural gas prices were in a long depression. Grain prices were falling too. The income advantage disappeared in 1987. By 1989, income per capita in Alberta was less than the Canadian average—$20,970 a year compared with $21,124.

The economic and political curves ran parallel. Conservative support in provincial elections followed the same rise and fall of individual income for nearly twenty years.

Boom and bust—growth and deflation—had been a continuing theme in the province's life since the 1880s. That made me think about Klein and his revolution in more historical terms. It made me think of Harold Innis, a giant among Canadian economists. Innis wrote about what happens to places at the periphery of the international industrial economy. He saw a continuing pattern in Canadian history. He saw that governments had invested in services such as railways to promote economic development, but at the cost of creating a crippling debt. They raised money during resource booms. The resource booms were always followed by recessions in which debt caused hardship and prevented economic restructuring. That sounded like Alberta too. Klein was partly swept along by events.

When I thought about history I also thought about someone who in most ways had nothing to do with Alberta—Lincoln Steffens.

Steffens was one of the first and the greatest of the muckraking journalists who exposed government corruption in the United States at the turn of the century. He was born in San Francisco in 1866 and died in Carmel, California, in 1936. He had spritely writing skills, a sunny honesty, an insatiable curiosity about the world, and a remarkable tolerance and readiness to like his fellow human beings. You could make a case to call him the patron saint of journalists in the twentieth century.

Steffens witnessed and helped nurture the establishment of public institutions the Klein revolution seemed dedicated to unravelling.

His world began to grant the decent pay and working conditions that are being eroded now. It was a world awakening from an era of wage cuts, and corporate reorganizations, and anti-union battles, and welfare cuts, and evangelistic calls for family values which had more to do with maintaining authority than with helping families. His world expanded public life and brought amenities such as parks and libraries to a wider population. It accelerated the spread of public education and started to experiment with public health care because both made sense. Nearly a century later, people have started to forget why building those paths of democratization made sense and are starting to let them slip away.

Steffens and his contemporaries began to believe in government as an instrument to improve their common lives. Many now want to deconstruct government, without putting anything useful in its place.

Steffens's world saw people trying to control the first of the giant corporations, such as U.S. Steel and Standard Oil, which now have outgrown national borders. Alberta in the Klein era did not think about control.

The Alberta government decided that low spending and low taxation were the way to adapt to a world of global corporations. Klein and his cabinet wanted the biggest and toughest businesses in the world to feel welcome in Alberta.

I saw that and thought back to Steffens's time and to his friend James B. Dill. Dill was the man who rewrote the corporate laws of New Jersey to create a welcoming home for the trusts, the great holding companies of the day. New Jersey's leaders in the 1890s thought in much the same way as Alberta's leaders in the 1990s. But Dill put the rationale more elegantly than any Alberta politician could. Steffens wrote an autobiography and in it he recalled, or reconstructed, Dill's words:

" 'Trusts are natural, inevitable growths out of our social and economic conditions,' he said often. 'You cannot stop them by force, with laws. They will sweep down like glaciers upon your police, courts and States and wash them into flowing rivers. I am for clearing the way for them.'"

So too with the Klein revolution. Its business consisted of clearing away—things, people, resistance.

I saw some of the upheaval first-hand—not one of the great revolutions of the century but a revolution of sorts nonetheless. I could have written a straightforward book about it. There were reasons not to.

I wanted to avoid preaching. I'm not an expert or an insider.

And I don't know if anything exists anymore which could be called a general audience. People go their own ways. We live in a sea of history but people seem to be aware mostly of separate moments. Our collective memory has come close to being erased. The Klein revolution took place in part because political leaders were able to take advantage of such separations, and it helped foster more.

So I wrote what follows to Lincoln Steffens, who lived at the beginning of the century. They still believed in print and in memory then—in words. Journalists should be prepared to answer to Steffens for what they write anyway. This is a personal account but eavesdroppers are welcome.

The story begins nearly two years before Klein became premier.

2

The Immolation of Faith

The Edmonton Journal
April 23, 1992

If we're going to go around barbecu-ing politicians for some apparently fat living expenses we at least ought to know why we're doing it.

I'd take some clues from the United States. It's getting difficult to tell them and us apart sometimes.

Bill Clinton is America's Brian Mulroney. Would-be presidential can-didate H. Ross Perot sure looks like America's Preston Manning.

And wouldn't you know it? The scandal over MLAs' living expenses in Alberta has a counterpart in the White House. A news release has just arrived, hot out of Time Magazines at Rockefeller Plaza. It's about George Bush and his income tax.

It seems a Time-Life publication called *Money* (motto: Where American Dreams Still Come True) found that Bush and his wife paid only $4,190 in state taxes in 1991. They claimed resi-dence in their home state of Texas, where they spent only three days in a hotel last year. Thus they avoided pay-ing state income tax to Maine, where they own a house and spent forty days. Texas is one of nine states without an income tax. The magazine says the Bushes would have paid the state of Maine $59,000 in income tax.

Is this the most important feature of U.S. political and economic life at the moment? When a multinational media giant starts touting a picayune Ameri-can tax story to Canadian political col-umnists you have to ask what's going on.

Obviously, the extension of Ameri-can pop culture is one item on the agenda. EuroDisney opens one week, the Time-Life conglomerate targets Ed-monton magazine racks the next. Every sale counts when you're building an empire.

Distraction is a factor. American readers have less time to think about how many tax dollars are being paid by Time and its executives if they are thinking about George Bush's tax. Ca-nadian readers have something to think about other than the way Warner Bros., a branch of the Time empire, joins other American firms in controlling distribution of movies in Canada.

But these stories have a broader function on both sides of the border. They give people something they can think about on an easily imagined scale, something that can be repaired at a time when other things in their lives are falling apart, someone they can blame.

Albertans can't roll history back to prevent the province from accumulating a $12-billion debt, but they can tell MLAs to stop taking $20,000 a year in living expenses. They can't easily secure an economic future, but they can make sure MLAs do not use their position to grasp that security.

One of the stranger facts about the subsistence allowance controversy is that the allowance ranks somewhere in the middle of the MLAs' perks, all of which have been public knowledge for some time.

There's a lot of richer gravy in the list. It should be trimmed. The trimming will not directly repair Alberta's problems.

So why the furore over living allowances, much of which should be paid to MLAs working away from home anyway?

I interpret it largely as an act of fear and revenge—fear that some people in society can fix the rules to get ahead of others, revenge against anyone who appears to be getting ahead while most people feel themselves slipping behind.

If we're going to barbecue anyone, politicians are a better choice than other minorities. At least politicians aren't trapped by skin colour or ethnic background or religious belief or occupation or social class. They can escape to private life. It's part of their job to take some heat anyway.

I'm more worried about what happens if we chew up the politicians and then start looking around for other people to blame.

Ah, if only you could talk, Steffens. Was this column good journalism or bad? It was certainly an accurate record of what I saw and thought at the time—a genuine entry in a personal journal.

It may have been too aloof. The better way might have been to join the hunt for fat little side payments and symbolic privileges. Journalists should inquire, not judge.

Yet you may have approved. You never troubled yourself about going against the stream. You ended up disowning the muckraking days on grounds that finding and changing surface abuses actually changed little.

If you had visited Alberta in 1992 you probably would have written one of your paradoxes: you would have called the extra payments for members of the legislature good as long as they were public knowledge, because extra pay would set a high standard for the MLAs to perform against.

I wish I had thought of that myself or stolen the idea from you. We need your kind of humour here. Alberta is a pretty grim place when it comes to politics. No one found any humour in the situation at the time.

People had grown plenty upset about politicians. Political leaders had too often been acting as if they answered to no one. The fiasco over the Meech Lake Accord in 1990 had worked out that way. Political leaders brought the country to the brink of a phoney crisis over the Constitution while the economy was falling apart.

The recession of the early 1990s looked like it might be more than a recession. It looked like a permanent destruction of hundreds of thousands of jobs. People were getting laid off and factories were closing despite a Canada-U.S. free trade agreement the prime minister had promised would produce thousands of jobs. Governments of all stripes were running up endless deficits. Changing those governments by voting in different parties seemed to accomplish nothing; people ended up with the same thing.

In Alberta, the economy had stalled. The government drifted from year to year apparently doing nothing much. Its leader, Premier Don Getty, had never lived down the day when photographers found him on an Edmonton golf course after his press secretary had said he was "working out of the office." That happened to be the day the Principal Group financial conglomerate collapsed. Getty spent each January in Palm Springs, California. He never developed the knack of communicating with large numbers of people. He led a government stuffed with middle-aged men who had developed their ideas during the 1970s and had been in or around the government ever since.

Some of them saw no need to change. Some desperately tried. Like would-be reformers of all entrenched regimes, they set their goals too low and their personal needs too high.

One thing they would not change was their grip on the power to fill their own pockets. In 1989, a few months after the election of that year, they gave themselves a 30 percent pay raise. Opposition members raised an objection or two, then went along. The pay raise automatically translated into a 30 percent raise in their lifetime pensions. The pension effect may have been uppermost in the MLAs' minds. Most people did not think about the pensions much until a few years later.

The raise drew acid comments for several months. The protest was spontaneous. The MLAs rode it out. They also seemed to begin concentrating on less visible benefits such as a maximum $22,300 annual living allowance for members from outside the capital city.

An unease hovered in the political atmosphere. You couldn't say it crackled. It just drifted around lazily and collected. A twitchiness had set in, a discrediting of old leaders with no notion of where to find or what to look for in new ones.

Revolutions must feel like this—a heavy, dull sense that things must change but with no sense of how; a piling up of clouds and humidity with no sign of where a storm may be coming from and no thought that it might not have to come from anywhere, that it might start right here, tomorrow, maybe today.

In mid-April 1992 a New Democrat backbencher named Gerry Gibeault found something interesting in the newly released public accounts for the fiscal year 1990-91. Gibeault showed a few reporters that Municipal Affairs Minister Dick Fowler and Economic Development Minister Peter Elzinga had received living allowances of about twenty thousand dollars each. They lived just outside Edmonton's city limits. Their neighbours included thousands of people who commuted twenty or thirty minutes to jobs in the capital each workday. Why did cabinet ministers need tax-paid apartments in the city when their neighbours did not?

The story appeared April 14. At first it looked like another small bite from an opposition gadfly, one of hundreds over the years.

Instead it ignited a frenzy. Within days, members of all three major parties were dragged in. Public outrage exploded. The anger spewing out in letters to newspapers and calls to radio phone-in shows astonished even some of the reporters who were finding new layers of padded income almost everywhere they looked. Rage over MLAs' pay and side benefits dominated political life for the next six weeks. The rage subsided but kept smouldering, feeding other fires until it burst out again a year later over pensions.

The list of commuters claiming the capital city living allowance expanded to include Tourism Minister Don Sparrow. He lived about half an hour's drive south of the city. Sparrow, Fowler, and Elzinga heard angry public reaction and all gave up their allowances within a week.

By then Liberal MLA Nick Taylor, the former party leader, had been drawn in. He had claimed the allowance although his constituency bordered the north side of Edmonton. Too late, the other New Democrats realized they were vulnerable too. Gibeault had not consulted them in advance. New Democrat MLA Stan Woloshyn from Stony Plain, about a half hour's drive west of Edmonton, had claimed $18,384 in 1990-91.

All parties were implicated. The affair was growing into an outpouring of rage against all politicians. The findings and confessions came one after another. A review found Alberta legislators received the highest living allowances and one of the best travel allowances—unlimited free flights between Edmonton and their home constituencies—of any provincial legislators in the country. Comparison with members of Parliament produced a pointed observation that MPs often roomed together while MLAs had their own apartments and condos. In fact, they often shared them with children attending college in Edmonton.

Conservative MLA Walter Paszkowski thought the implication that politicians should save money by bunking together went a bit far: "That's something that's really a way of living and if you want to live in a commune you're more than welcome to." But these were days when to be a politician was to be guilty.

Sometimes the politicians understood that. Most often they showed they simply did not. They seemed to have lost their capacity to judge; they thought everything they were doing was acceptable.

Jim Dinning was education minister and represented a Calgary constituency. He had received about eighty thousand dollars in housing and living allowance since first being elected in 1986. But he and his family had lived in Edmonton since 1984. He used the money to help maintain an apartment in his political base instead of for living expenses in the capital. He said he would continue to take the money because he was eligible for it. By April 25, after meeting outraged constituents, he confessed to arrogance. He said he would ask his colleagues for an independent commission to study the MLAs' entire package of pay and perks.

Calgary New Democrat Barry Pashak had been claiming the allowance to meet mortgage, tax, and condominium payments. He was one of several members who had used the money to buy rather than rent. He said, "When I bought the condo four or five years ago, I didn't think the housing allowance would be an issue."

By April 21, Woloshyn and Conservative Kurt Gesell, who represented a constituency at the northeast border of Edmonton and had claimed the full $22,300 in 1990-91, both said they would stop claiming a living allowance until the matter was reviewed. A waitress in Gesell's constituency, told reporters, "It's the pits. I don't think any of them should take it, not if they live within driving distance of the city, where most people would commute." The owner of a fish and chip shop in Woloshyn's area, said, "Why should they have privileges over anyone else?"

Treasurer Dick Johnston had collected the maximum allowance for two years on an Edmonton home he and his wife had bought in Edmonton in 1978. His mother-in-law confirmed that on visits to voters back in Lethbridge he stayed at her home rather than in an apartment or hotel. The housing allowance story began the same day that Johnston tabled a new provincial budget with a $2.3-billion deficit, a layoff of 287 government workers, and a warning that Alberta would have to rethink the way it operated. He had started claiming the allowance in 1989, one of the signs that MLAs had begun to think of it about then as an alternative to an even bigger pay raise.

Edmonton Liberal Percy Wickman had to explain why he had proposed in 1989 that the legislature's member services committee raise the living and housing allowance by twenty five dollars a day. "Maybe I'm too gullible," he said. "I was new to the system and I may have screwed that up." He said he wanted an independent body set up to write new rules.

On April 24, a television reporter in a legislature hallway tried to question Speaker David Carter about his claim for a full living allowance. Carter refused to answer, demanded the camera be shut off and pinned the cameraman against a wall. Two other cameras recorded the event. It was shown across Alberta that night.

Steve Zarusky, a Conservative MLA from Redwater, a town northeast of Edmonton, was found to own a three-storey apartment building in Edmonton. He rented a suite from himself and charged $500 a month in expenses. He said, "I'm so tempted sometimes to go to Canadian Tire and buy a tent and pitch it up at the legislative grounds. Maybe that's the way they feel politicians should live." Zarusky said the apartment was a revenue investment involving his brother-in-law and another partner: "Is it a crime to own property in this province? That's how this country and province were built, by people being owners."

By April 28, several MLAs were saying it was time to cut down on foreign trips. They often travelled with Speaker Carter to meetings of the worldwide Commonwealth Parliamentary Association. Carter had claimed $171,853 in travel expenses over five years.

People were calling media outlets with information. A neighbour of Conservative MLA Pearl Calahasen said Calahasen and her husband had been living in a new Edmonton house overlooking the North Saskatchewan River since before her election in 1989. In two years she had claimed $37,850 in living allowance. Her constituency president in Lesser Slave Lake said she visited often and deserved to have her expenses paid. He was surprised to learn she had also received travel expenses of $26,375 in 1990-91.

On April 30, Bob Clark, the province's new ethics commissioner, said he did not have authority to investigate complaints about allowances. The head of the newly formed Alberta Taxpayers Association said, "Is he just sitting around sorting paper clips?"

Klein managed to keep a curious distance from this shambles. He was not one of the old guys who should have known better. He did not talk as if he failed to understand the public anger and its importance. He always seemed to lean in the right direction without hardly trying. He owned a condominium in Edmonton and claimed $19,200 in living allowance for 1990-91. The number was large but it put him lower down the ladder than most of the Calgary members. Only two opposition MLAs had taken less. All the others had claimed at least $21,700.

Premier Getty finally gave in after a month of uproar. He had initially said no review of MLAs' pay was necessary. On May 12 he tabled a letter in the legislature asking the member services committee to obtain advice from outside experts. The gesture had the foot-dragging quality of any tottering regime forced to accept change. Getty said MLAs should be compared with judges, business executives, and senior civil servants. He said housing allowances should be reviewed quickly but nothing else should change for two years because salaries had been frozen until 1994. The timing would likely delay any change until after the next election.

Meanwhile, information about the MLAs kept spreading. No one had hidden anything during the 1980s. But no one in the public seemed to care much then. Now what was probably the fattest overall salary and benefits schedule in a Canadian legislature became embarrassing.

The MLAs all made a basic $57,500, one-third of which was classed as a general expense allowance and not taxed. Cabinet ministers received extra salary, pushing them to $104,000 a year. The Alberta cabinet, with twenty-six members, was one of the largest in the country. The Conservatives had developed a routine of naming backbenchers to committees and as nominal heads of government agencies. All these positions qualified for extra pay and many of them for government cars. With various expenses thrown in, it was a rare government member who did not cost taxpayers more than $100,000 a year. Some backbenchers earned more money than cabinet ministers. No receipts were required.

As the furore wound down the excuses multiplied. An all-party committee of the legislature agreed that MLAs living outside Edmonton but within one hundred kilometres of the legislature could not claim the living allowance. They could make an exception for days when they reported working at least fourteen hours, including travel time. Carter, in a widely published comment, said he worried about members being dead tired and trying to drive back home late at night: "It's just a great concern to me as Speaker because sometimes I am a mother hen as to how many members really are in jeopardy in terms of their travelling." Public Works Minister Ken Kowalski said working fourteen hours and coming back to the legislature for a 7:30 A.M. meeting was simply dangerous: "The last thing we want is these people on the road."

The politicians had apparently forgotten, those of them who knew, that any worker could pull a double shift or go to a second job. These people would not have a "mother hen" staking them to a free night at a hotel.

Now they had gone beyond greed to silliness, the final stage of any collapsing regime.

Hints of the bizarre had been creeping in more and more. Many voters were convinced that whatever information was turning up on the news, worse was being hidden.

One reader sent a letter of appreciation to a *Calgary Herald* reporter for a story on Getty's pay and said, "Now, how about doing some research and publishing the real perks etc. that our premier is involved in? Your article was good but it only touched on the real ripoffs."

Before the month was out the taint was spreading to Ottawa. A report came out showing that in the middle of a recession, with the federal government saying it was tightening its belt, ten cabinet ministers and sixteen senior bureaucrats had received new cars at public expense.

The daily revelations and accusations began to fade after Getty's request for an overall salary review. By the end of May the frenzy had played out. The anger remained. Liberal Gary Dickson won a summer byelection in Calgary. At his swearing-in ceremony August 26 he promised to write an annual cheque to the provincial treasurer returning 10 percent of his pay. He called this a small, symbolic gesture but one which had to be taken in a time when the provincial debt was getting out of hand.

Some of the people caught in this unsettled time had curious fates. The Calgary members who had claimed the smallest living allowances, Liberal Yolande Gagnon ($11,195) and New Democrat Bob Hawkesworth ($15,374) both lost their reelection bids a year later. Dinning had not only claimed a full living allowance, he had taken money from private donors to cover some of his expenses. His secret fund had raised $18,000 by the time it became public information in 1991. Dinning scrapped it on advice from the attorney general. He won reelection handily. Woloshyn, the New Democrat whose actions had dragged his party into the affair, jumped to the Conservatives early in 1993 and won reelection. Fowler lost.

The pay and perks affair put one more dent in Getty's badly battered government. Yet he easily survived the scrutiny of his personal accounts. Although he had represented the rural constituency of Stettler since 1989, a two-hour drive from Edmonton and far enough away to justify a full allowance for a second residence, he had claimed only $9,800 for 1990-91. He told reporters that was what he had spent: "I guess I just tried to keep track of what the costs were." His ambling, seemingly naive geniality kept him out of personal trouble. It just never won him many votes. People wanted a sharper operator. That was how things stood in mid-1992.

In the warm summer evenings, when cumulus clouds filled the uncompromisingly blue Alberta sky and the light lingered on almost to morning, an obscure Liberal worker named Andrew Beniuk knocked on doors in the middle of Edmonton. He was canvassing NDP Leader Ray Martin's Edmonton-Norwood constituency. Martin lived there. He had held the seat since 1982. Beniuk wanted to know what people were thinking. He found them unhappy with every party. They were even unhappy with the New Democrats, who had been drawn in and found culpable—not only on the pay issue but on two successive attempts to reform the Constitution. Beniuk wanted to run for election. He began to think he had a good chance to win on Martin's home ground.

Alberta had had trouble with politicians before. So had the rest of the country.

The political system had started to look as if it was out of control, as if no one had a real say aside from a vote every four years. A regular vote was a fine practice compared with much of the world but it was becoming increasingly inadequate. You could pick the people you liked to run the country or the province. They would use that one vote to justify all sorts of decisions you never had in mind.

And it was worse than that. Political leaders had learned they could say what was needed to win an election and then turn around and do the opposite. A Liberal, Pierre Trudeau, did it in 1976 with wage and price controls. A Conservative, Brian Mulroney, did it in 1984 with free trade and with his promise to cut Canada's budget deficits.

It was worse still. Changing the government with that one vote every four years hardly seemed to matter. All the parties seemed to end up doing the wrong thing. Sometimes they did the wrong thing because they were looking for votes and sometimes because—no one seemed to know why.

The Liberals seemed intellectually and morally bankrupt by the early 1980s. The New Democrats always went too far for many people when they won an election. The Conservatives promised financial responsibility but in Ottawa and Saskatchewan they ran up debt and governed badly.

Alberta knew the feeling of helplessness particularly well. Most of the province felt that the federal government's National Energy Program (NEP) of 1980 had represented grinding coercion and virtual theft.

The National Energy Program accompanied other impositions. In the late 1970s and early 1980s the federal government changed all measures to the metric system. The switch took some getting used to everywhere in Canada but it upset the most basic verities of prairie dwellers. The land itself came in units of 160 acres and square miles, and it was intersected by roads precisely one mile apart. Converting these wholes into odd new fractions meant turning the fundamental fact of the prairies into something alien.

Ottawa was extending the use of French, a language most Albertans did not think was needed where they lived. It was also taking the first steps toward tighter gun control. This may have made some sense in the cities but on thousands of farms, guns were less a weapon than a tool. A lot of Albertans saw a government in which they had no say throwing away everyday, familiar things which had helped make their lives certain and safe.

They saw it wasting money too. In the 1982 provincial election, more than one hundred thousand people, about one-eighth of everyone who voted, cast a ballot for a party called Western Canada Concept. The WCC drew attention mostly because many of its members flirted with the idea of western separatism. If you looked closely you could see a more or less direct offshoot of American populism from a few generations before. They believed in ideas like referendums and the recall of elected politicians.

A decade later, Albertans looked around and saw nothing much changed. They still had little apparent influence over political decisions and even less over economic life.

Hard-pressed taxpayers around much of Alberta watched teachers go on strike in the spring of 1992 to back demands for pay increases of 6 and 7 and 8 percent. The teachers were far out of line with other workers' reality, let alone with public budget pressures.

A lot of other Canadians were feeling the same impotence in public life.

They saw a prime minister whose nickname was Lyin' Brian. They saw hired experts consorting with political intriguers to rewrite the basic law of the country.

When the political leaders tried to rewrite the basic law a second time they sent a man named Keith Spicer around the country to find out what people were thinking. He reported there was "a fury in the land" and much of it was directed at the prime minister. Fury spills out of its channels easily.

Albertans were as angry as people in any other part of the country. This was peculiar and significant because Alberta and Quebec had put the Mulroney government into power for a second term in 1988. Albertans helped hand the party leadership to Mulroney in the first place in 1983. I kept wondering whether some of their rage came out of frustrated self-knowledge. They had helped make the situation. Maybe that only made them angrier at politicians.

But the political leaders of 1992 really did separate themselves from most Canadians. They held open constitutional meetings and then went behind closed doors for the second time in five years to draw up a document in secret. They wrote the Charlottetown Accord but they left out the ideas Canadians had raised with Spicer, ideas about changing elections and legislative procedures to make the political system more responsive.

And they tried to sell it to people in the worst way you could devise.

Mulroney poisoned the effort within days with fear-mongering and bullying tactics—sign this or watch the sky fall. The document itself was not ready for weeks. When it was released it proved to be full of unresolved issues. Some of the clauses people simply did not like. Nor did they like the overall feel of the thing, the emphasis on collective rights as opposed to individual rights. Nor did they see the need to be discussing these things at all when a million people were out of work and no government seemed able to control its spending.

The Charlottetown Accord went to voters in a referendum. There was a built-in incentive for voting No. Voting No was the only way the country could prove it actually had a choice.

The campaign drew some of the most inspired popular participation any Canadian election has seen. People figured things out for themselves and they spoke their minds.

Some wrote letters to newspapers and left a permanent record of their feeling of being fed up.

Helmut Beierbeck of Edmonton wrote, "These are the same geniuses who pushed the nation to the brink of bankruptcy. . . . I find it truly disgusting that even in a matter of such importance, our elected representatives toe the party line, rather than having the courage of their own convictions."

Eleanor Kelly of Olds: "Suddenly politicians are trying to brainwash us into changing history to appease Quebec's nationalism. . . . The present economic state of Canada can only be credited to one thing, and that is the financial incompetence of our leaders."

Gordon Ries of Spruce Grove: "The message is clear: people are sick and tired of elected members of governments misrepresenting them. No more deals behind closed doors."

Leonard Sanche of Whitecourt: "All this debate in this round of the constitutional talks has done, by thumbing its nose at the Spicer commission and steering clear of any kind of 'constituent assembly,' is radicalize public opinion. Unless you're associated with some special interest or identifiable group, you're nobody.

"The status quo is gone even if we gain the constitutional status quo back with a No vote."

And so it was.

I would not want to leave the wrong impression. Hundreds of thousands of Albertans voted Yes in the referendum. Hundreds of thousands who voted No had other good reasons for their decision. One reason the Accord failed was that it was not compelling; a reasonable person could build a sound case for voting No.

It was just that incrimination and stirrings of social revenge had infiltrated the debate.

Some people saw this fracturing. They wrote letters to editors too but not as many.

Brian J. McLeod of St. Albert wrote, "My business travels take me annually to many nations throughout the world. Assuredly, the highlight of every trip is the return to Canada's friendly shores. . . .

"[M]y return is normally spoiled by the constant shrill complaints emanating from the media. Whether it be print, radio, or television, the volume of complaining makes me wonder if I have landed in Alberta or Albania.

"Specifically, the attacks on all levels of politicians, whether they be municipal, provincial, or federal are becoming absurd."

Among the attacked was an exception of sorts—Ralph Klein.

He was named environment minister shortly after the 1989 provincial election. He always said he had genuine interest in the job. In fact, he called the environment one of his main interests during his 1980 campaign to become mayor of Calgary. As minister he had one major task. He had to lead the development of a new provincial environment law.

The old laws lacked force and credibility. They reflected a government that wanted almost desperately to guide businesses rather than draw boundaries for behaviour. They were notorious for never leading to prosecution no matter what kind of pollutants were being dumped or leaked or blown into the air.

Klein led a rewrite which turned into one of the largest public consultation exercises the province had ever seen. The department held public meetings. It gathered thousands of letters. It wrote draft bills and put the drafts out for discussion. The whole process took more than two years. By the time

Klein finally brought a unified, rewritten environment bill into the legislature, most of the complaints he was getting were about the delay .

Critics still saw shortcomings. One of the biggest was Klein's refusal to go along with a whistleblowers' clause—legal job protection for government and private workers who told environment officials about hidden things going wrong. There were tough fights along the way. But on the whole the exercise turned into a model of public consultation at a time when people were saying, with plenty of evidence to back them up, that politicians were not listening to the public.

Klein found himself caught all this time between two powerful forces. On one side were established cabinet ministers intent on overnight development of an Alberta pulp industry as one answer to the decline of oil and gas. On the other side was an environmental movement whose popularity those ministers and their officials had badly underestimated.

Klein's history as mayor suggested he would try to broker an accommodation. He would support development but try to get something for the opponents. That's how it worked out.

He came into the job as the biggest and most controversial of the pulp mills was winding through the government approval process.

The Alberta-Pacific project on the Athabasca River near Boyle, about ninety minutes' drive northeast of Edmonton, was to be the largest single-line bleached kraft pulp mill in the world. It was backed by Japanese investors. Many of the local residents wanted it, but some of the people living nearest to the site were leery.

The province would have to sign over much of northeastern Alberta, an area the size of New Brunswick, for logging. Reforestation could not reproduce the mixed aspen and spruce old-growth forest the mill would devour. Scientists had not yet learned exactly what lived in that forest or how. Other firms were developing ways to make pulp without the chlorine bleach which Alberta-Pacific proposed to use.

Al-Pac was the biggest of several projects and came along last. It got caught by growing protest and concern. The rules changed on the investors part-way through. The decisions were hidden in cabinet secrecy but Klein was apparently instrumental in forcing a broader and more public environmental review. The government responded with carefully plotted and at times inconclusive scientific studies.

Klein went up north to talk with upset residents at the mill site and arrange funding for them to make their case at an environmental hearing. Months later, he joined three of his senior cabinet colleagues at a news conference at the town of Athabasca to announce the go-ahead for the mill.

Both sides got some of what they wanted although the company got more and finally won most of what it wanted. Listening to the people was good. Knowing which people to listen to at what times was even better. Best of all was listening while staying onside with economic development.

It was a knack, or maybe an instinct. Klein had jumped into politics as the TV reporter who worked with bikers and rubbies and prostitutes. He became the mayor who drank with the ordinary folks at the St. Louis Hotel. Once he missed an 8 A.M. speech to 120 members of the Calgary Real Estate Board because he slept in. He also developed a reputation within his first year in office for being very much onside with land developers.

Klein was no radical. He was not even inexperienced although some cabinet veterans apparently thought he was green and unstable. He had spent nine years running a bigger government operation than any of them had been running, and he had been on his own.

He must have had instinct. More instinct than talent—whatever he did seemed infused by luck too.

He had run up one of the lower living allowance claims of any Calgary MLAs. Most Calgarians knew him as unpretentious "Ralph," the guy whose wife had quit her accounting clerk job to be available when he became mayor.

As for the referendum on the Charlottetown Accord, legal documents and abstract deals were not Klein's department. They were not his style and not his interest. No one used the words Klein and Constitution in the same sentence. He could talk about listening because the words sounded authentic from him.

He said in 1980 that he had decided to run for mayor because he was frustrated by Calgary city council's "people be damned" attitude: "Politicians have become an arm of the bureaucracy and I want to reverse that."

The last straw for him had been the development of a Civic Centre project that saw people forced out of their homes and businesses. "I just said, 'You can't treat people that way.' "

He could sell that attitude because he had lived it. By 1990 the only other politician talking that way was Preston Manning and Manning sometimes had to force the words. He had grown up as the son of a provincial premier.

Power cannot accommodate everyone. Klein arguably treated people "that way," at times, all through his career. He went along with allowing the Alberta-Pacific mill to be built in a settled farming and sawmill area but the ambiguity had started long before. In his first year as Calgary's mayor he took city council to a weekend retreat in Banff. Councillors heard a five-hour presentation from Ranger Oil on energy prices and the economy the first day there. The next, they made plans to start a pension plan for themselves and the mayor. The plan eventually became reality, with Klein complaining the Calgary media were talking about it too much: "The amount of money we're talking here is a fluff in the wind."

Yet when he walked blindly into a public exchange of insults with a political challenger in 1986, the owner of an aerial advertising firm sent a plane over Calgary with the message Ralph, We Love U Just The Way You Are. He got better than 90 percent of the vote that year.

He appeared to know something other politicians did not know. He appeared to be something they were not.

They knew people were angry. Klein had some idea what to do about it.

You know what public anger means, Steffens. You saw it a few times, and stood up to it, but not without cost. An over-eager prosecutor in a trial asked once whether you were an avowed anarchist and you replied you were far worse—you believed in Christianity. Politics based on the Golden Rule failed some of the people you were trying to help. It sank your own stock with just about everyone for twenty years.

But the idea of the Golden Rule has stood up for a couple of thousand years now and it keeps coming back. Sometimes it comes back with variations, separated from its Christian base. We are more likely now to hear a call for morality and civility. One of those calls came along as people vented their rage in 1992.

Vaclav Havel, the former president of the quickly unravelling Czechoslovak Republic, had written some essays a year earlier and collected them into a book called *Summer Meditations*.

They had a wistful sunniness about them. You could be lulled, as if listening to the buzzing of insects in a grassy field full of wildflowers.

Havel seemed to be up against most of what Canadians and Albertans were up against—economic and nationalist tensions and the invasion of crassness into public life.

He responded, "Time and time again I have been persuaded that a huge potential of goodwill is slumbering within our society. It's just that it's incoherent, suppressed, confused, crippled and perplexed. . . .

"It is largely up to the politicians which social forces they choose to liberate and which they choose to suppress, whether they rely on the good in each citizen or on the bad."

He said the politicians who angered him were not evil-minded. They were only inexperienced, and easily infected by whatever ill winds swept through the streets at any time.

His practical ideas could have found a home in Alberta. He sounded very North American. He envisaged a market economy with some role for the state, confident and powerful municipal governments, landscapes and cityscapes rebuilt on a human scale and with an eye for beauty, electoral laws changed to lessen the role of parties.

He insisted on simple decency and civility—on morality as the ground for public life.

It is not true, he said, that politicians must lie or intrigue. That was nonsense spread about by people who wanted to keep others out of political participation. He said what a politician has to count on is not a tactical sense or an education in law or economics.

Politicians need decorum, taste, moderation, an ability to talk to people. Those qualities have to be nourished in the population: "People need to hear that it makes sense to behave decently or to help others, to place common interests above their own, to respect the elementary rules of human coexistence."

Things did not work out that way here, Steffens. As you noted in your autobiography, public virtues come more easily to people who have money in their pocket and are sure they will still have some tomorrow.

This is a useful maxim, although in Alberta it carries a twist. Here it seems the poorer you are, the more morality and civility most people require from you.

3

The Immolation
of Dreams

The Edmonton Journal,
May 22, 1992

Some numbers you can say easily. But not $566 million. If you try to say $566 million it sticks in your mouth.

It lies there like an extra-large jawbreaker, or a big wad of cotton, or a thistle or a handful of chokecherries.

When you say $566 million it sits in your mouth feeling funny. And the number reaches your ears and you kind of gasp and the effect starts to spread.

Hearing that the government has lost $566 million leaves a sick, empty, sinking feeling in your stomach. It's like the feeling you get if you see two cars screeching toward each other and you know they'll never stop in time.

With that feeling in your stomach it's hard to be impressed when Treasurer Dick Johnston says that Alberta's deficit will not go up because the losses will be tacked on to last year's books.

You blink with disbelief when Technology Minister Fred Stewart says no one will resign because: "I believe in ministerial responsibility but . . . we've made the right decisions all along the line."

And when Stewart says the sale of NovAtel is great news because it makes Calgary's Northern Telecom plant a world centre in a leading-edge technology called wireless telecommunications, somehow that doesn't matter as much as it might on some other day.

The $566 million is still lying in your mouth and the hollowness is still creeping across your stomach. Good news does not feel like this.

It's simpler to understand New Democrat Leader Ray Martin when he calls this "the biggest bamboozle in the history of Alberta."

"What we've done," Martin says, "is sold AGT and got nothing for it, that's what it comes down to."

It is easier to follow Liberal Leader Laurence Decore when he calls the NovAtel experience "a dreadful investment for Albertans, a dreadful miscalculation by Mr. Johnston and Mr. Stewart and Mr. Getty."

Everything feels off balance. Back in 1990 everyone was hoping a German auto-parts firm would buy into NovAtel and develop a worldwide partnership to market cellular phones. All of a sudden Stewart is making that idea sound almost obsolete, almost like something we were lucky to avoid.

The wave of the future is wireless, he says. It's exciting that Northern Telecom would try to make Calgary a world centre for wireless manufacturing and research. They will have six hundred jobs; if it weren't for that, the four hundred jobs at Northern Telecom's switching plant would probably have disappeared into the U.S.

Meanwhile, an Austrian investor who does business in Hong Kong will pick up the cellular phone end of the business cheap, and try to keep those jobs in Alberta.

Maybe these are diamonds glittering in the mud. These are the kinds of enterprises everyone wants in the 1990s. It's hard to get excited. There are so many shadows getting in the way.

There's the mean trick of timing that let Stewart go a full day without having to answer in the legislature's question period. Even today he will probably not answer until his departmental budget estimates come up for debate. The opposition will have a couple of hours with him but none of it will be on television.

There's the way these shocks keep happening. It's only a month since the balanced budget blew into smithereens and Johnston announced a $2.3-billion budget deficit.

There's the fact that Premier Don Getty had reason to ask the auditor general to look into NovAtel's financial history at least a year ago but he waited until now.

No, it's all too much to swallow right now, and sometimes a person's stomach doesn't feel like it can handle much anyway.

All right, this was not a useful explanation. The only purpose was to record a sense of shock. It seemed like the best thing to do. Shock was probably the first reaction most people had. No explanations were possible. No justifications. There was only a stunned moment of disbelief, followed by disappointment, impatience, anger, sarcasm, rage.

NovAtel horrified the Conservatives. The company name turned into a one-word argument, an irresistible denunciation. NovAtel was an encapsulated history of everything that had gone wrong in the government's many business ventures. Whenever two people talked in Alberta and one of them said "NovAtel," the word flooded the conversation. It burst with meaning. It was a final proof of incompetence.

It should have been more. NovAtel was one of the conduits of the new world economy. The government wanted to support the company because the company tied into an emerging worldwide market for technology. It represented some morally blank power seeping into the streets of Calgary and Lethbridge and into the offices of the Legislature Building in Edmonton.

NovAtel would have been the face of technoglobalism in Alberta except that technoglobalism did not have a face. That was one if its characteristics.

An entrepreneur named Peter Pocklington had said six years earlier that workers staging a desperate and sometimes violent strike at his Edmonton meat plant should realize they were competing with labourers in Taiwan. Pocklington was not mean-minded so much as he was transparent. He would never stand in the way of economic forces or try to alleviate them. He always let economic priorities shine through him. But people could put his face on what was happening. NovAtel consisted only of plastic and wires in a couple of factories, and of unimaginably large numbers written down in the loss column of financial statements.

So people supplied faces on their own. When they looked at NovAtel they saw Premier Don Getty and Treasurer Dick Johnston and Technology Minister Fred Stewart and a government full of people who had in one bad deal lost nearly as much money as the Alberta government collected each year in corporate income tax. They lost so much money that you would have had to win the biggest lottery in the country three hundred times before you could catch up and pay off the debt.

Johnston stood up in the legislature May 21, 1992, and said the numbers. And that was that, a sentence as gentle and sure as a doctor pronouncing a relative's death.

He was out of character that day. Johnston was a high-strung beanpole of a man who had come into politics by way of an accounting degree and played the sophisticated intellectual trapped among rubes. Sometimes he resorted to lurid political name-calling. Usually he delivered a technocratic lecture. His lectures were never designed to make things clear. They were exercises in arrogance. He used economists' jargon for a weapon. If you had seen him in action you might have thought of a petty aristocrat harassing a peasant with a rapier. A lot of the peasants were in his own Conservative party and were smarter than he seemed to think they were.

The day he announced the scale of the NovAtel disaster he left his pose aside for probably the last time in his career. He simply uttered what had happened in a subdued voice. Everything about him said he knew this was serious.

He had already pushed the Conservatives' credibility to the brink with his budget speech a year earlier. Since 1986 the government had officially been following a plan to balance income with spending. In the spring of 1991, Johnston stood in the legislature and said the day had arrived: "This is a balanced budget."

If world oil prices had doubled it might have worked out that way. The whole province seemed to go along with the gag. There seemed to be nothing else to do once the government had spoken. People who had spent their lives not questioning provincial authority were not eager to start now. Johnston managed to put off an official revision for a year. Then he announced the balanced budget of 1991-92 had actually produced a $2.3-billion deficit, and 1992-93 would bring a deficit just as big. There was no apparent end to the losses.

But there was an end to faith. A month after Johnston announced the NovAtel loss he stood up in the legislature again. This time he was introducing a bill to end government deficits. If they could not control the government's finances they could at least have a law saying they were supposed to have control. Johnston said the Conservatives had been doing a good job on finances. He began with a double-edged phrase, "We have distinguished ourselves. . . ." The Opposition erupted into laughter, a devastating kind of laughter because it was utterly unforced. They laughed in one great spontaneous burst. And they kept laughing. They laughed in great guffaws of disbelief that spilled out of the chamber and rolled and echoed around the province. A small, rueful smile crept across Johnston's face.

I can't remember whether Getty was there and whether he smiled too. He had come to symbolize ineffectiveness even more than Johnston. At least Johnston had the know-it-all patter and a patronizing attitude. Getty never even acted arrogant. He just acted as if nothing bothered him.

In the end it all turned personal. People came to see the failures as a reflection of what they thought was Getty's view of running a government—it was an OK occupation as long as it did not interfere too much with golf. The disenchantment spread to some of the ministers most caught up in the deals that had gone sour. Fred Stewart, an earnest and respected Calgary lawyer, was one.

Connie Osterman had already had her turn. She came from a farm north of Calgary, brought a stiffbacked and widely admired rural Alberta attitude into the government, and eventually got fingered as the one minister who could be blamed in the collapse of the Principal Group financial business.

The biggest of the Conservatives' business failures was probably the pouring of billions of dollars into land and housing development during the boom years. The government boosted an already overheated market. Real estate prices collapsed between 1982 and 1984. People walked away from homes financed with mortgages through Crown corporations. Apartment developers could not walk away but could not make payments either. The province got stuck with land and buildings which it took a decade to sell.

There had been other intimations in the late 1970s and early 1980s— collapses of small mortgage and trust companies even while the oil boom was running strong.

But the first spectacular evidence of incompetence burst into view in the summer of 1987 when the Edmonton-based Principal Group collapsed. The group had several hundred million dollars in real estate and financial assets. The assets were held largely through two investment firms called First Investors Corporation and Associated Investors Corporation. Provincial regulators had been worried about the two firms for years. In mid-1987 the provincial treasurer made a final demand for injection of more cash by the owners. The owners asked for millions from the province too. Instead, the province got a court order putting the firms into receivership June 30, 1987 and leaving thousands of investors scrambling for their money. The collapse of the two crucial investment firms led to the collapse of the entire Principal structure.

Principal was owned by Edmonton businessman Donald Cormie and his family. Its headquarters were located in a downtown Edmonton skyscraper. Near the top, a curving staircase used by few people outside or inside the firm ascended toward the heaven of the highest reaches of management.

Principal Group ended up costing the province more than $100 million in compensation to investors and in the costs of an investigation that lasted more than a year. But it never cost much in terms of the government's self-confidence. You had to hand it to Alberta politicians there.

The firm was founded in Edmonton, nurtured in Edmonton, regulated in Edmonton. It represented local values and local pride. Financially, it was rotten at the core. It was allowed to exist for years by equally rotten government regulations.

The trail of mistakes may have stretched all the way back to 1975, when the great boom of the 1970s was just beginning and the Conservative government was hitting its stride. In that year, the province proposed toughening investment contracts law under which Principal's main branches operated. Cormie wrote to then-premier Peter Lougheed expressing concern about the changes. The official investigation into the Principal collapse concluded there was no evidence to show what impact, if any, the letter had on the eventual decision not to change the law.

The investigation into the Principal collapse began in July 1987. The Court of Queen's Bench appointed Bill Code, a Calgary lawyer, as an inspector. He was charged with looking into the reasons behind the failure of First Investors and Associated Investors. He spent the next two years unravelling a complex story which ended with his stating that he had found evidence tending to show dishonesty and fraud on the part of Donald Cormie. Cormie went to court in late 1994 to try to have the report quashed but that had no bearing on what Albertans saw in the late 1980s. Code said the firms failed because they had been sacrificed to parent firms and ultimately to the personal interests of Cormie. (The RCMP investigated for years and ended up not laying charges.) But Code found much more.

The rot in the foundations of Principal Group went beyond Cormie. It went beyond the collapse of the Alberta real estate market, which many Albertans conveniently pinned on the federal government's National Energy Program of 1980.

Code said the investment firms had never been solid and had been on the brink of failure as early as 1983. He said in his final report that a simulated earnings analysis showed "the investment contract companies were likely marginal operations at best, even if there had been no collapse of real estate in Alberta in the 1980s."

Instead, one of the significant causes of the failure "was the willful refusal of the regulators to act effectively." Much of this burden landed on Osterman. She had frustrated some officials in the Department of Consumer and Corporate Affairs and had even forced one into early retirement in 1984 after he persistently pointed out the Principal companies' weaknesses. It appeared she had acted alone but that a minister acting alone was out of character for the government of the time.

Code said Osterman had breached her public duty to carry out the purposes of Alberta's investment law. She had not wanted action against the Principal companies to shake the province's credit union system, itself in deep trouble. Code said she was neglectful, misguided, and even reckless. His findings effectively ended her career as a cabinet minister. But keeping up consumer and investor confidence in Alberta-owned financial firms was a policy of that entire government.

Code also wrote, "Osterman was prepared to allow the public to continue to invest in FIC and AIC when she had no idea whether the companies would be able to honor maturing obligations, because of what she perceived to be a greater public good. In the end, it was the investors who bore the risks of her decision and her policy and her hope that economic conditions would improve."

Similarly-worded sentences could have described a string of government-linked failures and losses in the late 1980s and early 1990s.

Some had germinated in the earliest years of the Conservative era, with the help of strong-minded ministers. There was a canola processing plant in the Peace River country of the northwest, a project which began in the mid-1970s under the sponsorship of then agriculture minister Hugh Horner, the second most powerful man in the Lougheed government. The plant's supporters kept saying it provided area farmers with an alternative market which improved their canola prices by about twenty dollars a tonne. It provided about seventy-five local jobs. But it drained about $68 million of tax money to cover investment and operating losses by the time it was sold to a private firm in 1994.

The pace stepped up in 1986 when the government watched the oil industry collapse and decided it had to pump up activity in other areas. One of those areas was transportation, particularly a privately owned port operation on the Fraser River, just outside of Vancouver.

Fred Peacock, father-in-law of future provincial treasurer Jim Dinning, helped set in motion the train of events there. He had willing allies in the government. Peacock had been part of the Conservative government himself in the 1970s. He had gone from business in Calgary to running the provincial industry department. In the 1980s he moved on to become Alberta's agent general in Hong Kong. There he met another Calgary businessman named Bill McKay and talked to McKay about the need for more port capacity on the West Coast.

One of Alberta's top economic priorities for years had been better transportation of export goods. B.C. was not helping, the federal government was not helping. Looking back a few years later, Peacock would still growl when he got onto the subject of British Columbia's port authorities: "Burrard Inlet was turning into a yacht harbour and they were an elitist group. . . ." But here was McKay, a businessman interested in getting something going. And Peacock was sure that private investors could not afford to develop ports with borrowed money: "It'll put 'em under the ground."

Larry Shaben, the newly appointed economic development minister in 1986, apparently had the same thoughts. The Alberta government provided the cash for a private group to buy and expand Alberta-Pacific Terminals. There was no sign that McKay or other private investors were putting in much of their own money.

By late 1990 Alberta-Pacific Terminals was headed for insolvency. Usually these firms just went out of business, the government recorded a loss and that was the end. This time, a court case intervened. Company papers were filed with the Supreme Court of British Columbia and available for public viewing. They told a rare inside story of how the Alberta government did business.

Several papers filed with the court referred to an impression that forestry and petrochemical exports from Alberta would be "directed" through Alberta-Pacific's dock at Surrey, B.C. No one ever explained who would do the directing and how. No one explained how many other things might be "directed" in the Alberta economy.

One of the most extraordinary documents was a handwritten proposal from McKay, then the chair of Alberta-Pacific, to new Economic Development Minister Peter Elzinga in October 1990. (Shaben left politics in 1989.) McKay was looking for ways to eliminate $12.4 million in obligations to the government. Alberta-Pacific had already made some proposals. The government had turned down one suggestion for a new $57-million investment in some form. McKay followed with a suggestion which included clearing $6 million off the table. He wrote, "This could either just be written off—or converted to a never-never pref[erred] share for political optics."

The provincial cabinet had made several direct government investments in preferred shares of private firms since 1986. Other loans or investments came from the Heritage Savings Trust Fund. Some were losers. No one ever explained this either—how many of the other investments might have consisted of "never-never" shares, simply a way to make a loss show up on the books as an investment.

McKay ended his three-page draft by noting he would send a copy to Peacock. After the document was made public in July of 1991, Peacock said that he probably received a copy because he had been acting as an adviser for Alberta-Pacific. The government resisted being drawn in further. But it lost $10 million when Alberta-Pacific Terminals finally went under a few months after McKay's handwritten appeal.

This was one of the few times a door opened on the way the government went about developing the economy, and losing money in the process. The details showed a remarkable tangle of private and public business.

A long string of investments marked the late 1980s. Often the government simply announced it had put money into firms, some of them poorly known. One of the most controversial was the Gainers meat packing plant, taken over when owner Peter Pocklington failed to make a payment on a $12-million loan intended to finance a hog processing plant in southern Alberta. By the early 1990s the Gainers plant was losing about $20 million a year, largely because of an overhang of debt. The government kept insisting the money was worthwhile because twelve hundred jobs were at stake, as was a ready market for hog producers around Edmonton. Cabinet ministers may also have wanted to guarantee security of supply for the Asian market which Gainers was cracking in the late 1980s. The firm was eventually sold for nothing much more than paper, after a loss of more than $200 million.

Other investments went into in a structural steel plant, a manufacturer of laser cutting machines, a computer design firm, and pulp mills. No one ever had a clear account of how the government ended up putting money into these firms. The auditor general eventually started reporting sloppy procedures in the granting of loan guarantees. By 1989 some of the investments were failing and taking government money with them. Getty and Elzinga and other ministers called these exceptions. NovAtel ended the ability to make excuses.

NovAtel itself grew out of the boom-era stage of investment. It was a creature of the Lougheed era's drive for "economic diversification." That was the magical phrase of its day, the life preserver which would keep Alberta prosperous when the oil ran out, which Lougheed kept saying would happen in ten years. He kept saying that year after year.

NovAtel was a reasonably early crack at high technology, a joint venture to produce cellular telephones. Nova Corporation owned half the firm. Alberta Government Telephones owned the other half. The owners themselves reflected decades of Alberta history. AGT was one of the provincially owned telephone companies formed by prairie governments to provide service when the Bell system proved reluctant to take on the task.

Nova was not government owned but it was a creature of the Alberta government and was government influenced. It began life in 1954 as Alberta Gas Trunk Line, a firm created at the direction of Ernest Manning's Social Credit government to act as the single owner of all natural gas collection pipelines in the province. It was owned by investors but the Alberta government retained certain rights, including the right to appoint some members of the board of directors.

Alberta Gas Trunk branched out into petrochemical production in the late 1970s and took the name Nova. The corporation spread around the world, engaging in ventures such as valve manufacturing in Italy. At home, where its crews roamed through the Alberta countryside far from telephone lines, it saw a future for cellular phones and joined AGT to form NovAtel Communications.

Nova decided to sell its half of NovAtel in 1988. AGT was urged by some officials to sell its half too. Instead it bought out Nova for about $40 million in January 1989. The province in turn began privatizing AGT with a share sale in the fall of 1990. NovAtel was supposed to be part of the deal. Several days before the AGT share offer closed, NovAtel's financial world collapsed. Officials hurriedly cut NovAtel out of the AGT sale. The government got stuck with the company and eventually sold it in 1992. That was when Albertans learned the firm had eaten up $566 million, a number the auditor general later estimated might reach more than $600 million.

You have to hand it to this place for one thing. The government can blow millions or even hundreds of millions of dollars at a crack but it produces some of the clearest and best written financial autopsies you could hope to read. Code's report on the Principal companies turned the numerical spaghetti filling an Edmonton skyscraper into 619 pages of magisterial and enlightening prose.

For NovAtel, Getty and his cabinet requested a report from provincial Auditor General Donald Salmon. This report left a few gaps because Salmon did not have the legal power to force anyone to talk. It told a convincing story all the same.

If you listened carefully you could hear the reverberation of the same themes which had come out of Principal—sloppiness, excessive trust, patronage, overconfidence, too much money in the hands of a government acting with little scrutiny, weak regulation, pride. There was personal weakness too. But mostly there was a way of doing things. NovAtel seared because it revealed the weaknesses of an entire political culture.

The company had never made money. It came close in 1989, bringing its net loss down to $3 million. The way the story unfolded, that relative success served mostly as bait to lure NovAtel officials into a cavern of debt and the treachery of circumstance.

Salmon said NovAtel was just plain poorly run and always had been. The firm developed products without checking markets. It usually missed its financial targets. Some of its managers did not understand elementary financial concepts. The firm as a whole often did not know where it was going. Managers from Nova tended to keep things in check. Their departure, Salmon wrote, removed "a restraining influence on NovAtel's operations, which, together with the perception that funds were accessible, encouraged expansion."

In the year that Nova pulled out of the company, developments in the cellular telephone market were pulling the company into the whirl of forces which finally blew it apart.

NovAtel could not compete with the biggest international players in U.S. cities, but U.S. officials approved a lottery system to hand out licences to run cellular phone districts in rural areas. NovAtel's managers saw this as a major chance to jump into the big leagues—to make the company a player on a world scale.

Jumping in meant financing small U.S. phone companies. The provincial cabinet gave NovAtel authority in early 1989 to make hundreds of millions of dollars in loans. Those loans caused trouble. So did a sudden collapse of sales in mid-1990 after the company had geared up for sharply increased production.

There were many ins and outs to this but the failures had a simple source. NovAtel's ambitious managers had too free a hand to do what they wanted. They had easy access to huge piles of money held by a government disposed to hope for the best, and were able to hand out money without facing up to questions in the legislature or elsewhere.

The appropriate staff were asking appropriate questions on the inside. AGT's financial managers raised warnings along the way just as some of the province's corporate regulators had raised warnings about Principal Group's investment firms. Politicians had brushed aside the warnings on Principal. This time the political effect was more subtle.

NovAtel had a board of directors but much of the board had a political background and little or no background in advanced technology firms. They were used to not rocking boats packed with their friends. Several directors were also directors of the parent firm, AGT. The AGT board was unlikely to question decisions approved by the NovAtel board. The provincial cabinet was the last stop but the ministers were part of the same management chain.

Salmon's central conclusion: "NovAtel's losses were made because the majority of the members of the NovAtel board and the AGT Commission either did not recognize the risks NovAtel was running or took no effective action to limit the risks."

And how could they? "With the exception of the president," wrote Salmon, "members of NovAtel's board did not have prior experience in electronics or manufacturing or the marketing of consumer products."

What a number of them did have was connections. Some came from the AGT board. That body was a hive of Conservative party or civil service insiders: AGT chair Harry Hobbs, who had played junior football in Calgary with Peter Lougheed; former deputy treasurer Chip Collins, who had come into the government from his job as controller at Mannix Corp., the Calgary construction and engineering firm where Lougheed had cut his teeth as a young corporate lawyer; former energy minister Merv Leitch; Lethbridge car dealer Fred Weatherup. The person least well-known in this group was NovAtel chair and AGT director John Burrows. He went back into private business in Calgary and never told his story to Salmon's staff or to anyone else.

The point seemed obvious: NovAtel had bled its way to disaster partly because of patronage.

Salmon made it glaring. He said, "I believe that the lack of previous appropriate experience of NovAtel's chair and non-executive directors was a fundamental cause for NovAtel's operating losses. . . . The fact that up to five NovAtel board members were also members of the AGT Commission hindered effective challenge of the recommendations made by the NovAtel board."

The political bosses of Alberta had been living in a world of illusions. An epitaph on NovAtel would have read the same as the epitaph over many another corporate grave where hundreds of millions of dollars of taxpayers' money lay buried: Too Few Questions, Too Many Friends.

Leaving the matter there would be easy, but some things in the NovAtel report suggested that powerful new forces were pushing on Alberta.

Salmon's report did not lay personal blame. Still, you could read it and infer that the key to many mysterious and costly decisions lay in the mind of John Burrows, the company chair. Burrows had apparently fought attempts to sell the government half of NovAtel when Nova dropped out. He would have been the person chiefly responsible for not reining in executives who paid more attention to research and production than to loans and markets. He held power because he had been chair of the company since its inception, and because he sat on the AGT board all that time as well.

The remarkable thing about Burrows was his background. He came into adult life in the 1950s, as had many other powerful players in the Alberta government and its agencies. He began his business life as a structural engineer with Canadian Pacific Railways. By the late 1970s he had settled in Calgary and had opened a travel agency, one of the hot businesses during the boom. He had some oil industry interests as well. His connections with the Conservative party are not clear but he ended up in positions of influence he would not have reached without party connections. In 1983 this former engineer who had taken on a decidedly low-tech business in Calgary, and whose background lay in the classic fifties-era fields of transportation and resources, took on a key role in an advanced technology firm.

Others in Alberta leadership ranks were making the same leap. Ken Broadfoot became deputy minister of Technology, Research and Telecommunications when that ministry was formed in 1986. He joined the government after a career as an oilfield sales representative. His deputy minister's position put him on the AGT board. As Salmon noted, no one in charge of NovAtel, aside from the operating executives, knew much about the business of advanced technology.

They were men from a mid-century economy trying to take Alberta into a new economy. And at exactly that time, history seemed to speed up.

By 1990, industries like telecommunications had become part of a vast economic globalization. NovAtel ended up competing against international giants, firms like Motorola, Northern Telecom, and Ericsson. It was a game where very few players had the stakes and the ability to survive. Global business had become so dangerous and tricky that even the dominant players were often forming joint ventures. Alberta's player in this game was still being managed by men from the past.

Albertans did not talk much about a changing economy or international investment. They knew someone had lost them more than half a billion dollars. The trail, as usual, seemed to lead to Getty and his pals, if they were pals.

Ralph Klein was off doing other things. NovAtel did not touch him any more than the pay and perks uproar or the Constitution had. He was in charge of an ambitious plan to rewrite Alberta's environment laws. He was also accepting speaking invitations all over the province.

4

Dreams of the Future

The Edmonton Journal
September 17, 1992
Calgary

Tuesday. A government with much on its plate visits the big city to talk about the Constitution, the Conservative leadership, the future.

Noon. Deputy Premier Jim Horsman visits the Rotary Club. Soup and sandwiches. Roomful of middle-aged men singing "Four Strong Winds," stolidly. Horsman peers at the lyrics through his reading glasses and joins in. Later he runs drily through the benefits of the constitutional deal, focusing on the Senate.

Most of the crowd stands to applaud afterward. Several just sit there.

2:30 P.M. Environment Minister Ralph Klein speaks in a crowded food court at Mount Royal College. He sells the Senate deal. His words, but Horsman's line of argument. The ministers apparently have a script. A teacher tells him with a breaking voice the deal is not her deal.

Students ask blunt questions. Klein returns his standard answers, complete with disparagement of "stinking, rotting, belching pulp mills" in B.C. and Ontario.

The toughest question is NovAtel. Never a good answer. Klein thinks, gives in to temptation, makes a crack about former Nova chair Bob Blair, now a federal Liberal candidate in Calgary. He stops. Perhaps he sees blank faces, perhaps he remembers that Blair got his shareholders out of NovAtel with more than $40 million.

4 P.M. Treasurer Dick Johnston visits the Austrian Canada Club. No crowd here. The club president would like more Austrian wine and beer in ALCB stores. Johnston looks excited and edgy.

He tells a reporter he has "never been more ready" and has been working on ideas for the province for the last five years. Subtext: things have been going badly, but we have miracle weapons on the way.

5 P.M. Ministers conduct seven round tables at the plush McDougall Centre, brainstorming with Calgarians picked by local MLAs. Noticeable PC contingent. The tone is urgent.

Tom Snell, party stalwart and head of a private vocational school, says public colleges add frills: "If it only takes two years to finish an accounting education why are we making them take four years? . . . There's nothing to stop students taking a liberal arts education on their own afterward, with their own money, not with my money as a taxpayer." Advanced Education Minister John Gogo listens.

Upstairs, Energy Minister Rick Orman, a few days away from his leadership bid, is asked why government can't slim down the way business has.

There are tremendous opportunities in health, education, and welfare, Orman replies.

He needs ideas. A man named Hal has an idea for him: "Go to hospitals. Say, 'I'm sorry, your budget next year is 10 percent less. You'll have to cut back. You'll have to fire people.' "

Someone else says one of Calgary's two cardiac hospitals could offer public service; the other could go private, selling care to British Columbia, Ontario, and the international market.

Orman says, "These are good ideas out there." He talks about teacher salaries.

A community league president named Moe Hartley poses awkward reminders about NovAtel and other places the government has been free with money: "There's a real perception at the street level that what you're asking for is free enterprise for the poor and socialism for the rich."

Orman says it would be easy to raise taxes but the government has to restructure itself instead.

I walk out into the Calgary evening, past thoughtfully designed office towers Edmonton cannot match and pioneer-era stone buildings like the ones Edmonton tore down. There are people on the street. Calgary feels like the mainspring of the province.

Ideas will come from here. Perhaps a new and brutally divisive form of Alberta politics.

In retrospect, these few hours in Calgary seem like an embryo of history.

Horsman was leading off the effort to sell the Charlottetown Accord, an aging politician in an uninspired setting delivering a flat sales pitch for a dead-end vision of the country.

Premier Don Getty had just announced his intention to retire. The leadership of the Progressive Conservative party was open. None of the ministers had announced their intentions but it was clear that Ralph Klein, Rick Orman, and Nancy Betkowski would almost certainly run.

Getty's successor would have to overcome years of hesitation, of disheartening financial failures, of government isolation. The next leader would also have to set about building Alberta on a far different financial and social foundation than the one Conservative governments under Lougheed and Getty had known since 1971. Now the money was running out. Now the great era of building and urbanization was largely completed.

The Liberal party had taken to using the phrase The Next Alberta to describe their vision of the future. The phrase had implications. Alberta has always found leaders apparently able to express the ideals and fears of an entire generation. Winning parties last a long time in power. They have tended to govern a generation or more. What nearly one-third of the Conservative cabinet ministers were doing that evening in Calgary was trying to bring together a Conservative vision of The Next Alberta.

Their round tables developed into a dry run for a technique used all through 1993. The meetings turned out to be prototypes in some deep ways. Some of the same people attended. And somehow, ideas casually brought forward that night in Calgary survived months of further public discussion. They became the government's guiding principles a year later.

The last element was Calgary itself. An energy radiated through the city that chilly September evening.

Calgary had money and it had confidence and it had power. It had life. Anyone who walked out of the thickly carpeted, hardwood-panelled government rooms of the McDougall Centre and along the downtown streets, past the golden glow of the new Bankers' Hall, toward the old Palliser Hotel, could have felt it. Even the presence of other people walking those streets that night signalled something; Edmonton downtown streets had come to be empty in the evenings.

But more than anything else Calgary had ideas. This was the city where oil and gas firms had discovered they could lay off hundreds of staff, sell off thousands of hectares of leases, and survive profitably. Many of the staff even went into business for themselves and began growing a new, flexible layer of enterprise.

This was the city where business organizations had been learning the practice of "downsizing" and the Thatcher-Reagan theory of political economy. Calgary was the place where people like Madsen Pirie, a theorist of Margaret Thatcher's privatization movement had been brought in for speaking engagements. People all over were reading a surge of economic and management theories from the likes of Peter Drucker, Tom Peters, Kenichi Ohmae, Ted Gaebler, and David Osborne, and others. But this was the one city in Alberta with the strongest white-collar milieu in which those ideas could thrive and strike off new ones. Calgary could support a new political movement because Calgary had the new intellectual theories to justify it.

The Klein revolution started in Calgary.

The consultants hired by politicians in these days talk about "paradigm shifts." The phrase comes from a landmark study in the history of science called *The Structure of Scientific Revolutions* by Thomas Kuhn. When the consultants talk about encouraging a paradigm shift they are really talking about encouraging a revolution. They mean that momentous changes happen when people start seeing their world differently, when they start using a new model as their basis for understanding their world.

Some historians use a far older set of words. They say, "When the shooting starts, the revolution is over."

When things have gone so far that people take extreme and irrevocable action, those people have irrevocably made up their minds. They have had enough. They will have change. There is no turning back.

Every revolution has leaders. The Alberta government tried hard to involve the people of Alberta. But the organizing cells were concentrated in the province's corporate world and inside the government itself.

The Klein revolution was very much a revolution from within. The Progressive Conservative party came to power in 1971 determined to make Alberta prosperous by making the government bigger. That leadership reinvented itself in the early 1990s, and held on to power with a determination to make Alberta prosperous by making the government smaller. Smaller in some ways but not in others.

The changes did not begin with Ralph Klein's election to the party leadership in December 1992.

They can be traced back at least a year earlier. Evidence surfaced at another meeting, this one in Leduc, a meet-the-ministers session sponsored by the Leduc Chamber of Commerce on November 7, 1991.

By this time, the Getty government knew the promise of a balanced budget had collapsed. Strains were developing in the Conservative party. Many members blamed what they called the government's communication problems, centred on Getty himself. The Reform party had been gathering strength for months.

The pressures came together in the annual fall cabinet tour. Ministers had completed their summer retreat several weeks earlier. They had apparently reviewed the budget situation and recognized what was happening. By late September, some ministers had already ordered departments to tighten up on spending. A formal program to save $100 million came a few months later.

The talk at Leduc made it clear that senior ministers had already been looking at the outline of Alberta's budget situation—chronic deficits in the range of $2.5 billion a year—and come to some wide conclusions. But now they were being carried along by events as well as guiding them.

Ministers spent the day of November 7 touring Don Sparrow's Leduc-Wetaskiwin constituency. Five of them, led by Energy Minister Rick Orman, had dinner in a basement meeting room of a Leduc motel that night. About one hundred and fifty people had been gathered by the Leduc Chamber of Commerce. The meeting turned into a revelation—of new ideas inside the government and of new public attitudes.

I had been covering Alberta politics since 1980. It had been a decade of watching adulation and tea-party politeness whenever the Alberta government spoke face to face with voters. On this night I thought I watched that era end.

Orman and Sparrow led a question-and-answer session. Orman was seen as an up-and-comer in those days. The session included Solicitor General Dick Fowler, Culture Minister Doug Main, and Transportation Minister Peter Trynchy. The crowd did not badger or belittle them. It did something more astonishing. People stood up to talk and treated the cabinet ministers as equals.

They offered compliments, skepticism, complaints, and honest suggestions. They seemed to have leaders. One was Len Zalapski. Another was

Leduc alderman Terry Kirkland, who ended up running for the Liberals in 1993 and winning election to the legislature. The attitudes and the ideas had a strong whiff of Reform.

Orman left looking invigorated. "There was electricity in the air," he said. He said he preferred this kind of atmosphere. It would help him make better decisions: "I don't want to live under a mushroom." One of the ministerial aides said the same spirit had been evident earlier in the day at stops in Wetaskiwin, Beaumont, and Millet.

The cabinet ministers had more to make them happy than the pleasure of plain talk. They heard a crowd ready for the new direction already being floated in cabinet.

Two hours in a Leduc motel made it clear: the Conservatives had brought their policies of the past three years screeching to a halt and were pondering a turn to the hard right. Orman himself seemed to be emerging as a major spokesperson inside cabinet for a small-c conservatism whose horizons included a wistful memory of medical user fees. His thoughts had come flooding out when someone in the audience asked, "Do we have the most expensive government in Canada or not?" He talked about Alberta suffering the economic fate of Argentina.

Orman told them, "Where we're going to have to bring it into line is the 65 percent that goes into health, education, and social services . . . the tough decisions are ahead of us and they're in education and health."

Cabinet ministers had been pointing out since the mid-1980s that about two-thirds of the province's spending went into health, education, and welfare. About three-quarters of all grants to such areas as health and education went into paying salaries. But the government had not gone after these areas since getting a bloody nose after 3-percent grant cuts in 1987.

The 1987 experience had shown two things. The government could not cut in sensitive social policy areas while it was pouring hundreds of millions of dollars into new economic ventures and losing hundreds of millions more in financial debacles such as the collapse of Principal Group. The 1987 budget also produced a fascinating split in reaction to the main budget decisions—strong protest against grant cuts for schools and hospitals, but a reluctant acceptance of $1 billion worth of increases in taxes and government fees. Over time, that reaction was reversed.

Orman took the explanation farther. He offered a rare glimpse inside the government's decision-making. Provincial budgets are presented in late winter or early spring. Much of the work of putting them together goes on in the preceding fall. In the fall of 1991, that work had already started for the fiscal year, which would begin April 1, 1992.

Orman said Treasury Board, the inner circle of cabinet ministers who make basic budget decisions, had taken a preliminary look at 1992-93. Its members had decided that the 35 percent of spending not directly funnelled into social services was "down to the bone." Relief would have to be found elsewhere.

The crowd focused on health. People urged more action on preventive health. Some suggested user fees. They found a sympathetic listener.

Orman told them, "My personal experience is that the biggest problem with the cost of the health-care system is that fact that it's free. We were the last province in Canada to have user fees and were penalized $40 million by the federal government for not taking it off. . . .That is, I think, one of the first things we have to bridge intellectually to contain health costs . . . So we are hamstrung by federal legislation, and if it wasn't there that is, I think, one of the first things we would address."

None of this signalled with certainty where the government intended to head. But Orman was sketching the mental framework of the Getty government, more than a year before Klein won the Conservative leadership. Other evidence followed quickly.

Getty spoke the following week to the annual convention of the Alberta Association of Municipal Districts and Counties. He talked to about five hundred leaders from the Conservatives' political base in rural Alberta.

Getty told them Alberta had strong services for people: "But if we don't have a strong economy, we are dramatically limited in how we can show that compassion." A few minutes later he talked about having to make "tough decisions" in health and education. Then he swung back to defending his government's interventions in the economy: "This is not a policy for the nervous nellies, for the timid . . . I know it's popular to point to failures. Negative thinking is the in thing these days. . . . We need to shake the negative thinkers off."

He fended off a rural councillor who asked about cutting the legislature's cushy pension plan. Getty said he knew it had become popular to take shots at governments: "That's just a cycle we're going through, and I accept that and understand it."

He was making his own attempts to overcome the separation between voters and politicians. The day after his speech, he departed from the usual protocol. He came back to the convention and sat down to lunch with the rural leadership, a job usually taken on by cabinet ministers while the premier went on to other things.

After this performance and the Leduc meeting the direction was clear. It was clear enough for me to write in a column November 14, 1991: "As for spending, when politicians talk about 'tough decisions' they mean things like higher medicare premiums, narrower medicare coverage, an extra kid or two in the average classroom. If they really work up their nerve, they might take on doctors with some kind of cap on medicare payments. Tough decisions? That's just a refined vocabulary for things like teachers putting off lessons for a while every morning so they can check their students for head lice because there's no money any more for a public health nurse."

The reference to the teacher checking students' heads came from a case reported at the time. The rest happened in time. The cuts of 1993 and 1994 were already in the cards.

Spending cuts which could have been made in the spring of 1992—and were apparently contemplated—were held off. The government ministers may not have wanted to hurt a fragile economy. They may simply have decided not to do anything hard the year before an election.

Between November 1991 and December 1992 something else apparently happened too. The government finally accepted there was a political limit to cutting social spending while pouring money into economic projects and into the hands of political friends.

The Conservatives had long said social programs had to be grounded on a strong economy. A 1987 social policy statement called *Caring and Responsibility* had put that belief into unusually clear and persuasive words.

During 1992 the government changed its view of how to build a strong economy. In late 1991, Getty and his ministers were still defending loans and loan guarantees and similar ventures. By the end of 1992, Klein was premier. He and some of the same ministers talked about getting government out of direct connections with business. Government would stick to creating a positive investment climate, mainly through less regulation and lower taxes.

How the change happened inside the Alberta government may never be clear. One part of the process was public, however. The government asked Albertans for their opinion, and that too began long before Ralph Klein became premier.

The government began with a novel project called Toward 2000 Together. It was a huge exercise in bringing together the people of Alberta to write a new economic policy for the province. It took months. It gathered ideas from thousands of people. It included public meetings with a broad invitation list, and private meetings for a leadership elite.

Toward 2000 began with an atmosphere of freshness and good will. It seemed a huge window had been thrown open for the province. Thousands responded.

One of the first public meetings took place in Medicine Hat on the last day of January 1992. An unseasonably warm wind was blowing across the southern Alberta prairie. People wore sweaters or light jackets as they walked down dusty streets, beside brown snowless fields.

Organizers had already sent more than seventeen thousand policy kits across the province. More than two hundred groups and business firms had become involved. This meeting had Horsman, Klein, associate agriculture minister Shirley McClellan, and Bow Valley MLA Tom Musgrove practising the new style of government—listening.

People came to the meeting with the same confidence that had surfaced at the Leduc dinner three months earlier. Some asked for lower taxes. Some wanted less red tape. One person complained about inadequate tourist directions. He wanted the plain brown highway signs directing visitors to the Royal Tyrrell Museum in Drumheller replaced with fifty-foot cardboard cutouts of dinosaurs set up on hilltops. A number of the presentations sounded like nothing the government had heard before.

Stuart Wachowicz, a teacher at Youngstown public school in east-central Alberta, offered what he described as a cry from the heart supported by fellow teachers. He said children need hard work, high expectations, and a feeling of discipline. In an era of broken homes, school might be the only place giving them that kind of environment. He said the Youngstown school persistently recorded far lower dropout rates and far higher academic achievement than the provincial average.

Nearly everyone who spoke was uneasy about the future of rural Alberta. The town of Brooks and the surrounding area had decided on cooperative regional development. They were getting advice from Wade Alston, a Harvard-trained planner running an international consulting business out of his home town of Magrath.

Alston told the ministers to forget handouts: "We don't need any for people to come to this province. We have too much to offer." He and the other Brooks-area leaders wanted the province to maintain first-class services, to support ways of raising local capital, to turn over more control to regions.

The small communities around Brooks tended to flounder individually. Put together, Alston said, they had powerful attractions—research institutions, pleasant lifestyles, strong tourist draws such as Dinosaur Provincial Park, the presence of major corporations, a huge tract of land controlled by one owner (the Eastern Irrigation District). He looked at that and saw a part of the world able to attract huge international investors such as Nestlé, the giant food processor. "It has all the major components for a twenty-first century, eco-industrial region. . . . We have the economics of scale required to do something that's really significant."

Ideas suddenly seemed important in Alberta. The views of unelected people suddenly seemed to count. Cooperation and consensus seemed to be possible. It did not take long for the image to fray.

Ten days after the Medicine Hat meeting, policy staff inside the Economic Development Department finished the third draft of a new manufacturing strategy for the province. It leaned heavily toward direct aid to manufacturers, lower taxes, and less regulation. Among its comments: "Alberta must ensure that there are no major growth impediments in such areas as corporate taxation, power costs, regulatory costs. . . . Consideration should be given to . . . R and D tax incentives, investment tax credits, lower corporate tax rates, or other options."

The department coordinating the gathering of ideas was already writing policy. It had apparently started sometime in late 1991, before the first public meetings for Toward 2000 Together were held. No one knew that until a leaked copy of the draft manufacturing strategy reached New Democrat members of the legislature that spring.

In mid-March another signal arrived. The Education Department had collaborated with the Alberta Chamber of Resources on a study called *International Comparisons in Education*. They released a document describing how Alberta schools compared with strong school systems abroad. It radiated a strong streak of self-serving, political-religious fundamentalism which always seems to be seeking an outlet in the province.

Good education leads to jobs and prosperity, the study said, "However, the quality of the education system product is not good enough."

Many of the little sausages coming off the school processing line had not been properly stuffed. Why not? Moral failure: "Societal values in North America and in Alberta over the last several decades have drifted towards self-discovery, individualism, sensual indulgence, pursuit of personal happiness and self-fulfillment. As a result, resistance has built up against the operation of a more rigorous educational program with higher achievement standards for all students. As well, teachers are increasingly faced with problems of student indifference, disobedience, unfavourable work habits, and non-academic distractions."

The study recommended an information campaign "to promote understanding of the linkage between education and economic prosperity, to foster work ethic values and to publicize and debate the value choices and their consequences for Albertans."

The words reeked of resentments which had been helping to stoke a certain kind of politics in many countries since the early 1970s. Yet they also spoke to some of the concerns Stuart Wachowicz had talked about in Medicine Hat. You could interpret them in different ways.

One thing was clear. Nothing in the report suggested that business contribute to technical skills by creating a more secure workplace or by taking on more responsibility for training.

The study called for Alberta to lean toward a German or Japanese model for science and mathematics education. It ignored the German model of industry-financed research, of industry-financed retraining, and of worker-industry cooperation aimed at producing long-term security.

It said Alberta students ranked technical careers low in their ambitions. Could this have been because some employers showed technical workers about as much loyalty as they would to a truck? The study said part-time work might be detracting from academic performance and contributing to a drop-out rate of about 30 percent from high schools. No education minister in Alberta has ever campaigned for less part-time work by high school students. Cuts to provincial education spending would increasingly demand more part-time work.

At the end of March the Conservatives held their annual convention. The delegates swerved back toward ideas the party had seemed to grasp in 1987, but had dropped in favour of no clear ideas at all. Getty led a government in trouble. Still, he was ready to rely on a will to win and on the blind luck which had served up two opposition parties lacking a killer instinct.

"We'll kick their butts," he told the delegates.

He told them how: "Our values are conservative values, and they parallel the fundamental values of Albertans. We should never apologize for being conservatives in this province."

A moral compass was always useful, even when it sounded as if it originated in a poll.

There were moments when the meaning of conservatism in the Progressive Conservative party remained unclear. A handful of older rural delegates actually proposed a sales tax. Others showed the party's streak of ornery liberalism; they narrowly voted down a resolution calling for daily recital of the Lord's Prayer in schools.

The most prominent delegates leaned in a far different direction. Dr. Dennis Modry, an Edmonton heart surgeon, told a session on fiscal policy that health insurance should cover everyone but did not have to be provided by government. He acknowledged the Canada Health Act banned user fees but called that an "extreme decision."

Provincial Treasurer Dick Johnston told Modry that health costs had been a growing burden and it was time for Ottawa to withdraw from setting health policy. Johnston said Health Minister Nancy Betkowski disagreed with the idea of user fees. He said debate would continue.

By now the party's annual conventions were becoming increasingly irrelevant on such issues. One factor was growing and unpublicized interprovincial cooperation. Major concepts for redesigning Canada's health system were no longer being spawned in isolation by individual provinces. A study commissioned by the country's deputy health ministers, for example, suggested that Canada could contain health costs partly by training fewer physicians.

Far bigger outside influences were touching Alberta.

Orman visited the Middle East in May 1992. He came back pronouncing himself convinced that oil and gas producers needed the lower royalties he had been resisting for the last year. He said his resolve had wavered when he saw first-hand the scale of Mideastern reserves, the extremely low exploration and producing costs and the Arabs' sophisticated tracking of markets and production costs in North America. Even allowing for some overemphasis on how much a two-week trip had changed his thinking, the argument was clear. Gerry Protti, executive director of what was then the Independent Petroleum Association of Canada, happily heard about Orman's remarks and summed up the pressures on Alberta: "I think the important thing is to have a competitive fiscal regime with other countries as well as being able to attract some equity."

Alberta was undergoing a reversal of the commodity boom of the 1970s. Producers of raw materials watched prices fall. They scrambled to maintain incomes by pumping out ever more product and by making life easier for multinational firms. This happened in oil, natural gas, and forestry.

At the same time, tax opportunities were shifting to the consumption side. In concrete terms, this meant that Alberta highway construction, once funded in part by oil and gas royalties, would soon be funded by vehicle licence fees and gasoline taxes. The question was not whether to move in this direction but how to sell the decision.

A Conservative party convention could not do the job. The government found other means. One was the Toward 2000 Together conference in Calgary at the end of May 1992.

Toward 2000 was meant to cross political and social boundaries. The project became compromised almost immediately. The Economic Development Department organized public meetings. It also helped organize private meetings for key corporate, bureaucratic, and academic figures. Many would go on to guide discussion at public round tables.

The Toward 2000 Together conference was held at the Calgary Convention Centre. The place was crawling with facilitators, people who have sprung into being in the last few years for the sole purpose of running meetings. They turned the Convention Centre into a nurturing oasis where everyone's idea was good enough to be written down. One participant looked forward to the process: "We do a little bit of blue-skying and sort of bust the paradigms, and throw everything into the cauldron and see what comes of it."

About five hundred and fifty people took part, divided into more than two dozen groups. Everyone had anonymity. Reporters were told not to use names unless participants agreed. No one would know who suggested what, or how many people supported any particular idea. Even the organizers would have only the summaries from the facilitators to work with. First came warm thoughts. People were supposed to describe their vision of an ideal future.

In Group 24, the vision of education in Alberta quickly boiled down to several themes: high quality of life, entrepreneurship, limits on bureaucracy, an emphasis on wealth creation, leadership, partnership between various institutions, respect for and enjoyment of social diversity. At this point, an older business executive pointed out that a Grade 12 student sitting by his side seemed unimpressed. Her name was Ladan Sadrehashemi and she was. To her the gabbing sounded like a waste of time: "This vision has been around for a long time. These goals have been around for a long time. And we haven't achieved it, have we?"

They did eventually talk about specifics. It seemed easy. Oil and gas executives at other workshops called for lower royalties and less regulation. Paul Boothe, an economist from the University of Alberta, said Alberta had to get its finances under control and everyone would have to contribute. He was told it would be better to lose some money than to lose an industry.

At a workshop on training, participants found that not having any teachers around made discussion easy. They called the Alberta Teachers' Association a major problem in the system. "Private schools do not have to hire ATA teachers," said one private school executive. "So that's one way to break the ATA." Someone else said, "Get rid of the bureaucracy, get rid of the bad, get rid of the ATA." A prominent rancher wanted to guard against people who "put down agriculture" by making agriculture courses compulsory from Grade 1 through Grade 12.

This cross-section of Alberta society seemed to favour close-cropped hair and blue suits. Some had pull. A government plane was on standby to take members of the Alberta Chamber of Commerce to a meeting in Edson afterward.

At its worst the conference turned into a rally.

And the worst arrived on the first night. Toronto financial journalist Diane Francis gave a keynote speech and stirred most of the crowd into loud applause with a flat-out attack on unions and the NDP, with calls for sharply lower business taxes, and with blame for anyone living an everyday life.

When a fifty-seven-year-old auto worker gets laid off, you have to ask why he hasn't been taking night courses to prepare for another career, Francis said. People were still repeating that line at workshops the next day. The crowd broke into moderate applause when Francis said, "I will give a lot to the first premier that has the guts to impose user fees on the health care system."

Most of the listeners jumped to their feet clapping when she finished. Hal Wyatt, the Royal Bank director serving as conference chair, congratulated her on a great address.

Doubts surfaced the next day. The few participants from outside the corporate-government leadership tried to let Francis's fans know they felt slighted. "I feel like an aboriginal," one union representative said after trying to make his point at one workshop. One of the conference wrap-up speakers celebrated Alberta's "classless society." By and large there had been only one class at the conference.

The tilt showed. One of the last workshops had people trading ideas to reduce the province's 30 percent high school dropout rate and to encourage technical training. They began talking about the merits of a weaker social safety net, and of a tax system more favourable to the wealthy and to business owners.

It took a small-town real estate salesman to say that people can not be forced into a life of technical servitude: "We won't have enough plumbers and we won't have enough waiters unless they feel they're equal." He did not sway them.

It was still possible to hope for improvements.

A few months later, Orman released Wyatt's report on the conference. Equality did not rate mention.

The report said, "Of all the suggestions put forward for a better economic future, improved educational opportunities was seen as a prime necessity." Yet the advanced education minister of the day was floating ideas about making people pay the full cost of postsecondary education.

The report said participants thought the provincial government was too big and too arrogant. Most of the participants had supported the big provincial government led by Peter Lougheed in the 1970s as a tool for forcing Alberta's economic growth. They had seen fiascoes such as the collapse of Principal Group and NovAtel develop precisely because the warnings of civil service professionals were brushed aside.

The report said, "Taxation must encourage wealth creation and so contribute to economic growth. . . . Royalties for the energy industry should be reduced sharply . . . A shortage of capital is a serious impediment to progress and must be addressed."

The scale of importance descended from there: "There was a clear recognition of the requirements of aboriginal people . . . Farmers are an important group as well."

But when it came to "the homeless, the poor, the handicapped, the sick, the abused and substance abusers"—there were so many of them. Programs for these people "cannot be sustained, let alone improved, unless new ways are found to finance them."

The report left out any mention of Diane Francis and her scorched-earth speech suggesting that unions, aging factory hands, the ungrateful poor, and others should be swept from the Canadian landscape—to be replaced by millionaire immigrants, preferably enjoying three-year tax holidays. The crowd had lapped it up like chocolate ice cream yet her speech disappeared in the final account. Did its spirit linger?

Wyatt wrote that the conference had not included enough women, minorities, environmental groups, or people "from the less privileged sectors of society."

He also said the people who were invited had made it clear that too many civil servants "have forgotten that they are servants of the people" and that "some members of our society have become too accustomed to the government taking care of their needs. As a result, we have a number of unmotivated individuals who could—and should—be doing more for themselves." The statement was possibly true in some cases, but it was a generalization from a body which Wyatt had just conceded did not have much personal knowledge of what life was like for "some members of our society."

The final report came out a year later. It had a stylized globe on the cover. It laid out in sweeping, generalized strokes the ideas which came out of the Calgary conference.

It was written by a committee of thirty-five people which had shrunk to thirty-four. One of the members, Margaret Duncan, executive director of the Alberta Association of Social Workers, resigned.

Duncan said the report formalized and legitimized a business-dominated province where the poor and the damaged were expected to keep quiet and go away. One committee member had called her a communist because she had used the phrase "social equity" during one of their talks. One told her Alberta would be a better place if it were more like Mexico, where people either worked or starved.

They were constructing a new mental map. They were putting Alberta squarely inside the Global Village, a place where much of the population turned out to be unnecessary.

The committee described its work as not just an economic strategy but "a broad-based strategy which addresses our society as a whole."

Toward 2000 was supposed to be the project of an entire society. By the end it looked more like an illusion—a plan written by a leadership class to justify its own actions to itself.

The illusion was being shaped into a serviceable political idea—the myth of Alberta as a "classless society."

The only people counted were "real" Albertans. The division between them and others who did not count was the line separating "good" Albertans from the lazy, from the bad, and from the pursuers of special interest.

The question was how to transform the myth and the ideas feeding it into a durable political structure.

On a cool September evening in Calgary that transformation started to become visible. The shape of the future began to unfold.

5

The Leadership

The Edmonton Journal
December 1, 1992
Calgary

All the famous lives and the invisible ones intertwine.

Nancy Betkowski beat Ralph Klein by one vote in the first part of the Alberta Conservative leadership election.

Every vote counted equally but somewhere a final effort weighed on that balance. Someone filled a last ballot and made a difference. It may well have happened in southeast Calgary, in the constituency of Calgary-Millican, where someone cast a ballot for Nancy Betkowski at 7 P.M., closing time for polls across the province.

The last voter has a name—Anthony Barnes.

He stood in a corridor in the Max Bell Arena on Saturday night as the stragglers drifted out chattering about the result that had touched off whoops of joy and amazement.

He was a slight man with a sandy moustache, a black Calgary Stampeders cap, a powder blue suit, a right eye shiny from a recent operation to remove a cataract, a friendly grin that revealed bad teeth. On his faded tie he sported a new pin slightly bigger than a quarter. It represented the provincial crest of Alberta. A party official had given it to him earlier in the evening for being the last voter of the night.

He had caught the No. 1 bus and made it to the voting station at Victoria Park Community Hall just in time.

"I had so many things during the day—trying to get my Christmas shopping, get home, try to get my shirt on."

A few politicos were still hanging around trading speculation on a cement floor littered with bits of paper, cigarette butts, and a stack of Rick Orman signs. Their voices were low. Barnes talked happily in the quiet.

He said he had thought about voting for Orman. He had talked to an Orman campaigner but had got a bad feeling: "Rick Orman, he won't listen to us. He's just like the prime minister. He won't listen to us. They believe in cheap living standards in Alberta."

He believes in Nancy Betkowski and in her smile.

"I feel strong that she's got some initiative in her, that she's going to help revive Alberta, heal some of the wounds Canadians have suffered in the last two years."

Brian Mulroney would love to see a provincial sales tax in Alberta on top of the GST, but Nancy will keep the sales tax out, he said.

He has met Nancy Betkowski twice. The first time was at the candidates' forum at the Stampede Corral. The second time was a couple of nights before the vote. That time he gave her a white felt cowboy hat with an I Love Calgary pin on it. "They were on sale, twenty-seven dollars. And that little lapel pin, that was only five dollars so that was thirty-two dollars. Thirty-three dollars with the GST."

He used to work as a janitor at a north Calgary motel, but all the full-timers got laid off three years ago. He cleaned up at a seafood restaurant for six months, but got laid off there too. His parents died about then within three months of each other.

He just turned thirty-eight and has been living on $534 a month from the province. "Now my doctor says I'm supposed to go on AISH, but social assistance . . . is taking their time." AISH is an income program for the severely handicapped.

He thinks Nancy can help. "I didn't mention anything, but one day I'll sit down and talk to her, because she's easy to talk to."

He would do much for her. The hat was an extravagance.

"I got mugged two weeks ago. I lost thirty dollars worth of groceries and two hundred dollars. A couple of young punks whacked me on the back with a skateboard. They grabbed my jacket, took a lot of things."

He got locked out of his room when he couldn't pay the rent and moved in with a friend. But he scrapes together pocket money by washing windshields in a local parking lot. There is no fixed price. He has made a big sign. People see it, give him a donation, and he cleans their windshield.

That's how he came up with five dollars for his PC party card late last week and with money for Nancy's hat. His face beamed at the memory of giving it to her.

"She loved it and it fit her really good too, right on the spot. She looked so good."

He can be tough. He opened the outer jacket decorated with two Betkowski buttons and revealed a tiny Reform party pin on the lapel of his polyester suit jacket. Reform will protect Alberta against Mulroney, he said. He has also noticed that people say he talks well about this sort of thing and he might do something about it himself. He has a chance to get somewhere, he said. "I could run for senator."

He thought again about how good it was he could get to the Victoria Park hall in time to cast that last vote for Betkowski. He lifted a hand and covered his mouth again with a gesture of amused astonishment at how things worked out.

"Nancy's been very nice to me, very softhearted to listen to me, and I gave her that lucky charm."

He gave her a vote too.

Her life has been much different than his. She talks to many other people. He has not noticed that of all nine PC candidates she was the one who refused to rule out permanently the idea of a provincial sales tax. She has had to order cuts in benefits under some aid programs. She has been part of a government that tightened the process of transferring into AISH. In return for his vote and his present of a hat she has given him hope, and memories of momentary friendliness. Maybe she will remember him when someone talks about what to cut from public spending next year. He needs an operation on his left eye too.

Anthony Barnes and Nancy Betkowski and the rest of us in between are bound together.

He gave me his story. I shook his hand.

He gave Albertans clean floors and now he gives them clean windshields. Sometimes he gets quarters or even a famous smile in return. On one special night he got the knowledge that his presence counted.

Havel's *Summer Meditations* had just been published. I must have still been thinking about his ideas. It was a long time before I wrote about warmth and growth and connections again. By then this story had revealed new levels of meaning, and Barnes had disappeared into the Calgary streets.

Even at the time the political climate was colder than it seemed. Some of Betkowski's supporters believed Anthony Barnes's story reflected her warmth and political generosity. I was skeptical and apparently should have made that skepticism more plain. She was the only candidate to start her campaign talking about Margaret Thatcher as an inspiration in financial policy. Hope and momentary friendliness might have made Barnes's life happier for awhile. They were unlikely to change it permanently. In the end it was never clear how much difference there really was between the leadership candidates, or what would be settled by their contest.

The leadership would be decided by popular ballot among party members. Betkowski finished one vote ahead of Klein in the first ballot November 28. Klein beat her easily in the runoff December 5, relying on strength in Calgary and the rural constituencies. The same coalition would give the Conservatives the provincial election half a year later.

Don Getty announced his resignation September 9. He had always liked surprises. He managed to make this a surprise too. There had been signs for months he was preparing to leave but who could have expected him to leave just as the national referendum over the Charlottetown Accord was getting under way? He had invested much of his personal reputation in the Accord. It needed a strong backer in Alberta. And he began the campaign by cutting off his own political legs.

People made disparaging jokes about Getty. This strange timing confirmed everything they said. Getty never seemed to care much about what outsiders said. He seemed to operate inside a binding core of loyalty. People could have said anything or nothing when Getty announced he was leaving. Deputy Premier Jim Horsman said, "Don Getty is in my view one of the most outstandingly truthful and decent people I have ever known." He said it effortlessly, the way people repeat one of the few things they are sure of in an uncertain world.

Getty's seven years in office saw him career through rough circumstances, occasional success, family difficulties, a ballooning government debt, a dangerous ulcer operation, trouble with arthritic knees damaged in his football career, gaffes like a wife-beating joke he told for no particular reason at the start of the 1989 election campaign, stunning displays of coolness and skill at Conservative conventions where his leadership seemed perennially in danger. He could stiff-arm people when he thought it necessary but he could also seem like a nice guy and maybe he was.

The Conservatives who wanted him gone—the most important were probably clustered around Calgary—seemed to think of him as some kind of goofy alien. You could argue it both ways.

He did things no one could understand. He did many other things which seemed to reflect mainstream Alberta. The things that went most wrong never seemed to be his fault alone. Financial disasters like NovAtel, Principal Group, and a failed magnesium plant in High River were the product of general government policy or an entire political generation's way of doing things. That generation's day was running out. The patronage and the insults like the 30 percent pay raise could be read as looting by people who knew their time was coming to an end. Getty was only their chief.

How much effect did he have on events? How much of a hand did he have in things like the decision to present a phoney balanced budget in 1991? How much of a hand did he have in the decision to back off from the cuts to education and health grants after the spring of 1987? Were such decisions ultimately made by one or two or three men? Exactly why were they made? It was astonishing that these questions could remain open. Albertans never really knew how they were governed.

All they knew for sure was that life had taken some hard shots at a man governing a province in a mean time. Getty had seemed to come out stronger. He walked away able to laugh at everyone who had called him the new Harry Strom, the gentlemanly but ineffective premier who had led Social Credit into political oblivion in 1971 after thirty-six straight years of power in Alberta. In the fall of 1992 it seemed that Getty would have the last and best laugh. Things were lining up for his successor to become the new Harry Strom.

Getty turned out to be the last of a Conservative dynasty all right, one that merely ended in a unique and unexpected way. Instead of being defeated, it was replaced by a recast version of itself. Getty arranged the timing. He was just a guy who liked Jack Benny and duck hunting and horse races and did the best he could, which was often better than most people thought.

Even in leaving he chose his own mysterious path. At his last news conference he had to comment on the rejection of the Charlottetown Accord. The failure of the constitutional agreement meant the failure of his personal dream of creating an elected Senate. His party had simultaneously lost a byelection to the Liberals in what should have been the safe constituency of Three Hills. He looked no more worried than if he had just spilled a little coffee onto an old tablecloth.

He said he was disappointed about the Constitution and it was time to move on; he had watched the returns on television until the result became obvious and then had switched to Monday Night Football. About the byelection loss he said, "As a matter of fact, while I've been premier we've won four out of seven. It's like the World Series."

Out of all the poignancy of the last few weeks he really remembered only one special moment—the decision to put his name and number up at Commonwealth Stadium with the greatest of the Canadian Football League's Edmonton Eskimos: "What a thrill to be on the Wall of Honour . . . My grandchildren and their grandchildren can see that."

He said Canadians seemed to be groping for their future but they would get by: "For me, I'm going hunting with my son, and my dog."

That was the last thing he said. He left through the side door of the shoebox of a news conference room in the Legislature basement. He never explained whether he knew what would come in his place. At the time, possibilities seemed open. They were all bound by certain realities. Maybe even by plans already made.

Klein was a mid-level minister but he gained ground quickly as the leadership campaign got under way. Agriculture Minister Ernie Isley and Tourism Minister Don Sparrow had already asked him to run and arranged meetings with other members of the legislature. Nearly half the Conservative caucus, in particular the rural members, lined up to support him. He already knew them and many of their constituents.

Klein cultivated ordinariness. Yet he was not ordinary. He had gone out to live some weeks or months—accounts were contradictory—at the Blackfoot (now Siksika) reserve east of Calgary. Not only was that unusual, he even adopted elements of the Native view of spirituality. As premier years later he would still pack an eagle feather in his suitcase when he travelled.

He was different from other people at work too. His reporting years became the source of newsroom yarns. Once during his time at CFCN, he treated a derelict to a night in the penthouse suite of a Calgary hotel, courtesy of the station. A stay in the penthouse included a free round of golf at a prestigious local country club. Klein went out the next day and did what witnesses called a hilarious story on the derelict touring the clipped greens and button-down clubhouse. He covered city hall but, instead of talking only to politicians and city bureaucrats, he picked up information from bikers, prostitutes, road workers. He built a reputation for knowledge. One story had councillors ordering a grate installed in an air vent because Klein was crawling inside and listening to closed-door sessions.

Alcohol was part of his life by this time. He admitted to interviewers early in his political career that he had been convicted of impaired driving in 1977 and paid a $300 fine. Police were called to his house in December 1978 and he ended up spending the night in the drunk tank. A guard said that Klein cooperated going in but started to rattle the cell gate, holler at the staff, and demand cigarettes and a phone call to his wife. An official report had him betting the guard that the guard beat up prisoners, and inviting the guard to come into the cell and "mark him up." The guard said he later saw Klein standing in a stupor and turned the lights up and down with a rheostat—to check for a reaction, he said. Klein got out that morning. Two hours later he telephoned in a complaint, saying the guard had antagonized him with the lights and with obscene gestures.

Once he was supposed to do a live report from a convention he was covering but he went missing. His boss was frantically searching for him by telephone. Klein's cameraman and a radio reporter found him lying in a hallway, halfway into an elevator, the doors squeezing against his legs. The radio reporter happened to be Dennis Anderson, who later became a Conservative cabinet minister. A hand up, a quick trip to a washroom for a splash in the shower, and Klein was on the air fifteen minutes later giving a first-rate report on the weekend's happenings.

If you concentrated on the drinking you could miss his ability to get the job done well. In his last year at CFCN he wrote and produced a half-hour story about a dying cancer patient's reaction to a new chemical treatment. It won a western Canadian television award.

Behind the ability to get the job done was a strong streak of sheer determination. He liked to win. His brother Lynn remembered, "Ralph was the marble king at school. You didn't play marbles with Ralph unless you wanted to lose all your marbles."

He could take advantage of situations and now he had one he could exploit. The Conservative party had switched from the traditional system of electing a leader at a delegate convention to a provincewide vote open to any party member. Memberships were for sale up to the closing of polls December 5. The leadership vote had been recast as a popular election. Only Klein had been taking extra trouble to meet voters across the province.

The campaign started slowly and was overshadowed by other events in the first few weeks. Auditor General Donald Salmon released his report on NovAtel September 25. Rick Orman released the interim report on Toward 2000 a few days later. He had been acting as chair of the cabinet's economic development committee and this seemed to be his political baby.

On October 13, Orman and Getty announced the most sweeping changes to Alberta's oil and gas royalty system since 1973. It was easy to read the royalty announcement as a sweetener from Orman for the Calgary energy establishment to which he had strong ties. But the announcement struck much more deeply.

This was the final admission that the great boom of the 1970s and early 1980s was over. It had been some ride—a wild ascent and heart-stopping fall of energy prices and real estate values, all wrapped together with the rise and fall of Conservative party support and of a policy of provincial empire building. Now the Alberta government was introducing a permanently lower royalty for any new pools of oil as well as other concessions for existing or inactive wells. The announcement amounted to a tortured admission that the days of easily found oil were gone.

No one explained where the province would find the money it was giving up. Johnston had said in his spring budget speech the province would have to find $275 million a year over the next four years to balance the budget. He implied the money would be found through spending cuts. Now the province was cutting royalties by an amount nearly as large. The royalty cuts were estimated to take nearly $240 million a year out of provincial revenues. The cuts approximately doubled the budget pressure. If the province wanted to balance its budget with spending cuts it was looking now at cutting more than $500 million a year.

At the same time, oil and gas firms were finally enjoying dropping interest rates and the falling value of the Canadian dollar. A lower Canadian dollar was good for the industry because all exports to the U.S. were priced in U.S. dollars; the lower the value of the Canadian dollar, the more Canadian dollars each unit of exports brought in. The industry's own figures suggested the dropping dollar would bring in more cash than the royalty cuts would.

Two weeks after the royalty announcement, the Conservatives lost a byelection in central Alberta. On the same night, Albertans, with voters in most other provinces, rejected the Charlottetown Accord, which had been supported by the entire Conservative hierarchy.

Every strain in the Alberta political system—the economic strain of the end of the oil and gas boom, the civil and political strains embodied in the constitutional debate, the crushing of the image of competent management after NovAtel—had come to a head in the middle of the Conservative leadership campaign.

But within the apparent collapse new ideas were emerging.

The day after the referendum and the byelection loss, Klein signed a letter to Bob Saari, vice-president of the Canadian Manufacturers' Association. He said he was responding to a CMA request of September 28 for answers to ten questions posed to the Conservative leadership candidates. Klein did not frame the answers himself. He attached his letter to a six-page statement prepared October 19 by the policy development and co-ordination branch of the Department of Economic Development and Trade.

Klein may never have read the entire statement. He never really explained how a party leadership candidate could get campaign help from a departmental policy unit.

There were clear political links, however. Economic Development Minister Peter Elzinga was working for Klein. Elzinga had earlier installed his former fellow member of Parliament, Stan Schellenberger, as head of policy development in the department. It was this department which had been writing a new manufacturing strategy and coordinated Toward 2000.

How much earlier had the work begun? Who was doing it? What links had been formed between government policy analysts, politicians, and outside advisers? Those questions too were never answered. Economic Development was one of the most silent departments in an unusually secretive government—and the one most obviously employing the government's political friends. The letter set out what became the agenda for Klein's government.

The letter to the CMA said it was time to end the machinery and equipment tax, a $170-million annual property tax on major industrial plants.

It said corporate tax rates were competitive but might be brought down more.

It talked about a smaller cabinet and fewer government departments; less overlap with federal agencies, particularly in environmental regulation; less regulation for private industry; privatization of government operations. The last point came with the added thought that some parts of government could pay more of their own way through user fees.

It held out the possibility of a sales tax: "Before new sources of revenue such as a sales tax are considered, every effort must be made to reduce the deficit by cutting expenditures and improving the productivity of program delivery. This means some hard decisions will be required as to the level of health care, education, and social services which Albertans expect and how these services will be financed."

It suggested an independent commission could review Alberta government finances and make recommendations about where revenue should come from, adding, "There is a serious structural imbalance which will further deteriorate unless a clear strategy for action is developed and implemented in the near term. There is little room left for increased taxation on income if we are to remain competitive. The larger issue as to whether in principle we should be taxing wealth creation activities or consumption should be dealt with by this independent review."

It said the government, as a matter of principle, should not bail out struggling businesses, but might still help kick start key projects: "Oil sands development, for example, may require some degree of government participation. . . ."

It outlined an economic policy based on global trade, on attracting international investment, on linking education more directly to employer needs and on upgrading resources instead of plunging into industries completely new to Alberta.

There were several remarkable things about this letter.

It set out the map which the Alberta government followed. Virtually everything came about and became the centre of the government's public strategies. Within eighteen months the only element missing was the oil sands plant.

It must have been based on extensive policy work already done, possibly as early as 1991. It indicated how economic development had become the core of the government's thinking and purpose—social policy would be made to fit around the economy's need for targeted education and low taxes.

It was anonymous. It was far more complete than anything Klein ever said during the leadership campaign to a general audience. It was written months before any of Klein's public consultations, although it did come after the initial work on Toward 2000 Together. It seemed to set out a common ground for all nine Conservative leadership candidates—none seriously differed with the ideas in the CMA letter and some spoke in ways suggesting they too had been exposed to some of the ideas in it.

None of this policy advice became public until months later, after the letter had made its way to the Liberals.

The campaign meandered along. The first month slipped by in a snooze. Only a few hundred party members seemed to be paying attention. Fund raisers were finding it difficult to pry money out of anyone's hands, creating an advantage for the candidates with the wealthiest backers and best connections.

Klein had shown himself tougher and smarter and better prepared than many had expected. His first major appearance at a forum in Grande Prairie saw him talking knowledgeably—presumably on the strength of a briefing from local MLA Walter Paszkowski—about the area's canola industry. Canola was not a subject he would normally know anything about. All through the campaign Klein showed an ability to soak up briefings and to reproduce the information in a personable and easily understood way on a platform.

Betkowski had shown strength, too, and was doing surprisingly well on Klein's home ground in Calgary. She had not been making much impression in rural Alberta. It was largely foreign ground to her. Early in the campaign she visited Stettler and, among other stops, was scheduled to tour the livestock auction mart. The plainspoken cattle crowd did not know she was supposed to be coming and did not seem impressed. One twenty-ish cowboy called the forty-three-year-old minister an "old bag" and lumped her in with everyone else he saw running down the whole country: "If she's a politician she must be drunk." She was late. Her staff said she finally did visit but the stop could not have lasted more than a couple of minutes. Betkowski had spent her life in affluent west-central Edmonton. Now she had to wander among people wearing jeans and quilted vests, people with open and watchful eyes and hockey-player toughness. She never did that as convincingly as Klein.

The other candidates were Rick Orman, Consumer and Corporate Affairs Minister Elaine McCoy, Social Services Minister John Oldring, Culture Minister Doug Main, former education minister Dave King, professional futurist Ruben Nelson, and Lloyd Quantz, a farmer and agricultural consultant who lived in the country but worked in an office in Calgary.

Their campaign teams were trying and largely failing to raise enough money for telephone sweeps through the Conservative membership list while the candidates tried sporadically to talk about the future. Nelson was trying to indoctrinate the party into the theory of change and adapting to change. Main and Oldring were cabinet ministers in their early forties apparently staking political ground for the future. Orman launched his campaign with a barrage of 1990s buzzwords—innovation, excellence, strategic alliance, diversification, global marketplace, and the like.

The odd woman out was McCoy. She had stood apart from the government since her election in 1986. She was a lawyer and a veteran activist in former premier Peter Lougheed's constituency of Calgary-West. In government she had cut a marginal figure. McCoy was the minister identified with unpopular causes such as adding homosexuality to the list of prohibited grounds for discrimination under Alberta's human rights act. She had been known to make fun of Getty's bald spot after camera operators were told not to take shots of him from behind. She regularly spoke for women's right to equality in the workplace. She repeatedly talked about the importance of women, immigrants, and various minorities to Canada's future labour market. And she was routinely ignored by most of the Progressive Conservative caucus.

Yet when the leadership began she staked a position as the only candidate to offer a detailed plan. She kept a stack of copies of Ted Gaebler and David Osborne's book *Reinventing Government* in her office for handing out to anyone who was interested. She talked not only about the changing economy and work force but about reorganizing the government. She proposed having each department run by a board consisting of the minister, the deputy minister, several members of the legislature, and people from the private sector. She wanted to balance the budget with the help of $1.5 billion in new user fees. She floated ideas for a radical restructuring designed to shrink the government permanently. That could be accomplished partly by having private industry build projects such as roads and pay for the investment with tolls or other fees. She ended up largely ignored by Conservative voters, just as she had been by the Conservative caucus.

There was more than talk in McCoy's plan. She had apparently pioneered in 1986 the budgeting method the entire government would adopt eight years later under Klein.

In the Consumer and Corporate Affairs and later in the Labour Department she went to budget approval meetings with a departmental business plan. It was remarkable that one minister could go her own way with a radically different budgeting technique, and that no one outside cabinet would really become aware of the experiment until someone leaked a copy of the Labour Department's five-year business plan to the New Democrats in 1992.

The change began a few months after she was elected and named minister of consumer and corporate affairs. McCoy said she had been scheduled to take the department's 1987-88 budget proposal to the cabinet committee known as the Treasury Board on September 1, 1986. She saw the plan on the last Friday in August: "They showed me a budget and I said this isn't a budget. . . . There was no relationship between expenditures and revenues . . . I looked at it and it just made ultimately no sense. So I phoned them and said, 'I'm sorry, you're not filing this. We'll get together and go over this and I'll explain to the treasurer we're going to be late.' "

She said she wanted to apply standard business methods. She wanted objectives, measurement of results at the end of specified periods, and changes in staffing policy such as performance appraisals.

In 1987 she hired as her deputy minister Robin Ford, an Oxford graduate who had drifted into government after immigrating to Canada. He later changed departments with her. Ford had begun his life in Canada as a teacher. Then he worked for three years as a producer for the Canadian Broadcasting Corporation. His later career took him from the federal civil service in the Northwest Territories to advising for the United Nations on Africa and the Caribbean, then back to senior consulting and civil service jobs in the Territories before joining Alberta's Municipal Affairs Department in 1979. "He cottoned on to my ideas, which was very gratifying," said McCoy, "and then implemented them and then got very good at it."

McCoy said, "We were able to reduce management by 50 percent . . . We were able in some instances to raise revenue." The revenue came from user fees. She and Ford also started spinning off what were called delegated regulatory organizations. One of the first was the provincial insurance council. The idea was to have regulation done by bodies ultimately answering to the minister but acting independently in their dealings with the public. They never got to full self-funding in either department although their plans headed in that direction. Still, McCoy said the business plans clarified what departments were doing and helped in financial decisions: "It does make cutting easier. It also makes it very much more evident when you're cutting too close to the bone."

During the leadership contest McCoy had seemed a lonely arguer for strange, new ideas. She said later it was not her position to tell others what to do.

In a number of ways, the Klein revolution resembled the McCoy plan. Was it only McCoy's plan? Some of the ideas were hers. Some may have been discussed in cabinet.

Betkowski took a different path. She had come up through the "soft" ministries of education and health. She had worked most of her life inside the government, starting as a ministerial aide in the 1970s. She said she would end patronage, ask for a cut in legislature pay, and recruit back to the party the members who had strayed—as close as any of the leaders ever came to criticizing Getty. She left an impression of liberal tendencies but talked about winning back the natural conservatives who had drifted from the party. Like Klein, she talked about commissioning a report on government finances, making symbolic cuts in the size of the cabinet and going from there. She always stayed one step away from being pinned down. She went through the campaign saying things like, "I am going to ask our party to change, not to attack our past but to address our future at the most fundamental levels."

Klein talked as vaguely about the future as Betkowski. He said he wanted to build a consensus in Alberta on how to balance the budget. He said he would like to persuade local authorities—health, education, municipalities—and their unions to sign up for a few years of pain. He talked about an economic policy founded on the notion of building on Alberta's existing strengths.

No one knew in detail what this meant. Klein stayed away from providing more detail. He allowed himself to say he liked the idea of user fees in health care. He carefully appealed to rural voters in ways the other contenders could not or would not do; he even promised to fight for an expansion of southern Alberta's costly irrigation systems despite his tendency to look at cuts elsewhere.

How did he plan to sign people up for a program of pain when his party had created NovAtel and other disasters and had let deficit spending get out of control? He had a simple answer: "We'll just have to say, 'We all learn from our mistakes.' "

To sell a message like that the government needed a leader people might willingly forgive. It was a matter of sheer personality. Klein had a track record in public forgiveness. Of them all, he was the one candidate who had made mistakes in public, and come back. People tended to trust him.

It was a good thing. At a rally in Edmonton at the end of November an unknown woman wearing an Orman button stood up and asked, in front of fifteen hundred people, whether Klein's wife had ever been admitted to a battered women's shelter. The question apparently arose from a vaguely worded report on Klein's night in jail in 1978. The report mentioned delaying his release until his wife was "able to move out of the family home" but there was no suggestion that this had in fact happened. Anonymous people had been trying to peddle a copy of the document to reporters and had been smearing Klein with other rumours in calls to his supporters.

Klein shouted back, "It is absolutely not true, and that is absolute baloney and crap. It is the most vicious kind of smut that I have been subjected to, me and my wife."

He denounced the "nameless, faceless, spineless, gutless individuals" spreading the rumours and won loud applause. Colleen Klein later said, "I think that the person who said this comes from a very desperate camp and it's not worth comment. It's garbage."

Other politicians have been sunk by dirty tactics. Klein had the crowd on his side, the media on his side, and no one mentioned the incident again.

On December 5, the Conservatives gathered in Edmonton's Agricom to hear the results flowing in from the runoff ballot. Betkowski had astonished the Klein camp the week before in the first ballot by finishing one vote ahead. The outcome seemed uncertain but Klein won easily in the resulting head-to-head contest.

The theories followed fast. Some said Albertans could not abide a woman leader. Others said that Klein workers had telephoned the rural party members with a dirty whisper campaign, spreading stories about lesbians working for Betkowski and a secret plan to shut down rural hospitals. No one really knew.

Klein had a streak of toughness. He could draw on many qualities, which is one of the signs of leadership. When he jumped up on hearing the clinching announcement that made him leader, the man who stood by his right shoulder was Herb Belcourt, a Peter Elzinga supporter who had campaigned hard for Klein and who, a few weeks later, received the first minor appointment from what was supposed to be a government free of patronage. When the candidates climbed up on the Agricom stage, Klein looked around at the celebrating crowd and said, with either calculated or accidental cruelty, "Wasn't this fun, Nancy?"

But no one needed stories of dirty campaigning to explain this win. Klein took most of the vote in Calgary and the rural constituencies. He had taken more than 90 percent of the vote the last time he had run for mayor of Calgary in 1986. He had confidants in the city's corporate offices. He had the backing of most of the rural Conservative members of the legislature. He had the only rural-oriented campaign and the only strong history of showing up in rural constituencies. He came across as ordinary at a time when Albertans and other Canadians were celebrating a constitutional referendum result which many interpreted as a defeat for the country's "elites."

Betkowski had grown up in the family of a prominent Edmonton physician. She had studied for a year at Laval University in Quebec, had spent most of her working life at the top levels of provincial government, had spoken for the Charlottetown Accord, had been the only cabinet minister to question Getty when he suggested it might be time to scrap bilingualism. She belonged to those "elites."

She also had a campaign team organized around some of the biggest heavyweights in the party—people like former provincial treasurer Lou Hyndman and longtime federal party official Susan Green. And the hospital stories had grounding in fact. Betkowski had just put in motion a plan to create regional health boards. She had not consulted the rural MLAs. They and their constituents were left wondering how many hospitals might end up shutting down or being converted to other uses. They would look for someone else they could trust.

The leadership would not be the last election decided like that.

Betkowski never settled with Klein. He dropped her.

She might have become treasurer. In her place, Klein installed Jim Dinning, who had worked his way up through the ministerial offices in the 1970s with Betkowski and who had been one of the few government members to back her leadership bid. He had been isolated on the presumed "liberal" wing of the party as well. Now he found himself riding a fast "up" escalator. Just as fast he emerged as a leading spokesperson for hard budget cuts.

Klein dropped Main from the cabinet too. Klein kneecapped anyone who had opposed him, and Main had made a particular impression during the campaign with a crack about nobody wanting a "smoking, drinking, paving" premier. But Klein later appeared at a fund-raising dinner to help Main offset campaign debts likely in the fifty or seventy thousand dollar range. Main seemed the worst off of the candidates financially and he became a radio talk-show host.

Quantz said he had lived up to the principles he was preaching and spent only about fifty thousand dollars. He had also said in the last week of the campaign he would support Betkowski. His explanation took on a heavy colour of ambiguous irony over the next few years: "I think Ralph's a fun guy, but he's backed by a lot of people who want to keep the province the same as it's been."

None of the contenders said exactly how much they spent. Party rumours had Betkowski and Klein spending well over $300,000, and perhaps none of the major candidates breaking even. Klein did release a twenty-page list of donors who had given him $359,000. Among the heaviest contributions were $10,000 each from Tony Koo and K. H. C. Ngan of Calgary, $7,500 from Atco of Calgary; $5,000 from Bennett Jones Verchere, Peter Lougheed's law firm; $5,000 from Stewart Green, a large Calgary-based retail landlord; $5,000 from the law firm Field and Field Perraton; $1,000 from developer Trizec Corporation; and $1,000 from his father Phil. Klein said he had not seen the more than five hundred names on the list and had not been involved in raising money.

Oldring had to cancel a fund-raising dinner but went to Mexico on subsequent consulting contracts for Economic Development. The first contract was explained as the result of a commitment made by Don Sparrow shortly before Sparrow's death in a car crash.

Orman returned to the Calgary oil industry. He became director of a firm developing oil spill cleaning technology. The firm became one of the last recipients of a provincial loan guarantee. Orman's campaign team also ended up in an unusual business deal with Orman's Calgary-Montrose constituency association. The constituency executive paid more than twenty thousand dollars for assets from Orman's leadership run. The primary asset was a list of supporters. The next constituency president found the cupboard bare when he looked for campaign money for Orman's successor as Conservative candidate in Montrose in 1993.

McCoy quickly set up shop as a management consultant. King and Nelson went back to private careers.

Don Getty took a suite in Edmonton's tallest office tower and began sorting his papers and writing his memoirs. He had gone virtually unmentioned through the last weeks. There was no official goodbye. The party newsletter ran one small photograph of him in its postleadership issue.

Several days after the final ballot, Klein won $100,000 in a hospital raffle. He was one of those people, the lucky kind, the kind other people say have an aura around them.

6

Government

The Edmonton Journal
December 12 1992

If Ralph Klein has enough time he may leave as deep an imprint on Alberta as Ronald Reagan left on the United States.

The thought of a Klein Revolution may boggle the mind.

For one thing, the new premier appears to lack the full-blown ideological agenda that Reagan brought to the presidency, and cannot influence as many things. He is not even as good as a communicator.

But he is being pushed by circumstances. . . .

December 16, 1992

We thought we had a new government and we got the Calgary Stampede instead—a wild, brawling, ragged, bruising extravaganza full of show-biz, manure and people getting hurt.

It was Premier Ralph Klein's first day running a government. Sometimes it was rough, always it was a spectacle.

There were mix-ups. Klein started introducing the wrong ministers at the swearing-in ceremony. Release of the cabinet list was delayed a couple of hours, purportedly by last-minute legal issues surrounding the amalgamation of some departments.

There were Indians in full regalia at the Legislature Building reception—a crowded affair that felt like a midway and looked like the inauguration of a shirt-sleeved populism. The coffee ran out early but the tables were loaded with more than enough shortbread and Christmas cake.

There were stunning accidents. Nancy Betkowski's political career seemed to crash in flames after a week-long nosedive. Jim Dinning, a more or less forgotten man for six years under Don Getty, a sidelined minister who backed the wrong leadership candidate (Betkowski), filled the gap and became the tenuous link between Klein and the Betkowski wing of the party. He finds himself unexpectedly with the opportunity of a lifetime.

There were scenes of dogged determination—Bob Bogle, the unfortunate former minister of social services, has come back to the innermost circle of power like some tough Russian diplomat back from Siberian exile.

There was drama—a newly promoted Dianne Mirosh gave Dennis Anderson (former minister of consumer and corporate affairs) a heartfelt kiss and hug of encouragement in the hallway of Government House as he dealt with the sudden end to his cabinet career.

As always, there were telling little snippets.

Klein promoted some clearly talented backbenchers such as Halvar Jonson, the new education minister from Ponoka-Rimbey, and Brian Evans, the new environment minister from Banff-Cochrane.

He neglected some courtesies, however. At least one former minister, Elaine McCoy, learned she was out by reading the news release that went around to government offices Tuesday morning.

Public Works Minister Ken Kowalski could have asked for a new portfolio. Instead he intensified his holdings in pork-barrelling and propaganda—a reflection of his interests, one assumes.

Deputy premier Peter Elzinga will run a new Government Reorganization Secretariat. The news release acknowledged that moving to fewer departments will result in "human resource issues." Effective translation: civil servants will disappear.

If they disappear mostly in Edmonton, the local paranoia about Klein will fester. Klein apparently puts a high priority on handling layoffs well: he named himself responsible for the Personnel Administration Office.

It all looks interesting. Still, Klein is stuck dealing with some long unacknowledged disasters.

Gainers looks to be high on the list. Two of the ministers in on that deal from the start—Elzinga and Agriculture Minister Ernie Isley—are top figures in the Klein government.

There is also the embarrassingly long and expensive goodbye of Don Getty.

Who would have thought that Getty would hand out the last patronage crumbs to himself?

Refusing to represent Stettler in the legislature, setting up an expensive suite at the top of Manulife Place to sort out his papers and start his autobiography—it's tawdry, it's insulting to taxpayers. These guys get too many ideas watching U.S. presidents.

It looked almost American, Steffens. A lot of things in Alberta look almost American.

You could look around the main rotunda of the Legislature Building and imagine what the records describe as a similar scene in the White House in 1828 when Andrew Jackson was inaugurated and western frontiersmen came to the party enjoying, among other things, a cheese as big as a wagon wheel. Or possibly the scene resembled the excited coming and going of young reformers in a new century when a vigorous Theodore Roosevelt took over a drained and self-satisfied capital.

You were there for Roosevelt. You would have recognized what was going on in Edmonton.

Those were passing impressions. In the end the scene was pure Alberta.

It looked like rural populism but there was something else afoot.

Klein had become premier because he swept the rural Conservative vote in the party leadership ballot. He had worked with the support of nearly every rural MLA. His government began its life by throwing open the doors of the Legislature Building and letting the people in.

Four months later the same government was travelling on a course laid out largely by government insiders and a network of business executives, themselves all coping with a world which had changed.

Klein showed a rare ability—the ability to cross into those different worlds and remain credible in each of them.

He could fuse people and power. Between December 1992 and May 1993 he did exactly that. He grasped the two discontents which had corroded the old Progressive Conservative government—a crumbling faith in politics and politicians, and a crumbling faith in the government's ability to manage. And he began to soothe them. Sometimes he exploited them. That was visible.

He also began to oversee the creation of something new and far less visible. I made it out only a piece at a time.

Klein had been elected Conservative leader December 5. He effectively became premier of Alberta at the same time. One week later he was imposing change so rapidly that it became possible to think in terms of revolution. After everything that had happened in 1992 I should have been more sure, and more aware, of how fast the restructuring could come.

The basics came directly from the plan he followed when he first beat incumbent Ross Alger to become mayor of Calgary.

He cultivated local business leaders and leaned on long friendships in places like Calgary's Chinese community.

He practised a political leadership based largely on communication. A lawyer attracted to his campaign team said, "The city has lacked the common touch. And Klein will bring politics back to the people." Klein saw the mayor's job in much the same terms. He went into office saying exactly the sort of thing he would say later in provincial politics: "I interpret my mandate as a vote of confidence in me to be able to talk to people, to listen to people, to become somewhat personally involved in their problems, and to act on their behalf."

He also showed from the start he could be hardnosed. The civic unions disliked Alger and endorsed Klein's mayoral campaign. Klein did not embrace them. He said the unions had little influence in his win. Half a year into his first term, some bus drivers walked off on a one-day wildcat strike. Klein said any drivers who did so again would be fired and the city would hold the union responsible for the work stoppage. Three months later some neighbourhood opposition cropped up against a proposed site for the new arena which would become the Saddledome. Klein said the real people were not opposed to development. He said the only criticism was coming from "community mercenaries" and "misguided academics."

He scored his first international coup when Calgary was bidding for the 1988 Winter Olympics . Klein called on his Blackfoot friends to go to Montreal with him and make Olympics head Juan Antonio Samaranch an honourary member of their nation. Others in the Calgary delegation worried about the imposing Samaranch's reaction. But Klein knew how to reach people. Samaranch got the title and a headdress, and was delighted. The local leaders on the Olympics committee were delighted too, and impressed by Klein's insight.

He had been in office only three months when a national television crew taped a documentary on him. They described him as one of Canada's most unusual mayors.

After a year, skeptical city officials had developed respect. So had others. The director of a coalition of inner-city communities said, "He seems to be a very, very fast learner. He picks things up quickly and has had better control of council than Alger did." Alger had been watching from his new job at an office furnishings firm. He said, "I think he's done well, to tell you the truth."

Klein spent most of the 1980s as mayor of what was becoming an international city. He won his second and third elections with more than 90 percent of the vote. One of his big tasks was to help the city prepare for the Olympics. He did for the Games what he was doing for local politics generally.

The local organizing committee was running into trouble. Volunteers were dissatisfied and communications were poor. Klein helped shake the committee out of what some read as aloofness and arrogance. A few years later he had exactly that task to perform with the province's aging Conservative government.

But his biggest test was probably the first drying up of the boom which had seen tens of thousands of people migrating into the city and the city spending money fast to keep up. In Klein's first year as mayor the National Energy Program rocked the petroleum industry, the U.S. natural gas market dried up, interest rates soared over 20 percent and a worldwide recession began. Calgary's rapid growth stopped. The city brakes screeched on in 1982. A few days before Christmas that year, the city announced it would lay off more than five hundred workers.

Klein said the staff and spending cuts would result in less service: "It won't be a Cadillac service but it will be a good, adequate level of service and still offset our deficit." The soothing words about an "adequate level of service" would also have echoes a little over a decade later.

Klein led an effort to have some of the cutting take place with the cooperation of city workers. It ran into trouble but on the whole he thought it worked well. Years later he seemed to look back on the experience as a model. Watching him were other community leaders such as alderman Art Smith, a businessman who later won election to Parliament as a Conservative and later still became one of Klein's close advisers in provincial affairs.

Klein got into his share of scrapes. His mother said, the night of his first election, he was too thin-skinned to be mayor. But he got out of the scrapes too. The most famous recovery followed his complaint about the eastern "creeps and bums" coming to Calgary during the boom in search of easy money or easy crime; the controversy led to a well-received speaking tour in Central Canada and a public relations coup for the city. But it was more than that. He had a knack for living down failures, and for smoothing things over with potential enemies. He verbally attacked Municipal Affairs Minister Marvin Moore a number of times for not handing Calgary hundreds of millions of dollars to finish a light rail transit line. He said Moore represented rural Alberta and obviously knew little about Calgary's needs. Ten years later, Moore enthusiastically became Klein's provincial campaign manager.

Between August 1980 and the end of his first term in late 1983 he demonstrated nearly every instinct and every political tactic he would use as premier of Alberta.

The rest were tailored to new circumstances.

Klein began by announcing a new legislature committee system. The committees consolidated the position of backbench MLAs who had powerfully supported Klein's leadership bid. The new system involved them more in the creation of government decisions. It clarified what much of the party had rejected when it voted against Betkowski. It also signalled Klein's intention to keep firm control—all members of the new standing policy committees were Conservatives.

Under Lougheed and Getty, the Conservatives had always prided themselves on running a government in which major decisions were cleared at meetings of all the Conservative MLAs. No outsider could ever really be sure how decisions were made.

By 1992, if not earlier, the caucus discussion sometimes amounted to nothing more than being presented with a bill or a policy decision and being asked, "How do you like it?" MLAs said after Klein's victory that they had not even known at times what questions to ask. The mechanics of changing a decision were complicated. It took a back and forth discussion between a caucus committee and a cabinet committee plus final approval by both the full cabinet and full caucus. Al Hyland, a veteran MLA, said, "You could change it but it would take a lot of work."

One of the most grinding irritants had been Betkowski's plan to remake the health system by creating a small number of health regions. The proposed regional boards would almost certainly close an unknown number of rural hospitals—a source of jobs, pride, and feelings of personal safety across rural Alberta. One MLA who wanted to stay anonymous even after Klein's win said, "The process was out in the community before the MLAs knew about it."

Klein cemented in place a new decision-making path to prevent the same thing from happening again.

The rural MLAs felt they finally had their day in the sun. Stan Schumacher had been a Conservative member of Parliament for eleven years, one of the Albertans disaffected by both Joe Clark and the Ottawa establishment. He won election to the Alberta legislature in 1986.

"I've waited all my political life to feel really comfortable," he told an interviewer that January, shortly before being elected Speaker of the legislature. "Now I really feel comfortable. I've never had any influence. Now I have some influence."

The coalition which made Klein premier also moved to cement its place politically. A few days after the leadership vote, a committee of four Conservative MLAs released their newly drawn map of provincial electoral boundaries. It followed the rules the Conservative-dominated legislature had laid down—giving more weight to rural voters than to urban voters.

Klein took his first public step on January 21, 1993. He had Dinning appoint an independent financial review commission.

The commission broke the government out of a tailspin of confusion and distrust. By 1993 several stories about Alberta's financial state had been embedded into public talk. Some were contradictory. The province was hugely in debt; no it was not. The $12-billion Heritage Savings Trust Fund was generating $1 billion a year in investment income; the Heritage Fund had virtually disappeared. The province had a plan to balance the budget; it never had a plan.

The government turned to old acquaintances for help. Dinning appointed a respected figure from the Lougheed years to chair the commission— Marshall Williams, recently retired chair of TransAlta Utilities. The executive director was George Cornish. He had been a city commissioner in Calgary while Klein was mayor but had later joined the University of Calgary's management faculty. There were also five partners of accounting and management consulting firms, four of them from Calgary. Two oil industry executives and the financial head of Nelson Lumber Company in Lloydminster joined the team.

They did not hold public hearings. They studied the government's books and talked to government officials. They studied management changes undertaken in British Columbia. They also studied the financial statements of New Zealand, the first hint that anyone in Alberta might be looking at New Zealand as a possible model.

Meanwhile, Klein made Vance MacNichol, his former deputy minister in the Environment Department, the deputy minister of cabinet. They had built a loyal working relationship during the struggle to create a new environment law. MacNichol's appointment put a Klein ally in charge of the entire Alberta civil service.

Much of what was happening and would happen had been sketched out during the leadership campaign in the letter to the Canadian Manufacturers Association. The policy branch of the Economic Development Department had prepared that.

Another influence was Auditor General Donald Salmon. Salmon spent years recommending sharp changes in the way the government handled and reported its finances. He ran into stalling, but stalling was hardly a realistic option after the NovAtel report. Salmon said later that NovAtel had given him an opportunity to speak out more. Many of the changes Klein and Dinning brought about in their first months at the financial helm reflected Salmon's recommendations.

Six days after the financial review commission came the announcement of a far different body, a round table on the budget.

This round table would be the first of several. They would become key political tools—the crossover point between grassroots populism and decision making by an invisible leadership of corporate executives, cabinet ministers, and key bureaucrats.

Dinning appointed Norm Wagner and Ralph Young to co-chair the round table on the budget. The official material identified Wagner as a former president of the University of Calgary and Young as a well-known Edmonton business leader. They had other connections.

Wagner had grown prominent in the Calgary business world. He had been a volunteer with the organizing committee for the 1988 Winter Olympics in Calgary. That project had brought many Calgary leaders together and had been a grand success. It may have left them wondering what other enterprises they could take on—perhaps the reform of a provincial government?

Wagner was also a member of the provincial government's audit committee. These were private-sector observers who received the auditor general's report each year and commented on its findings for the treasurer. Wagner was no outsider.

Neither was Young. The vice-president of Melcor Developments of Edmonton, he was closely linked with Conservative circles. He had joined, for example, the board of directors of the Canadian Football League Edmonton Eskimos. The Eskimos were on a shuttle line between the Edmonton business community and the Progressive Conservative party; the same Conservative names kept popping up in all three organizations. More significantly, Young was a member of the provincial audit committee too.

The round table was supposed to function as an independent advisory group. The government had strong links with it from the start.

On February 6, Klein announced plans to cut six deputy ministers from the government's organization. The cut was supposed to help symbolize a determination to shave costs at the top levels of government first. Reducing the number of deputies was supposed to save $2.4 million but that number included entire office budgets. Some of the deputies could and did end up in other jobs. The cut of deputy ministers may have saved money mostly by a layoff of secretaries. The government never produced a final accounting.

At the same time the government said it would cut one thousand positions out of its approximately thirty thousand jobs in the civil service. It offered government workers bonuses for early retirement, voluntary quitting, and job-sharing.

This was the kinder side of a phenomenon that started in Alberta in 1983 when the construction industry suddenly shrank to about half the workforce needed during the boom. By the late 1980s, layoffs and wage cuts had become part of an international economic shift. Peter Pocklington had tried to tell Albertans the new era had arrived in 1986, when he informed workers on strike at his Edmonton meat packing plant they were competing with cheap labour in Taiwan. By the 1990s, small employers and large supermarket chains were demanding wage cuts all over Alberta. In 1993 the movement had spread to the Alberta public sector.

A few days after the civil service announcement, an Edmonton hospital group named Caritas laid off several dozen registered and licensed practical nurses. Caritas simultaneously announced it was hiring nurse attendants, and would be happy to take back licensed practical nurses in this role for $2.11 an hour less than they had been making. Smaller hospitals around Alberta had already started the same job shift.

Many events pointed in the same direction. About half the province's annual spending went to paying salaries in schools, colleges, universities, the health system, and municipalities.

This was the budget bull's-eye. The people living in it were teachers, nurses, assorted other professionals, and their support staff. There were not many ways to reduce what these people earned.

Klein had promised to balance the budget in four years and had ruled out tax increases. He had few choices left. At the time a 20 percent cut in spending seemed possible, but too brutal and damaging a method to be likely.

They kept up the pace. On March 1, Klein and Dinning announced a 5 percent cut in cabinet ministers' salaries. It applied only to the portion of their pay covering their ministerial duties, so it amounted to more like a 2 percent pay cut overall, but the government kept saying 5 percent. They cut deputy ministers' salaries by 2 percent. They said they wanted to freeze all civil service wages in upcoming negotiations. They said they would freeze all grants to schools, colleges, municipalities, and hospitals in 1993, despite an earlier promise that hospitals would receive 2.5 percent more.

Someone at the news conference asked Klein why he was breaking the previous year's commitment to hospital boards. He replied with an answer that would become a hallmark: "I wouldn't put it that way. That was then, this is now." Someone else asked whether the Conservatives could win an election on a platform like this. "Yes, sir," Klein said. "You just watch."

The opposition parties watched too. The Liberals were busy organizing for the coming election.

The New Democrats, hurt by the public attack on MLA pay and perks, discredited by lining up on the losing side of a constitutional debate for the second time in five years, had taken weeks to realize that Klein might be serious about his promise to eliminate the provincial deficit in four years.

At first they had scoffed. They had begun putting out position papers of their own. By early 1993 they had largely been written off. Their papers showed they did not have any idea about how to deal with more than about $1 billion out of a deficit chronically in the range of $2.5 billion.

Now they blundered into a nomination battle in Edmonton between veteran MLA Alex McEachern and prominent environment critic John McInnis. It should have been a showcase. It turned into one all right—a showcase of unhealthy pessimism.

The fight had been forced in part by a redistribution of electoral boundaries. New Democrat MLAs were concentrated in Edmonton and had been squeezed by the changes. There may have been personal rivalry between McEachern and McInnis as well but neither ever said so.

Four hundred people sat stifling in a hot, overcrowded school gym in west-central Edmonton March 13. It was one of the biggest nomination meetings the party had ever held. But people in the crowd were unimpressed.

"I don't think the NDP's doing that well," one man said. "I think Klein really has people enthused about the Conservatives. People think he's personable and they like him." A McInnis supporter liked Klein as a party leader— "probably the best of the three." An older man said, "I think people are looking to Decore for leadership. Of course, he doesn't really turn my crank."

Another older man wondered about the future: "I think the party needs a forceful leader."

That was not Ray Martin. Everyone called the former high school counsellor a nice guy. Almost everyone. Some active party members thought an insiders' group around him kept too tight control of the party. He sometimes stumbled over words. He spoke in a collection of stock phrases and no one ever said he had an aura around him. None of this had mattered so much until Klein took over the Conservative leadership.

Still, the party had other problems. You didn't need to see the campaign signs to know this was a New Democrat meeting. A woman hoping to win a nomination in another constituency wore a button reading Dead Men Don't Whine, a sentiment which appeared to write off half the electorate. A week earlier, one prospective Edmonton candidate had dropped out of the running because he could not get a no-smoking rule applied in the hallways at party meetings.

NDP fiscal policy boiled down to a version of "tax the rich" although it had become burningly clear that taxing the rich would not come close to balancing Alberta's budget. Every time New Democrats held a meeting they left reason to wonder whether this was a political organization or a self-help group for people with odd public fetishes.

McEachern won the nomination. He ended up spending several thousand dollars more than he raised for the spring election and lost the seat.

The budget round table met at Red Deer College March 29 and 30. At first the exercise seemed a curiosity. By the end of the second day it seemed somehow fraudulent, staged, dangerous.

Klein stayed away because Alberta people were supposed to be hashing things out for themselves. He arrived at the end and told the crowd, with equal parts of guile and charm, "To me, this is the fulfillment of a political campaign promise . . . and I thank you very much for helping me further my political agenda." Maybe it came out differently than he had intended, but with Klein you never knew.

The structure was simple. Dinning put the meeting into Wagner's hands. Wagner invited 140 participants. A handful of union leaders and others showed up. Most of the crowd represented the corporate and professional leadership of Alberta, with some municipal figures thrown in.

They broke into discussion groups of about a dozen, working their way through gaggles of college students into classrooms and small theatres. Each discussion group had a token representative or two to speak for the social services which stood to be cut or the people who stood to lose wages and jobs.

People spoke, moderators took down comments. No one could know exactly who had proposed what or how much support any one idea had generated. Ideas filtered through the moderators. The loose method left room for argument afterward. Some participants, including some of the business leaders most likely to be onside with the government, talked about probably having to turn to higher taxes or heavy user fees in about the third year of the four-year budget plan. Some even talked about a sales tax. Others would deny later that higher taxes had been seriously discussed. That was a sidelight anyway. The message coming from most of the discussion groups pointed to deep and fast cuts in government spending, as much as 30 percent in some departments. Klein said he would study the outcome.

No one in the government clarified the point of this meeting. On the surface it was a consultation with Albertans. But the participants did not represent a cross-section of the Alberta population.

Was it a false front of consultation? Was it an attempt to engage opinion leaders in a debate and send them back into their communities armed with information and purpose? Was it an attempt to gauge their mood? Was it an attempt to sell what had already been planned in a general way as early as the late summer or fall of 1991?

The round table may have filled any or all of these purposes. It also set a pattern for other round tables to come, a refinement of the Toward 2000 project probably combined with experience gained during the rewrite of the environment law. This was a new way of doing public business and conducting public debate. But for Alberta it was also an old way.

The round table essentially attempted to strip politics out of a very political task—the allocation of public money.

Alberta had always been a place of single-minded politics. There was always dissent but it was often squelched. Often Albertans were trying to close ranks against the federal government. One observer compared the province to a musk-ox herd always circling, facing outward to challenge intruders.

There was always a common economic interest; first wheat, then oil and gas. There was a local culture of boosterism and conformity.

The round table reflected and measured Alberta's political life.

What emerged was a picture of interested and talented people coming to grips for the first time with how their government operated. Their first instinct was to call for simple, across-the-board cuts in all departments. That fit the new management theory already emerging from the government side. It was borrowed from business experience in the recession of the early 1990s and it was called cutting The Stupid Way.

The theory was that refined methods took too long and created their own obstacles. What worked was announcing how much money was available and letting the organization adapt to harsh reality. The workbook handed to the round table participants quoted Michel Belanger, former chair of the National Bank, as saying, "I favour the stupid way."

The round table introduced another slogan: Hit the Wall. It was borrowed from New Zealand. Governments "hit the wall" when they wake up one morning to find out that international lenders will no longer give them more money. In New Zealand their choice when this happened was sudden and drastic spending cuts. To reinforce the message, everyone at Red Deer attended a showing of a CTV television documentary on what had happened when New Zealand "hit the wall." Cutting the "stupid way" and "hitting the wall" were not passing thoughts. These were ideas being endorsed and spread by two conference organizers who sat on the government's audit committee.

Not everyone was buying the package. When participants from different worlds disagreed it was like watching aliens meet at a convention on some faraway moon. Heather Smith, president of the United Nurses of Alberta, saw the pressure for public-sector wage cuts. She told her discussion group that many nurses had already been forced into part-time and on-call work without pensions or other benefits and were unhappy. Rod McBride, president of a Calgary oilfield service firm, told her, "I beg to differ. I think most women find it a nice way to do work."

But there was another lesson most of the participants did absorb, without even questioning what had happened. Along with the benefits of cutting "the stupid way" and the dangers of "hitting the wall" they learned that they were experts and most other Albertans were not.

Sherrold Moore, the Calgary oilman who had closely supported Klein through the leadership race and advised him even before that, came to Red Deer as one of the discussion moderators. He spoke the first day. He wondered whether Albertans really understood their situation: "The people in this room, sure, but the other two and a half million people outside in Alberta, we don't think they all understand."

At Red Deer, the government seized the budget deficit as its own issue. Since the late 1980s the government had been denying Alberta had a chronic financial problem. It had arguably lied about the province's financial state in the 1991 budget. The 1992 budget speech had edged toward admission. All through this time the people of Alberta had been far ahead. They had been drifting toward the Reform party, partly because of worries about public debt.

After the Red Deer round table most Albertans were followers again. From then on, members of the government and their closest supporters told the people of Alberta what was good for them.

Klein said the government was listening. He was its friendly face.

The government had another face that never went away. One day at the round table it appeared in the person of Community Development Minister Dianne Mirosh. She was watching a workshop, her arms folded and lips compressed. Ron Lajeunesse of the Canadian Mental Health Association told the other participants the government was planning to spend too much money building new hospitals. Mirosh interjected, "They're only replacements." Someone tried diplomacy. He noted the group's advice was hasty, free, and only partly informed: "Take it for what it's worth." Mirosh stared and said, "We will. I don't notice any of you have your name in for running this year."

The financial review commission reported March 31. The commissioners set down in writing what had become reasonably plain by 1989 or 1990, what former treasurer Dick Johnston had hinted at in circumspect language in his 1992 budget, what Klein's letter to the CMA had said in late 1992, what Dinning had come out and said in early 1993: Alberta had a structural deficit—revenues permanently smaller than expenditures.

The commission also put a final figure on the province's loss in loans and loan guarantees since 1985. It was $2.1 billion, the kind of number government ministers had been scoffing at in the legislature a couple of years earlier.

The key findings were stark and easy to understand:

The province is spending more than it can afford, has done so every year for the last eight years, and the rate of overspending is increasing. . . .

We must adopt a plan to eliminate annual deficits completely. Just reducing the annual deficit is not enough, since that only reduces the rate at which the level of our debt is growing. . . .

The province's annual deficit for 1992-93, forecast at approximately $3,170 million, continues a trend of increasing overspending on an annual basis since 1985-86. . . .

The problem can be linked to the dramatic drop of $3,040 million in resource revenue in 1986-87. Although there was a partial recovery in resource revenue in 1987-88, the downturn in oil and natural gas prices has kept resource revenues essentially flat, averaging approximately $2,300 million a year. The downturn in 1986 was not a cyclical move which can be expected to reverse. Indeed, it must be recognized that resource revenue will inevitably decline over the long term owing to the natural decline in producing fields.

There was no reduction in expenditures corresponding to the dramatic drop in revenue and, in fact, they have grown at an average rate to 1991-92 of 5.1 percent. Although this rate has been below the combined rate of inflation and population growth, it has been from a higher base, and at a higher rate, than revenue growth.

Klein and Dinning now had a believable bat in their hands to beat the message of the deficit and debt into Albertans' heads.

Yet even this authoritative statement on Alberta's financial position left room for argument. The commission's estimate of average spending growth included the astonishing rise in the cost of debt payments—from $36 million in 1985 to about $1.4 billion in 1993. By 1993 these payments accounted for more than 10 percent of the budget. The biggest and fastest increase in Alberta government spending had resulted from the government's own failure to control its debt.

Dinning usually avoided mentioning this. When he did mention it he lumped the debt payments in with health, education, and welfare spending.

Was Alberta's problem too much spending or not enough taxation? Tax rates were by far the lowest in the country—less than 80 percent of the average across the ten provinces. Klein and Dinning said the answer was too much spending. Government polls backed them up. Albertans did not want to cut education or health, but emphatically did not want higher taxes. The state of public opinion was handy. The government's economic policy makers did not want higher taxes either. They wanted lower taxes if possible.

The workbook prepared for the Red Deer round table had said, "We hear almost ad nauseam that we are facing a new economic order. We need to brace ourselves therefore not for modest alterations of longstanding patterns, but for fundamental paradigm shifts which will startle and challenge our assumptions and our practises . . . . The course we help set for Alberta can lead the way for the rest of Canada."

There was one more job to do first. Klein had to convince Albertans a reborn Conservative party existed and was worth voting for. But he had to work with the old Conservative government, full of old politicians—old in age and old in spirit. He had to cross the bridge of the present with the old government to get to the future.

He remade the legislature committee system and opened some of the workings of government. He purged old ministers and leadership rivals from the cabinet. He literally opened the door to the premier's office suite and kept it open. Passersby could look down the central hallway of the government's executive centre for the first time since Peter Lougheed had walled it off two decades earlier.

Other things were not so easy. Klein and his two deputy premiers, Ken Kowalski and Peter Elzinga, had never run government business before. There were times in the spring legislative session when business would stall while they looked at one another apparently figuring out what happened next.

Klein left many day-to-day details in Kowalski's hands while he toured the province speaking weekly to Conservative constituency meetings, something Getty had been criticized within the party for never doing.

Some of the former ministers appeared now and then like smiling wraiths. Other veterans who had been on the winning side hung on grimly. The legislature took on an air of a lunatic carnival stranded in the middle of a struggle which no one understood, and by which everyone would be damaged.

The Conservatives' annual party convention in April had drawn hundreds fewer people than usual. It was heavily produced, complete with a stage set consisting of a partly framed house representing Alberta under construction. A video crew recorded proceedings at random and showed the delegates the edited final tape, which was a far more exciting convention than the one the delegates had actually lived.

There were signs of a hard swing in the delegates' frame of mind—talk of sending able-bodied welfare recipients "out sweeping sidewalks," and approving references to Canada Safeway's successful recent campaign to slash the wages of its store clerks.

Klein delivered a rollicking speech which promised reform and had the crowd cheering his bites at the opposition parties and their policies: "You can find them in the Yellow Pages. You'll find the Liberals listed under 'demolition contractors' and you will find the New Democrats listed under 'bankruptcy counselling.' " The main excitement for outsiders was watching a skit event in which Mirosh ad-libbed bawdy jokes at the expense of fellow MLA Stockwell Day, a fundamentalist Christian.

Dinning presented the 1993-94 budget the first week of May, a month later than usual. Minor parts of it seemed contradictory and caused confusion. Some parts were astonishing blanks to be filled in later; the Health Department budget included a promise of more than $100 million in spending cuts with no firm indication what area of the department's spending would take the hit. Most other areas were merely frozen.

The biggest message was a four-year plan to balance the budget by cutting overall spending by about 20 percent. No one would say which spending would be cut, only that overall spending would go down. If this was true, if this was the plan, then the government had to slash education, health, and welfare spending by almost unimaginable amounts. First they said they were hoping the welfare rolls would shrink. Then a few months later they admitted reality and simply cut what people received.

No one talked much about the underlying assumptions. Interest rates would have to stay low for several years. It would have to be possible to lay off or slash the wages of public-sector workers and not hire more or raise wages for a number of years. Other costs would have to stay in line.

This looked very much as if the government was counting on the continuation of a new kind of economic depression, or at least on continuing high unemployment. It amounted to creating a policy based on destruction.

People hardly reacted at all. They had expected a hard stand and saw only mush, or perhaps a campaign pamphlet.

But even all this did not get Klein across the bridge. He had to react to fierce public pressure to cut the pensions going to the approximately thirty MLAs planning to retire along with Getty. The 30 percent pay raise they had granted themselves in 1989 translated into a 30 percent raise in their lifetime pensions. The oldest of them, elected with Lougheed in 1971, stood to collect more than eighty thousand dollars a year. For voters stuck with the financial consequences of that group's failures, for voters already unhappy with politicians and other former leaders in society, the pensions became the symbol of incompetent, self-serving arrogance.

Klein eventually saw no alternative. He asked the MLAs to roll back legally authorized pensions. The caucus meetings took hours. The retiring MLAs and former cabinet ministers of the Getty era, several of whom had been bounced from office by Klein, had to be persuaded into going along. He finally stepped out of his office on a Friday night in mid-May and told reporters the 30 percent pay raise had been cut out of the pension formula.

A few hours of deciphering the carefully worded statement and checking with officials uncovered a hitch. The cut applied only to the last four years. Actual pension amounts would go down by only a few percentage points. Klein compensated by wiping out the MLA pension plan entirely as of the coming election. That seemed less a concession to the public than the price for an agreement; Klein apparently had to sacrifice his and others' pensions before retiring members of the old government would agree to a small cut in theirs.

John Gogo, one of the Conservatives not tarred by stories of mismanagement and one of the few Conservative MLAs who had publicly shown an independent streak during the long years of conformity, went home to Lethbridge to meet his constituents. He said a few days later that people told him Klein's pension cut would win the election. He said he believed that.

7

Election

The Edmonton Journal
May 20, 1993

The best explanation I ever read of how elections work came from a novelist named Robert Kroetsch.

He wrote a book called *The Words of My Roaring*. Its setting strongly resembles the 1935 election that brought Social Credit to power in Alberta.

In the novel, farmers are suffering from years of drought. The old politicians say the weather is uncontrollable and everyone has to cope. The hero of the piece runs for election by promising rain.

He doesn't worry about making sense. He understands what people need, lets them know he understands, and promises to do something.

This worked in the real Alberta election of 1935. Most people desperately needed money. Social Credit promised them $25 a month.

How would someone apply this apparently simple formula to Alberta in 1993?

Maybe no one can. Alberta has become many different places and many different people. Here's one example. About one in every 10 workers can't find a job. It's a tragedy. Yet whenever someone offers an early retirement deal all sorts of people snap it up.

Political communications are changing. Voters tend to be tougher on politicians than journalists are. They often ask more specialized questions, know more about local issues and more consistently demand clear thinking.

Premier Ralph Klein ran into that Wednesday during an open-line radio show. A caller asked why he was trying to tar the Liberals with the National Energy Program of 1980 while saying his Conservatives have nothing to do with the last twenty-two years of Conservative government. The call could have been planted, but it's the sort of question ordinary voters ask these days.

More importantly, no one has a clear idea any more of what constitutes "an Albertan."

A typical Albertan of the Lougheed

era was born here, distrusted Ottawa and believed everything would be all right if grain prices held up and particularly if the oil and gas industries stayed healthy.

Now, about four of every seven people living in Alberta come from somewhere else. They mostly live in cities. They distrust politicians in general. They don't expect any job to last and don't see their future tied to any commodity; but they probably believe in sound education. There is no common image.

That's why this election can be read as a collective search for identity. The question is not so much "Whose policies should I vote for?" The parties won't be running that kind of campaign anyway. The question is: "Who am I and who best reflects the person I am?"

As usual, there's a strong economic underpinning.

The Lougheed-Getty party lasted in power from 1971 to late 1992. Oil prices took off in 1973 and crashed in 1986. The personal income of Albertans took off in 1974 and slumped back to the national average in 1987.

The province still does well compared with the rest of Canada, but the decline has left fear. What if we keep falling?

Albertans want prosperity. Every political party acknowledges that somewhere in its choice of words.

NDP Leader Ray Martin began the campaign saying Albertans are "looking for some security and some hope." The Conservatives put much the same thought into a general slogan—For A Better Alberta. Liberal supporter Nancy Power put it into precise words when she introduced Laurence Decore at an Edmonton fund-raiser last week: "The good ship Alberta needs a new captain to get it turned around and sailing back to the land of prosperity."

For nearly two decades everyone knew how to get there. Now they don't. Political life has become part of the search.

There was a place called Prosperity. It was too small to be named on any map.

It was a place where old dreams collided with new ones, where an old local economy got supplanted by the new global one, where a community fractured.

Klein had been there. He had gone to meet people being confronted by the new economy and give them a human face to talk to.

Prosperity was a collection of farmsteads in central Alberta, near the south bank of the Athabasca River. It lay at a geographic edge where the last farms faded into a bush that sprawled all the way north to the tundra.

The area had been cleared and settled in the 1930s by Ukrainian families and others whose immediate descendants still farmed, ran small sawmills, or worked outside but kept homes in the area. The little community lay about a twenty-minute drive east of the town of Athabasca. It was remarkable for nothing. Then Alberta Pacific Forest Industries, a consortium of Japanese-owned firms, selected Prosperity as the site for what it called the largest single-line bleached kraft pulp mill in the world.

The Al-Pac mill grew out of one of the Alberta government's most successful economic initiatives of the 1980s. In the mid-1980s the new government led by Don Getty saw oil prices collapse and searched for new industries to nurture. Forestry officials identified the tens of thousands of square kilometres of mixed aspen and spruce forest in central Alberta as one of the last and largest unallocated stands of easily exploitable timber in the world.

Alberta forestry officials took this raw material and added the government's determination to back up development with large loans or loan guarantees. They sold Alberta internationally and created a land rush. In effect, the government created a new forest industry in a few years.

The developments created new environmental concern. The mills were approved and built so fast that little protest was organized. Al-Pac was a different story. It came last. It was biggest. It planned to use an old chlorine-bleach process which other mills were bypassing. And it was being set down in the middle of a small farm community where some residents liked the idea of a new industry but others feared what would happen to the local roads, air, and water.

Klein had become provincial environment minister after the 1989 election. He found himself in the middle of the Al-Pac fight at a time when he was also trying to get a rewrite of Alberta's much-criticized environment laws off the ground.

In the spring of 1990 he drove to Prosperity to meet several families who had been organizing a local protest and looking into legal action. He came in a jacket but tieless to the house of Emil Zachkewich. Klein took his boots off at the door and went downstairs into a carpeted rumpus room to talk with angry and fearful people. He listened. He took notes. At the end he said he could not tell them the mill would not be built at the chosen site. He could promise to try to come up with money to help pay for a local intervention in an environmental review of the mill.

He kept his promise. The environmental review raised several serious concerns about the effects of the Al-Pac project and the other pulp developments. Several months later, another review commissioned by the government cited recent tests and a proposal by Al-Pac to change its processing method. The second review swept aside much of the earlier objection. There were questions about some of the statements in this second review. There were signs of tension between Klein and the forestry minister. But Klein's role in the eventual decision never became clear. Only the outcome was clear. Klein had successfully gone into the heart of the local protest and come out with something to offer. Several months later the mill went ahead, albeit with apparent improvements to the environmental acceptability of its technology.

The go-ahead announcement took place in a four-hundred-seat theatre in Athabasca. It was a raucous affair—a gloating celebration for local mill boosters, a chance for a final show of defiance by protesters. Klein was there too, on the stage with Getty, Forestry Minister LeRoy Fjordbotten, and Economic Development Minister Peter Elzinga. An Edmonton environmentalist sitting in a front row gave them the finger.

Most of the ministers took it but Klein gave his own middle finger back. His emotions always seemed to run closer to the surface than those of other politicians. Someone caught the moment on film and the image of an irate Klein with an upraised middle finger became common in magazines and on street-corner posters. It never seemed to hurt him much. People did not take it for arrogance the way they had interpreted a similar gesture by Pierre Trudeau years before.

He was the only member of the government who had gone to the mill site and talked to the people and given them some of what they wanted. He crossed more borders than other politicians. But he always ended up sitting beside power.

In May 1993 the Al-Pac mill was nearly complete. It loomed out of the horizon, surrounded by a cordon of bought-out farmland. At its flanks lay the gatherings of raw material—tree trunks stacked into piles as high as two-storey houses and as long as city blocks.

Some families had moved out. Emil Zachkewich was still around and had been nominated to run for the NDP. Down the gravel road about four kilometres east of the mill stood a newer house belonging to one of the local mill supporters, Casey Bizon. He talked about the downturn in farming and natural gas production. He worried that the local Grasslands School had lost more than half its student population in recent years and might not be able to hang on to its Grade 12 classes long enough for his children to go there. He saw empty spaces where there used to be a farm family on every quarter-section of land.

"It was a depressed area and we were losing our population," he said. "In my opinion it wasn't so much [a case] of getting a boom as to reverse the trend."

He did not remember much about Klein. He talked instead about supporting local Conservative candidate Mike Cardinal: "He's a down-to-earth person, not a stuffed shirt. The good thing about him is it's usually doctors, lawyers, run for MLA, people with the big bucks behind them. Mike, he's got two fingers missing from working in a sawmill when he was a kid."

Many others said much the same. At Amber Valley, another tiny community east of Athabasca, Juanita Hetherington bent over a gently sloping garden with her daughter and granddaughter setting out cantaloupe and watermelon. Both were unlikely plants for the frost-prone climate of central Alberta. She had planted them before. Tenacity, a little imagination, and some hard work paid off. If it did not, then not too many people would have been living around here in the first place.

Hetherington could take on the land and the climate. Politics had her discouraged: "I don't think it would matter much what party gets in. . . . It amazes me the way they call people down. . . . I'd vote for Mike because he's Mike and as far as political parties they're all the same thing anyway."

In Athabasca itself, builders were happily hammering nails and tamping earth in a new subdivision. Work was steady with the new mill coming in, although no one was calling this a boom.

Yet here the same alienation had set in. A young motel handyman in a red checkered shirt said, "I've never really had much faith in politicians of any kind. They all talk big when they want to be elected. . . . I don't think that they can make things any better. I think the whole world is bankrupt."

At the local Esso station, owner Jim Paterson sat behind his cash register and considered: "Personally, I'm so tired of all the fighting, I don't know who to trust any more." Liberal Leader Laurence Decore may have been a good mayor in Edmonton but liked to "shoot his mouth off at everybody." Ray Martin and the New Democrats were always saying taxes on big business were going to solve all the problems. Paterson had been thinking about Klein: "I think to a certain point Ralph was starting to impress me but then he said we're going to cut two and a half billion dollars in four years. Well I don't care who you are you're not going to do that. I don't like being lied to. That's a pretty big whopper."

A lot of other people had not noticed how much Klein had promised to cut from government spending. Or they had noticed and thought he was telling them a whopper and did not care.

Many seemed to be looking for an honest man, but one with enough brains to know which whopper to tell them when he had to.

Klein always seemed to be looking for something too. A resort owner near Lac La Biche told me that back in the 1980s he had walked out on his beach about nine o'clock one morning and found the mayor of Calgary sitting in a lawn chair with a beer, staring across the beauty of the lake. Klein told him there was no finer place in the world.

It had been billed as a campaign likely to turn into a bruising, mud-slinging brawl. I had expected it would. Nothing much was happening. Martin had started down a long slide by talking about spreading the tax load onto more sources of wealth. People were already saying that more taxes on the rich would end up meaning more taxes on everyone.

Decore had spoken to about one hundred people in Leduc and brought along his secret weapon. He called it a "CD player," the letters CD being an abbreviation for Conservative Debt. It was a gadget in a brief case. A black box with blinking red lights kept inexorable track of the increase in provincial debt from minute to minute. It did not impress the audience any more than Decore's wooden and aloof presence on the speaking platform—or his vague assurance that a new government could easily find $1.1 billion in wasteful spending to cut almost immediately, then work from there.

Klein spent the first Saturday of the campaign in Edmonton. He was scheduled for an afternoon jog around the cinder track at Coronation Park. The party billed this event as Run With Ralph. There were to be many more runs with Ralph in other cities through the campaign—an apparent compromise between the need for photo opportunities and Klein's desultory commitment to exercise. Or maybe even a compromise with some inner reluctance. Klein was the politician who, on the eve of his first election as mayor of Calgary, had confided to a reporter, "I hate asking for votes. I think it's cheap."

None of the voters showed up for the run. There were only some local Conservative candidates, party staff, a few kids, a couple of dozen people in all. Most of them passed Klein on the first lap.

He jogged at a determined little pace which almost became a trot. He never actually became airborne between steps, but he never slowed down. He wore long grey socks. The residue of thirty years worth of beer clung around his belly. His T-shirt had a fist-sized knot tied into it on the right side. He kept plugging along. After half an hour he had outlasted all but the youngest and slimmest of the other runners.

If an election were going on it did not seem to be going on here. The concrete stands capable of holding a few hundred spectators were virtually empty. Even the TV crews were not keen on recording this. No one in any party was explaining exactly how they planned to wipe out Alberta's $2.5-billion budget deficit although they all talked about doing it. Voters were saying they had not thought much about the election and planned to brush up on the issues later.

I'd met someone named Al waiting at the Edmonton Food Bank the day before. He said he was going to a casual-labour office every morning and getting about one day's work a month. He disliked politicians: "What have they done for me? They've done nothing for me. They sit pretty in their offices making a hundred, hundred and fifty thousand a year." It was a common line, not unlike the story from a small contractor who had been tamping dirt around a house at Athabasca: "Me, I'm working just about every day and I still can't make ends meet. I've got a mortgage and two kids."

This was not shaping up as a clash of ideas, let alone insults. There were only people. They gathered in places like the Callingwood mall, an over-grown Edmonton strip mall Klein had visited earlier in the day, before his jog. The drive to the mall had displayed the panorama of everyday life in Edmonton—a city which boasted an opera company and every weekend turned into a land of garage sales.

A guy in a gaudy jacket watched with a satisfied smile as his German Shepherd squatted on the boulevard grass. An older couple—the man with white hair and the woman with burnished copper—took two small children across the street against a red light. At the mall itself, folks dropped in for coffee and chocolate-dipped ice cream at a Dairy Queen. A sign out front read Order Your Cake For Father's Day Early. Three Toronto-Dominion Bank employees were selling hot dogs and pop in the parking lot; they were raising money for a foundation trying to establish a children's hospital in Edmonton to match the one in Calgary.

Klein was late. Thirty or so people were waiting to see him. Among them were John Slana, Mike Ryan, and Mary Ryan, all middle-aged refugees from the Cassiar mine shutdown in northern British Columbia. Slana wondered whether Klein would arrive in a limousine. He said he was looking for politicians who put themselves on the same level as ordinary people—maybe Conservatives, maybe Liberals.

Slana had lived in Edmonton once. He had gone to B.C. twenty-six years earlier to run heavy equipment. He had come back in February. He was looking for any kind of work: "My UIC's going to run out and then I'll be on welfare like the rest of great Canada."

Mike Ryan had worked in the Cassiar mill. The New Democrats were looking for people like this but they did not stand a chance in this group. It was the British Columbia New Democrats who had shut down the Cassiar mine, faster than they had said they would. They had run over some people pretty roughly. Slana had bought a home there in 1970. He said the B.C. government bought it for exactly the $14,000 he had paid those two infla-tion-ridden decades earlier. Ryan said, "They carry their socialist dream a little bit to the extreme. They get in there by saying they're for the workers and then they turn around and prove they're not for the workers."

Klein showed up in a short motorhome, maybe a twenty-footer. He got out and walked around shaking hands, looking at people with his wary but hopeful eyes, working his mouth into the broad crease of a nearly shy but friendly smile which always took over the lower half of his face.

He stepped through the crowd. He kept saying, "How you doin'?" He wore a grey jacket, jeans, and grey cowboy boots. It looked like the same outfit he had worn on his visit to the pulp mill protesters at Prosperity. Slana stuck himself into the small crowd on the sidewalk, an excited smile on his own face. He shook the premier's hand, a politician's hand, and came out of it still smiling.

"He's a decent guy," Slana said. "He came in blue jeans just like me."

I could have stopped covering the election right there and still have had a lot of it figured out. But it was tough to believe things were that simple. That was only the fundamental part of it anyway. There was plenty more going on.

They held a TV debate a few days later. It was structured for television—a scriptwriter's idea of a debate. The questions came from people who were supposed to represent the general public. Their questions were prescreened. The leaders' answers came in one-minute segments and faded out to prompted applause.

They had been well prepared but they largely avoided the most far-reaching question of the night. Gerry Wilkie from Banff asked whether the province should set limits on growth to protect the environment. This was deep water. Klein, Decore, and Martin barely dipped their toes. They had more immediate issues.

Martin kept asking Klein and Decore the question about spending cuts that neither wanted to answer: "You have to be specific, both of you. . . . Where are the cuts going to be?" They never did answer. Martin himself never explained how he was going to deal with more than the first billion dollars of a $2.5-billion deficit.

The core of the debate—the ideological core of the election—emerged from a brief clash between Klein and Martin. It lasted less than two minutes. Klein said the province had to keep taxation low if it wanted to compete in a global economy. Martin said corporations got the most benefit from Alberta's health and education systems and had better pay to keep those systems running well. The audience applauded for both of them.

Klein ended the show by looking straight into the cameras and telling viewers, "This is all about trust, folks." He said he aimed to keep taxes down and eliminate the deficit while creating jobs and protecting core services such as health and education: "That, folks, is what you have been saying you want and that is what we are committed to delivering to you."

It was hard to see how he could deliver. It sounded like a whopper. It also sounded like the whopper many voters were trying to sell to themselves.

The campaign fell back into its somnolent early state. The election was nearly invisible. It was ten thousand conversations in a thousand different towns and crossroads.

Klein's photograph was plastered on billboards and campaign pamphlets all over the province with the slogan He Listens, He Cares. The phrase seemed to sum up what people wanted in a political leader. It was borrowed from some of the advertising copy for Don Getty in the 1989 campaign. No one noticed the recycling until after the election was over, which tells you about the disintegration of public memory.

I went out in early June. Along highways in southeastern Alberta, in communities strung together by lines of asphalt looped around the dinosaur-bone beds of the Red Deer River valley, people were feeling a quiet and uncertainty. One of the old regulars walked into Elmer's Garage at Hanna. It was a place where you could look at a tool bench and then turn around and look at a deserted stockyard and the edge of the prairie. The old guy said, "You don't hear any talk in the coffee shops. Seems like none of them have any idea what to do if they got in."

But if you pushed the talk along just a little bit, you could see an outline of hope, frustration, evasion, and trust taking shape.

At the Laughlin Brothers garage in Youngstown a morning-coffee crowd of mechanics and travelling sales reps gradually settled into a consensus. One of them put it this way: "Ah, everybody knows old Ralph. He'll probably get in. At least he tries to do something. Doesn't always do it right but at least he tries, like on the pensions."

Old Ralph had not been around there much but everyone had seen him for years on television, first as a reporter for CFCN in Calgary and then as Calgary's mayor. They liked what they saw. They talked as if he were their next-door neighbour. People in other parts of the province might like him or not but in southern Alberta people talked as if they knew him. Klein cast a political shadow which seemed to reach just as far as CFCN's broadcast signal.

Something else came up in the garage, a sentiment cropping up all over Alberta about where to find the layers of fat which could be sliced out of the government with pain to none but a few people who did not count for much: "They should fire the top eight civil servants in each department and then hire back the ones that are needed. That's what happens when a business changes hands. I'll bet it would save us billions."

But one of the people at the table worried there was not enough money going into student loans. A student in the family was studying in Calgary. He was depending on regular deliveries of groceries from Youngstown to get by.

At Oyen, a farm service centre on some of the driest and sparsest agricultural land in Western Canada, sisters Connie Chaplin and Lucy McLaughlin had the same worries. "They'll cut something that really affects a person, like hospitals," Chaplin said, "then they'll turn around and have a committee on something like how many pieces of garbage there are between here and Hanna."

At the north edge of town, in a low-lying building, a former carpenter named Cal Johnson had followed his dream and built his own wax museum. He thought he liked what Klein was saying too, especially after the MLA pension cuts. Johnson could have had a crack at a government grant to develop his museum but said he really did not want to take it: "I myself feel that I should start off on my own, and if I can't make it. . . ."

He was learning his craft as he went along. He had made display stalls in the building by tacking black polyethylene sheets onto two-by-fours. He had Dracula, John Wayne, Ricky Nelson, Elvis and a bunch of others so far, and had mounted some of the displays with keen humour. He was being lured by civic officials from Drumheller and planned to move because there he would have more tourist traffic coming through to see his work. That was on his mind. As for the election, he thought he might like to see a new crowd running the show in Edmonton but he was tired of hearing Laurence Decore saying the same old things everyday like a parrot, always running down Klein. And while he might like a new crowd running the show in Edmonton, he did not want it too new: "I don't know a new government so much as a changed government."

Kathleen Smigelski liked what she heard from Klein about cuts too. But grain farming was an exception: "Help the farmer more, give us a better price for the product."

Still, there were plenty of signs that this election was not turning on tough economic times. It was more like the other way around.

Wheat farmers were losing money and some had turned to canola in recent years. It seemed like a strange choice given the local climate and soil but there was an incentive. Wheat was guaranteed $80 to $120 an acre on crop insurance, depending on an individual farmer's record. Canola would bring either a good cash payment or crop insurance at $145 an acre. Some farmers said that crop insurance officials were telling them they could move on next to lentils, guaranteed at $180 an acre.

Cattle prices were booming. Oil and gas rigs were hiring all through the area and down west toward Brooks. Any community more than half an hour's drive out of Edmonton seemed to be doing well. The official statistics explained why several months later. Soaring cattle prices in 1993 led to the highest net farm income in a decade. The widening export market for natural gas led to the busiest drilling year since the days of the boom. The number of oil and gas wells drilled in Western Canada jumped from 4,772 in 1992 to 9,398 in 1993, and most of those were in Alberta. It had been the busiest drilling season since 1985. Winter employment on the rigs had jumped to 8,000 from 2,500 in one year.

At Brooks, cars and half-tons filled the roads. Brooks was a bigger town, on the verge of becoming a sort of rural metropolis, the biggest centre between Calgary and Medicine Hat. It had farming, oilfield service work and other advantages like a meat packing plant that represented the new Alberta.

The plant was one of the survivors of a decade and a half of packinghouse closures throughout Alberta. It had successfully ridden out a strike and held down wages. It had attracted the giant Japanese trading conglomerate Mitsubishi into making a 15-percent investment. Brooks was entering some new world of a more urbanized economy in a rural setting. Its attitudes were more impatient than those of the surrounding countryside. For every few people saying, "I'm going to vote for Ralph," there was someone saying it was time to teach the government a lesson: "Every time you move 'em out it gets a little better."

There were also the larger themes playing out again and again all over the south. "Don't talk about elections," said one old man, "it's all junk anyway."

Cindy Sobertson, sitting in a Dairy Queen, worried about the state of her son's school and worried more about who was getting ahead in Alberta: "I'm sort of tired of paying and these big outfits not paying. There's no middle class any more."

But all around the circle of road from Hanna to Oyen and back toward Brooks the image of the "big outfits" had more to do with government and its unions than with Mitsubishi or the oil companies at the town doorstep.

Sobertson added, "We should have never let the wages get to where they are. I'd rather see a cut in some of the wages than cut some of the programs."

One woman, one of the economic refugees from Saskatchewan who were filtering into the town, said she liked Klein's cutting of MLA pensions and other decisions: "I like what he's done since he's been in there. Some of them are a little bit scary like user fees, but if that's what it takes. . . ."

Over at Bassano, outside the Legion Hall, people were saying that Klein was "down to earth." That was the phrase they mostly used. I heard it over and over.

Bassano was changing too. Its commercial centre and its jobs had drifted down the TransCanada Highway to Brooks. Bassano was turning into a retirement community and a home for commuters. Its underpinnings were different from what generations of Albertans had been used to.

Instead of the local farm economy and feed mill its underpinnings were now a good school, cheap real estate, the promise of an advanced technology firm, and the attractions of small-town life. The most colourful of the latter was an old billiards hall with a faded metal *Star Weekly* sign out front and a counter with antique wooden seats where the regulars and the occasional tourist could order a three-scoop ice cream cone for eighty cents.

Marg Scott was serving up the cones. She said she had met Klein and his wife once years before at a soccer game in Calgary. Scott said she had spilled the contents of her purse in the stadium washroom "and a lady helped me and it was Colleen." She was impressed: "I thought, 'Here's this lady, wife of the mayor, and she's helping me pick my purse off the bathroom.' "

Central Alberta was a different story. In the populous farm area north of Red Deer, the border area between the two historically different political zones of northern and southern Alberta, anger and uncertainty played through the streets.

Bernice Luce lived in Ponoka. She was running for the Liberals. She had a record of community work and had taken part in the province's review of labour law in the mid-1980s. That kind of work was a training ground for Conservative candidates. She had received hints she might want to look into the party. She did, and disliked the view: "Chauvinistic, male-dominated, and full of very arrogant people."

The social geography here was changing. Middle Alberta had been a farm-oilpatch setting, a place where some children carried on the family business and others left for the city. Now, in 1993, many people were staying here or even moving into small communities by choice. They found niches. They were comfortable with computers and with international trade.

Oilpatch technical experts routinely flew to jobs on the other side of the world. Small shop owners talked matter-of-factly about bringing flowers in from the Netherlands or lawn and house ornaments from Tijuana. Artists' shops dotted the region. Style had come to complement cash. There was a capuccino bar by the foothills in Rocky Mountain House and a clutch of marina-front homes at Sylvan Lake that looked as if they had been taken out of a picture book about Cape Cod. Acreages sold fast. People changing their lives might find it easier to change their politics.

They might, but it was a struggle. They wanted to make the Conservatives pay for years of financial misadventure, to hold the governing party to account at least once. Yet they had not found a convincing alternative. And they were angry about a political system they could not control because their only control was the right to put an X on a piece of paper every four years.

"Time for a change," people said.

"What will we get that's any different?" came the call back.

An older woman in the village of Bentley put it most graphically: "If they was a bunch of cats and you took them down to the river you don't know which one you'd pull out of the bag to save."

In the end, most of them decided to save the one with the broad, engaging smile and the record of at least having done something with pensions. Maybe they liked what they saw. Maybe they did not really want change, and would have grasped any reason not to plunge into something unknown.

There was a place called Prosperity. There was even a church of prosperity. You could find it at the south end of Edmonton, on Ellerslie Road. It seemed a place to look for the election when the official election looked hollow.

Technically it was not a church. It was called a Christian Centre. It lacked the usual Christian symbols. The interior had blank walls, intense stage lights, theatre seats with no racks for Bibles or hymnals. The service opened with a half-hour floor show by a seven-piece band and well-trained singers.

The pastor came out in a sharply cut downtown suit. He mentioned that the grand piano behind him cost $35,000. His money pitch lasted a good half-hour. The idea was to "throw money at the altars" although this place had no altar. Sowing a sacrifice of money every week would produce success and rewards. This would happen supernaturally.

The church of prosperity had no comfortable place for the weak and the failed. "I love to be on the right side," the pastor said. "I hate to be on the losing side."

When he finally began his hour-long sermon it had a strangely disconnected structure. He jumped from one chapter of the Bible to another. He said the Word was reality. But words were missing from his sermon. It was all noise and picture. Sometimes he tried to revise the meaning of words. He said that "peace" in one Bible passage meant "success." Sometimes he babbled in tongues.

This was not religion. This was television taking on the form of religion. The church was a television studio. The Word had become sound bites. The congregation was part of the stage set. They had mostly arrived in the parking lot in cheap compact cars and six-year-old sedans. They were there to buy hope.

It all looked familiar. The election had not been a political campaign seen in part on television. Television had become politics. The visual and emotion-based thought processes of television, its ability to project a strong personality from an assembly of dots and sounds, its detachment from any sense of context or history, its fragmentation of the audience into unconnected individuals receiving an apparently spontaneous but thoroughly programmed message from what looked like an authoritative and personal source — all this had become the method of politics.

But even in the church of prosperity, where ushers roamed up and down the aisles staring at the congregation, there had been moments of quiet dissent. The pastor got into a complicated analogy about mirrors. He started joking about wives having a daily ritual of looking at themselves. They spend four hours a day in front of mirrors, he said. He had the crowd laughing for a good five minutes. One woman who appeared to be in her sixties held her Bible, looked at him and kept her lips pressed tight. She finally muttered something that sounded like, "That's stupid."

The Conservatives looked strong but there was only one sure prediction to make: a party would win with less than 50 percent of the popular vote on June 15, and would govern as if it had received much more.

Afterward the result seemed inevitable. Too much had pointed in the same direction. Klein won on more or less the same terms he had fashioned for the leadership campaign. He won big in Calgary and the rural areas and that gave him a majority. The Conservatives took 44 percent of the popular vote to the Liberals' 40 percent and the New Democrats' 11 percent. They had fifty-one seats in the legislature to thirty-two for the Liberals; the NDP, the official Opposition for the last decade, was shut out.

Other factors came into play. Many Albertans had been voting Conservative for decades. Political scientists still single out previous voting patterns as the best guide to any individual's vote in any given election.

Large sectors of the economy were growing more healthy. It was probably no coincidence that the Liberal opposition was concentrated in Edmonton, where the province's heaviest unemployment rate, around 11 percent, was concentrated. The New Democrats had been self-destructing for a year. The Liberals under Laurence Decore had proven unclear and indecisive.

There was also change in the electorate. Several thousand voters in bedrock populist country in the central foothills and in the southwest had gone back to Social Credit, the nearest stand-in available for the Reform party, which had refused to be drawn into provincial politics.

One Social Credit candidate from Hanna had put up probably the most evocative signs of the campaign. They read: Waste Not, Want Not. Young voters had shown a streak of resentment against getting stuck with poor job prospects and the fallout of heavy government debt. Some leaned toward Reform federally and the Conservatives provincially. Voter turnout climbed significantly. Perhaps a quarter of a million people voted who had not voted in 1986 or even in 1989.

But Klein seemed the biggest single factor. His personal presence loomed everywhere. He had probably injected the most important policy decision by fighting for the cut in MLA pensions just before the campaign.

I had heard the myself. I had read it again and again in other stories about the campaign. The words always had a familiar ring. They were virtually interchangeable. Louis Massicotte, a Petro-Canada dealer in the foothills town of Caroline, had said, "He's the best damn politician we've ever had, and I hate politicians. I've got a lot of faith in that boy. He's just like one of us, came up from nothing through hard work." Hendrik Stuut, who had been forced to give up farming because of the economy, had leaned over a cup of coffee in Huck Finn's, in the irrigation farming centre of Bow Island down south, and said, "I'd rather vote for Ralph than some lawyer. Let's see what he can do in four years."

Decore, the Edmonton lawyer, watched Klein's ability to separate himself from the last Conservative government and said toward the end, "It's the most perplexing thing that I have ever tried to sort through."

The choices were emotional and intuitive. Maybe that was the best resort. Elaine McCoy had given a talk on politics a few months earlier and suggested that logic-based critical analysis might be giving way to what she called "critical feeling."

Change came hard. One woman had said the Conservatives had created the mess in the province and they could darn well clean it up.

Yet Klein had managed to convince people he stood for change. He had said so when the budget came out: "Change is what we offer. And change is what we will deliver."

He had successfully reinvented the Progressive Conservative party. A faltering political party had broken into pieces, put itself back together and succeeded itself.

Klein said he was deeply disappointed that Martin—"a good, kind human being"—had been beaten personally. He had a simple explanation of this campaign and all others.

"It's people," he said. He said he had learned as mayor of Calgary to deal with people on their home ground, not to make them come to a stuffy office for half an hour and be told that what they said would be considered: "It's a very simple kind of politics but that's what politics is all about."

On election night, about three hundred or four hundred Conservative activists celebrated in an Edmonton hotel banquet room owned by former Conservative cabinet minister Julian Koziak. They cheered the arrival of Klein, who had flown up from Calgary. Klein was hoarse but gave them the rousing speech they had come to expect.

Gloating was in the air. The party's top field organizer would say a few days later that Decore could never beat Klein and the election had settled matters for at least eight years. People were already feeling that way.

Hugh Dunne, a Calgary television producer who had handled Olympics coverage and gone on to become the press secretary who oversaw many of Don Getty's communication failures, emerged from the crowd. He would soon be on his way to Calgary as Klein's director in McDougall Centre, the southern cabinet office. He said over the noise that Klein had won a great victory. He agreed the government faced a large challenge but said Klein had the ability for the task.

"That's the man who can do it," Dunne told me, pointing to the rumpled figure surrounded by well-wishers on the stage. He fixed a stare and added, "Now we all have to get on the ball and get behind him and stop being so negative all the time."

The party had won its weakest election victory since 1971. That hardly mattered. Power tasted more tempting than ever before.

8

The Red Market

The Edmonton Journal
July 9 and 10, 1993

The lines between government and private business are breaking down. Technology flows in new paths and politics change too.

It's worth keeping an eye on the new maps as they form. People are making up the rules as they go along and the new ways of doing things could be with us for a long time.

One area is government information. Governments produce large amounts of information.

It used to exist on paper in government buildings. Now it goes into computers. Information stored electronically becomes mobile. It can even become a commodity, sold like coffee or cigarettes or liquor.

And liquor makes a good comparison. Information can become a commodity controlled by government but managed or sold by private firms working in association with the political side. You could call this system a red market. It forms a kind of counterpart to the idea of a black market.

The red market economy keeps growing.

Significant questions need to be asked about it—and answered. Are the goods involved essentially public or private? Who owns them? Who should own them? What does ownership mean? How do private firms enter this market, which is not a free one? Since the market is not free, what are the appropriate controls? Do the private players in the red market become clients of political machines? Does their technology overwhelm the political side and shape public policy?

The Alberta government does not usually take on such questions.

A small example from Ottawa demonstrates what is happening.

Two years ago, you could call a federal office and find out quickly who owns a patent. Now you would be directed to a private firm which would charge about $100 for a basic patent search.

There's a more complex story unfolding in Alberta. The province has been negotiating to join Ottawa in a contract bidding system managed by Information Systems Management Corp. of Regina.

Alberta would supply information about contracts to ISM. The firm sells subscriptions and computer time to anyone interested in government business. Ottawa began this open bidding service in an arrangement with ISM last July, and left the door open for all provinces and territories to come in later. As of April this year, 922 Alberta companies had subscribed.

This system is open, honest and economical. It replaces the inefficient mail-out of huge amounts of paper to lists of registered suppliers.

It also makes public information a commodity held in the hands of one private firm. The firm becomes a monopoly supplier regulated by a government contract. The provisions of the contract may not be public. A big firm could over time choke off growth of competitors.

ISM itself has features which make it hard to classify.

It began under another name with heavy involvement by Saskatchewan government-owned SaskTel. IBM Canada bought just over half the firm after a recent merger. Shares in the remainder are traded on the stock exchanges.

The open bidding service involves ISM's federal arm. But the firm has created several subsidiaries to handle much of its other work. These cross public-private lines. BC Tel owns a majority interest in ISM-BC. Telus Corp. (the recently privatized corporate parent of Alberta Government Telephones) owns half of ISM-Alberta. A subsidiary in Moncton involves NB Tel and Blue Cross of Atlantic Canada.

You end up with a federation of public-private hybrids handling information for a mix of private and public customers. This group manages AGT's computer network, prints all the telephone and power bills in New Brunswick, manages information systems for the City of Regina, runs the electronic message system in Shell Canada's office in Calgary. Where are the boundaries here between public and private?

The creeping privatization of liquor sales subtly changed the face of Alberta in the last year.

Hotels all over have set up wine and liquor stores. Many exist hand in hand with the sudden bloom of video gambling machines. Anyone touring the province during the spring election would have been surprised how fast these sights have become fixtures of Alberta life from Edmonton to Empress. But you can see them only at hotels.

They form a prime example of the red market—an economic sphere in which private firms operate as clients or licensees of the government.

The red market is not private enterprise. It represents a largely unexamined spread of political influence into the everyday life of the province.

Why have hotels been granted most of the private alcohol trade and the video gambling rights? None of the excuses used by the government—the usual is They Know The Business—holds up.

The public-private tangle grows worse when you consider that government lending agencies have provided much of the financing for Alberta hotels since the mid-1980s. The government has a financial stake in their success.

The whole alcohol trade is full of this crossing of boundaries. Last September, the government said it would start allowing alcohol sales in small rural stores. A liquor board spokesman says about 30 rural stores have licences now.

What's fascinating is the way the board determines public support before issuing a rural store licence—customers' signatures, support from the local municipal council, support from the local MLA. No matter how innocently this may work in practice, the system builds in a political client relationship.

The red market often spreads quietly. No one knew—until an opposition MLA asked about it in the legislature last spring—that two businesses and one individual were acting as employment agents for the Distance Learning Centre in Barrhead. There was no competition. The Education Department simply decided who might be able to do the job and offered it.

No one knows how many similar deals have been made around Alberta.

The ripest red market commodity is computerized information. The province intends to plunge much further into information sales.

Municipal Affairs Minister Steve West has said the government will present a business plan this fall for consumer registry services.

Private agencies supported by user fees will provide driver's licence renewals, birth and marriage certificates, land titles, corporate registry information and more. A free market would see this business thrown open to all bidders. We're more likely to see one-time handouts of long-term contracts, with perhaps some potential for eventual domination by one or two firms.

Maybe none of this will cause much protest. Albertans seem more likely to look for government favours than to question the system these days.

Still, a spreading red market looks as if it has potential to corrode public morality, just like anything Eastern Europe dreamed up in the last 40 years.

By the time the government announces its plan for consumer services it should be ready to take a much broader look at the context.

Albertans can legitimately ask for some public policy direction. Among the issues: How big is the red market? What areas, if any, are appropriate for it? How can political influence be kept out? How can competition be preserved and encouraged in these sectors? If it is appropriate to run any business under government licence or concession, can or should any part be channelled to unemployed Albertans or to worker co-ops?

🏛

We are not alike, Steffens. But I have found as you did that learning about the world is a lifelong proposition.

Life reveals itself by steps, and through persistent attention.

Starting in the 1890s you spent several years uncovering the links between business and politics. You tried to persuade people that those links corroded public morality.

The first of the great muckraking articles of 1903 concentrated on city governments. At the time those governments were crossover points. They linked the political machines with the great trusts that monopolized commerce and with the privately owned franchises that ran most public services. Nearly a century later the idea of private franchisers running public services has taken on a new respectability.

While Ray Baker was examining the underside of organized labour and Ida Tarbell was telling the world about the real history of Standard Oil, you were trying to expose the links between political and economic leadership.

The muckraking days have been forgotten. The East European example speaks more loudly to people now.

You have been so well forgotten that people were much impressed when Jane Jacobs published a book a couple of years ago delving into ideas like yours. She traced fundamental social-political problems to a difference between political and commercial ethics. She called them commercial ethics and guardian ethics.

You had clearly identified the split by 1910 although, typically, you did not develop the idea in much detail. Jacobs seems in some ways a successor to you but she works harder.

You thought that hiding the link between two spheres—each operating with its own set of ethics—caused the corruption you saw all around.

Has anything changed between the 1890s and the 1990s? One thing seems conspicuously different. People talked then. Now they do not.

It is astonishing to look back at your end of the century and read how political bosses and corrupt police captains told you about their business. Some became your friends. Many privately worried, once they began talking to you, about what their system was doing to public morality.

There are connections between your time and ours. Albertans know the name Weyerhaeuser. It is a major forestry company. Recently it bought a pulp mill near Grande Prairie. The company is the one you knew, except that you also knew its founder, old Frederick Weyerhaeuser himself.

By the time you met him his firm was already one of the great American business enterprises, with huge landholdings spread from the pine woods of Georgia to the great fir and spruce forests of the Northwest. It had grown with the help of bought politicians. It had successfully exploited legal loopholes. At one point it opened vast new regions to logging by obtaining a court ruling that any small stream able to float a log was navigable; thus the trees alongside it could legally be cut.

Frederick Weyerhaeuser created an empire in the woods. He looked back and was troubled about some of the ways he had succeeded. But succeed he did. Now his corporate legacy continues in Alberta and in other places, stripped of the human being who began it.

Business and political leaders do not seem to doubt themselves these days. Maybe they have less cause.

But I think the structure of modern commerce has also tended to eliminate the process of doubt. If questions exist they are answered by public relations specialists. The specialists' job is not to philosophize. Their job is to make businesses and politicians look as good as possible in any circumstance.

Albertans never worry much about the links between commerce and politics. The province has usually embraced such links. Klein's government embraced them, without debate.

Debate has never really been the point of Alberta politics.

Do you want to know about grassroots Alberta? A rural couple came to the legislature in 1993. They took part in a news conference organized by the Liberals shortly after the first round of minor hospital spending cuts. They complained about the husband's recent experience in hospital. They thought his care had been poor and had led to complications.

It turned out they had been longtime Conservatives. The wife had played key roles in Conservative campaigns around Wetaskiwin. If anything, she told reporters, she had thought the long years of party work would have qualified them for a little preferential treatment at the local hospital. That is grassroots Alberta. Politics and favours go hand in hand—in everyone's perception if not in fact. None of Klein's reforms touched this way of life. The spread of new technology tended to entrench it instead.

Some of the gluey connections were blatant and some were only guessed at. Hard evidence surfaced almost by accident.

At the end of 1992 a committee of Conservative MLAs was drawing up new constituency boundaries for the province. They decided the town of Lac La Biche should be lopped off its longstanding ties to the north and grouped with the east-central communities around St. Paul. Many Lac La Biche residents were concerned. The local economy depended on northern links. Those links depended in part on their member of the legislature, who for the last three years had been Mike Cardinal. The concern was jobs.

Lac La Biche Mayor Tom Maccagno said, "Invariably, the local MLA will give preference to the local truckers."

John Karpetz hired out trucks and heavy equipment. He said MLAs look after their own: "You usually get a lot of information from your MLA. He'll give you tips, let you know where things are happening."

Archie Gladue of Lasso Contracting said about 90 percent of the work in Lac La Biche was tied to oil and gas, and the local contractors depended on their MLA: "I call my MLA, Mike Cardinal, he talks with oil companies. He opens gates for us . . . I'll say, 'Mike, call Mr. So-and-so to let us in on some of this work. . . . And I'm sure a lot of our work is done politically.'" Gladue said he had tried it on his own once. He went to Calgary and could not even get straight whose office he should be in. He was left with a simple conclusion: "Politicians own the country."

Cardinal was Klein's minister of family and social services. His own career had symbolized the mix of private and political pursuits typical of the Alberta government. He worked in a variety of jobs in social service and housing agencies starting in the early 1970s before running for election in 1989.

He became minister during a time of privatization. At least one of his own department's ventures represented the strange hybrids growing in the political landscape.

In 1993 several employees in the department's northeast region, where Cardinal came from, went to the Public Service Employee Relations Board to ask for back pay and other benefits. They won, and were awarded tens of thousands of dollars.

A few months later the department decided to privatize their jobs. In-home counselling work in the region was contracted to a new firm. The department awarded the $2-million contract to its own former manager who had been supervising the work, Keith Tredger. It did not ask for competitive bids despite interest from two established community agencies. There was never a satisfactory explanation. And no one ever explained why an MLA like Cardinal would be the middleman between small contractors and oilfield servicing firms, or what role he would play in trucking.

These small interventions were rarely visible except to the people involved, who usually understood them to be simply the way things were done. Albertans finally got a glimpse of some of the interventions in 1994, more than ten years after the fact, when stacks of government memos were made public in a contractor's lawsuit against the government.

The suit stemmed from the construction of the Paddle River Dam in the early 1980s. Some of the memos involved Deputy Premier Ken Kowalski and Transportation Minister Peter Trynchy. By 1994 they were not only cabinet heavyweights but the two strongest links with the Conservatives' past. Their political careers stretched back into the peak of the Lougheed era.

In 1981 Kowalski had already served an apprenticeship as an executive assistant to Hugh Horner, Peter Lougheed's rural lieutenant. He had become an assistant deputy minister under Horner in the Transportation Department, then succeeded Horner as MLA for the Barrhead area. Trynchy, a farmer and small business investor, had represented the neighbouring Whitecourt area since 1971.

The Paddle River Dam touched both their constituencies. Among the documents in the lawsuit were memos indicating the young Kowalski's shocked surprise at finding out some of the noncontract jobs at the dam had been earmarked for heavy equipment operators in Trynchy's constituency. Kowalski negotiated a written agreement which said that work in their respective constituencies would be split 75-25. Seventy-five percent of the work done in either of the constituencies would be earmarked for operators in that constituency; 25 percent could come from outside. The memo read like a peace treaty. It was sent to the environment minister of the day, who was in charge of dam construction.

Trynchy's name showed up again later on documents related to the allocation of two months of noncontracted earthmoving work on the dam. He reviewed a list of equipment operators lined up for the work, writing "OK" beside some names and in one case specifying that work should be split with another operator. He was also involved in confirming that local truckers would receive nine dollars a load for earth hauling rather than the going rate of six dollars and fifty cents a load.

No one ever explained how many MLAs engaged in this dabbling and how often. It was a style of governing which could begin to create a population of political patrons and clients.

The Klein revolution refined and extended the connections between business and politics. Some of these connections had parallels elsewhere. Some were decades old. Some were small, like the communication between MLAs and grader operators. Some were large and economically strategic, the Alberta equivalent of the American military-industrial complex.

One of the oldest was Nova Corporation, theoretically a private firm but one with deep political roots. Nova owned the gas transmission system to the Alberta border. Ownership by a provincially chartered firm made it impossible for the federal government to regulate natural gas movement inside the province. That was a major reason why Ernest Manning's old Social Credit government had created the company. Klein's government repealed the Nova legislation in 1994 when the firm split into four operating parts, but continued to stipulate that Nova's head office had to remain in Calgary.

The public-private province building lay behind some of the financial disasters of the 1980s. NovAtel was part of that strategy. So was the Magnesium Canada plant at High River. Don Getty's government had tried to interest three or four private firms in the magnesium smelting project before it finally found a taker in Alberta Natural Gas, a pipeline firm which was branching into other businesses. Some of the biggest forestry projects of the late 1980s involved hundreds of millions of dollars in provincial loans and loan guarantees. Some of the loans went out on easy terms and even then were shaky. By 1994, the government was conceding that tens of millions of dollars of a huge loan from the Heritage Fund to the Millar Western pulp mill would probably not be repaid.

Klein liked to distance himself from the projects of the Lougheed-Getty years. Swearing off turned out to be tough.

The most obvious backsliding was a $50-million loan guarantee to Calgary-based PWA Corporation as part of a deal for American Airlines to make a rescue investment in Canadian Airlines International.

There were less noticed deals too. Off to the side, generally ignored because of its location and its corporate structure, sat the Alberta Special Waste Treatment System. This was a curious hybrid set up to operate a hazardous waste disposal plant in the small community of Swan Hills, about two hours' drive northwest of Edmonton.

The plant linked the Lougheed era to the Klein era. It demonstrated how Alberta in the 1990s was elaborating on old policies. It also reaffirmed that the province never ran into financial disaster without being warned of exactly what would happen.

The treatment plant was built in the mid-1980s and operated by a separate entity called Chem-Security (Alberta). The province owned 40 percent of the plant through a Crown corporation called Alberta Special Waste Management Corporation. A firm called Bovar owned 60 percent. Bovar also owned 100 percent of Chem-Security.

The plant was a joint venture between the government and some of Alberta's top business leaders. Bovar actually began life as Bow Valley Resource Services, a subsidiary of a firm named Bow Valley Resources, one of the largest and best connected players in the Alberta oil patch. The joint venture became one of the classic tales of Alberta government entanglement with a business firm. An Environment Council of Alberta panel toured the province in 1980 to gather opinion on treatment of hazardous waste. The panel reported to the government that the safest route was to create a Crown corporation to do the job. There were other warnings.

After Bow Valley bid for the right to build and operate the plant, an independent analysis by the consulting firm Woods Gordon concluded, "Given that the project is not presently seen to be economical using the current estimated costs and revenues, it does not appear practical to establish this project in the private sector."

The government pressed ahead anyway. The directors of Alberta Special Waste Management Corporation resisted. Environment Minister Fred Bradley fired the corporation's chair who later released minutes of board meetings showing Alberta Treasury officials also had concerns. Two other directors quit within weeks. The corporation's vice-president of finance left at the same time, after she was shut out of negotiations with Bow Valley.

A Bow Valley official insisted the plant would make money. Some government ministers suggested the Alberta Special Waste Management chair might have been incompetent. Bradley said the government's policy called for a private operator and that was that.

Bow Valley Resource Services virtually collapsed in 1988 when its offshore drilling arm ran into deep trouble. Creditors took over. Trimac of Calgary bought a controlling interest from one of the creditors, the Royal Bank, and changed the company name to Bovar.

The idea was visionary—use a public-private venture to build and operate a plant capable of incinerating or otherwise disposing of a wide range of dangerous substances. The method perversely twisted any of the usual private-sector incentives for a tight financial operation.

The government agreed to subsidize annual operating costs and guarantee Bovar a yearly return on investment. The return was calculated at three percentage points above the going prime interest rate.

Between 1986 and 1994, the province poured about $250 million into the plant's operations. The Alberta Special Waste Treatment System became one of the huge hidden drags on Alberta finances, silently burning up more money each year than the government would eventually save in 1994 by eliminating half its funding for kindergarten.

In 1992 Chem-Security spent $80 million on an expansion. Klein was environment minister at the time. That led to manoeuvring to let the plant import waste from outside the province. It would still need scores of millions of dollars in public subsidies for at least another five years; possibly it would need hundreds of millions and never make a profit.

In the meantime, the Swan Hills plant had also become part of the government's new international sales push. China, Korea, Taiwan and other countries on the Asian Rim were finding that rapid economic growth led to a rapid spread of pollution. The Alberta government spotted a major potential market for engineering services or technology. Klein made a three-week sales tour through Asia in the fall of 1993. Among his priorities was helping develop the market for environmental services.

There was no untangling public from private interest here. Bovar needed subsidies and government help in selling technology overseas. Any sales to Asia would generate money for Alberta Special Waste Management Corp., but would also bring extra revenue to Bovar. Klein acted as a representative for both.

None of this business had quite the tang of government's more direct licensing of alcohol, lotteries, and registry offices.

All of these suggested a client-patron relationship. They suggested a new political order—a government apparently getting out of business but in less visible ways becoming more entangled in it.

Governments have run the alcohol business in Canada since the prohibition movement began dying out in the 1920s. The first chair of the Alberta

Liquor Control Board was Robert J. Dinning. He went on to chair a crucial commission which led to the approval of natural gas exports from Alberta. He also became the first chair of Alberta Gas Trunk Line and president of the Burns meat empire. His grandson Jim became provincial treasurer in Klein's government. Political structures may change but the same people often end up working on the top floor.

The liquor board had a strong political component. In 1993 the board's chair was a former deputy minister who had once run the Alberta jail system. The other two members were a former Conservative MLA and a former executive director of the Conservative party.

On September 3, 1993, Klein's government became the first in Canada to announce it would get completely out of retail liquor sales. The surprise privatization would cost about fifteen hundred liquor store workers their jobs. An unknown number ended up working in the private stores, sometimes for close to their former pay and sometimes for only half. No one had even whispered the possibility of liquor store privatization during the election campaign three months earlier. Klein, who was making a fetish of public consultation, said everyone knew privatization was coming so there was no need to discuss it. The Opposition said it had heard of government polls indicating strong support for privatization.

The government began a half-year campaign to sell its 210 liquor stores. Selling the stores would guarantee that no future government could afford to revive the publicly owned system. Virtually anyone without a criminal record would be allowed to apply for a retail licence to sell beer, wine, and spirits.

Some people had a head start. About thirty private agencies had opened in rural Alberta in the preceding year. Hotels had been allowed a couple of years earlier to begin selling take-out beer and liquor. Cabinet ministers had said at the time this was not part of a creeping privatization. They had also said it was not a form of subsidy for a hotel industry under pressure because of declining sales.

Several private wine stores had opened under special licence. They were clustered in Edmonton and Calgary. The liquor board had granted some of the wine store licences to well-known Conservatives in the face of dozens of other applications.

The government explained the privatization as a mix of money and ideology.

Privatization let the liquor board dump about $67 million a year in operating costs. Most of that cost would be passed on to private store owners, who could presumably make up some of the difference by paying their clerks lower wages.

Municipal Affairs Minister Steve West, the man in charge of the board, made it clear that ideology played a role too: "There are certain elements in government that would be just as well served by a free market system."

People seemed to like the idea. For a lot of Albertans this was part of the general attack on bureaucrats which had fuelled their thinking during the election. Liberal MLA Percy Wickman held a town hall meeting in his south Edmonton constituency a few days after the announcement.

A middle-aged woman told him that she backed the government's move because she thought it was time to put unionized liquor clerks in their place: "I'm not a drinker but I believe the government should never have been in the liquor business, and I agree with what they're doing. I have a daughter who graduated from university this fall. She can't even get a five-dollar-an-hour job. And here these people without education are getting eighteen dollars an hour to stock liquor shelves? Give me a break."

Here spoke the authentic voice of the politics of social revenge, complete with exaggeration of the store workers' pay.

But politicization of the industry followed almost immediately. The new retail store owners had been in business for only a few weeks before scores of them formed a retail liquor store owners' association that would act as their voice. One of the association's first jobs was to fight to keep alcohol sales out of the free market, contrary to all the rhetoric accompanying the privatization.

West had made it clear the first wave of licences would go to small operators, although one owner could apply for many licences. The big supermarkets were explicitly shut out. By January 1994 the supermarkets were asking for the right to apply for retail licences. They had their own organized voice, the Canadian Council of Grocery Distributors. The council's Alberta office was run by a former executive assistant to a provincial agriculture minister.

Top grocery executives went to the Legislature Building January 25, 1994, to talk with a policy committee of Conservative MLAs. West was there too. He told them the government had promised the smaller operators a four-year head start on sales, although it was not clear when the promise had been made or in what form.

West explained the limits in a redolent choice of words that summed up the Klein-era way of doing business: "That is the free market that we have allowed."

The next few weeks produced more of the make-it-up-as-we-go wobbling which had become a hallmark. Klein announced that the government had changed its mind and would allow the major grocery stores into the retail alcohol market. Within two days they were out again, and the issue put off for reconsideration in the fall.

That fall, West announced flatly that alcohol would be kept out of grocery stories for at least five years.

Beneath all these manoeuvrings lay very old impulses, ways of doing things which stretched back far earlier than the Klein era and beyond even the days of Getty and Lougheed.

Albertans thought of themselves as hardy free-enterprisers. Their history spoke otherwise. They were always ready to bend market rules if they could gain some advantage. The Social Credit experiment of the 1930s had been a radical assault on the market economy, one which frightened the country's bankers and mainstream politicians.

The Alberta Treasury Branches acted as the only government-owned retail bank in English-speaking North America. The Alberta Energy Resources Conservation Board regulated the province's oil and gas industry more closely and with more power than any similar agency in Canada or the United States. Alberta Gas Trunk Line had been one of several public-private economic hybrids running right into the Klein era.

Albertans had demanded hundreds of millions of dollars in government grants during the 1980s to subsidize high-interest business loans, farm loans, and home mortgages. Albertans had nearly voted for government takeover of the private electrical power companies in 1948. A provincial plebiscite defeated the proposal by 151 votes. The vote split on pragmatic lines: the further away people were from existing power plants, the longer they thought they had to wait to be hooked up, the more they favoured public ownership.

The MLAs on the policy committee looking at liquor sales spoke in the raw voice of that more basic Alberta. The executives from Safeway and other chains listened as rural and small-town MLAs explained why they would not readily approve of letting the big stores in on the market.

Clint Dunford from Lethbridge told them he had grown up living in the back of a small grocery store that failed. He said his father had been run out of business by the big chains. He said he might listen to his local

Safeway's request to sell beer and wine but he would listen harder to independent grocers.

Don Tannas from High River said the big chains did not show much compassion or understanding for local food suppliers. He said honey producers and small meat processors were crushed by demands to pay for shelf space and to provide caseloads of free samples for handing out to customers. He could also see the small distillery in his home town getting beaten up if it had to compete for supermarket shelf space.

The same politicians who wanted everyone exposed to economic forces were still using government to protect a few people. It had to be the right people.

They did not talk about crime but they could have. The small new stores had less security than the government stores. Five months after the privatization announcement a robber hit a store in Olds. Several weeks later the owner of a store in nearby Didsbury was held up on the town's main street as he walked to a bank to make a night deposit.

By April 1994 all the government-owned stores had closed. A major opinion poll early in May found that people tended to think prices had gone up and selection had gone down. They still tended to favour the privatization.

The free market was not working its magic the way it was supposed to. It seemed Albertans did not care. Practising the magic was good enough.

The government turned the alcohol business upside down in the middle of another social shakeup. It brought a form of slot-machine gambling into virtually every bar of any size in Alberta. It accomplished that in a silent partnership with the province's hotel owners.

Albertans liked gambling. The province regularly led the way in Canada in betting on bingos, raffles, government lotteries, and other types of gaming. Community groups kept the profit from bingos, casinos, and smaller games. The province earned millions from lotteries.

In 1992-93 the Alberta government took $113.5 million into its lottery fund. Two years later, lottery income hit $500 million. Various volunteer agencies took a large share of that money but increasingly the profits went into general government revenues—$25 million in 1992-93 but $340 million in 1994-95. The government's net take multiplied more than tenfold, at a time when the government said it was not increasing taxes. The money came from the deployment of video lottery terminals.

These machines could be programmed to mimic poker, blackjack, mechanical slot machines, or other forms of casino gambling. At the start of 1992 Alberta had none. By April 1994 Albertans were playing on 4,516 of them. They were all in hotels, bars, and restaurants licensed to serve alcohol. The government planned to increase the number to 8,600. The government owned them all.

They were under the control of Ken Kowalski. He explained the rationale for government ownership to the legislature on April 25, 1994. His language was a shade on the florid side on that occasion, but that was Kowalski.

He had a master of arts degree in Chinese history, a manic delight in using showy wording whenever he thought he was on solid ground, a habit of pursing his mouth into a hurt sort of pout when the opposition caught him off guard or asked him a nasty question, and a reputation for walking into departments and letting the civil servants know he was boss. He had a bad back and used an extra cushion on his seat in the legislature. He did not carry the cushion into question period himself. One of the women in his office carried it in ten minutes before the day's sitting started.

He had usually been effective in whatever he had done—from his youthful days editing a magazine for junior Kinsmen to coaching a high school quiz team in Barrhead to running government departments.

I met him during the 1982 election. We sat in his office in Barrhead and he told me he was going into the cabinet. Modesty and humility had not entered his mind; they were waiting for a traffic signal which never came. He made up for this with an openness about his style and with a surprising sense of humour. He even managed to keep smiling after his taste for personal power brokering made him outdated and Klein pushed him out of the government in October 1994.

Here is what Kowalski said about the province's insistence on owning all the video lottery terminals and keeping control of the money: "Nobody else owns the machines other than the province, and that's been a policy of the province of Alberta. There's only going to be one godfather in the province, and it will be the province. . . .

"I can assure honourable gentlemen and ladies in this assembly that if there were private ownership, there would be a lot of people walking around with black suits and they'd have black shoes with white tops on them and they'd wear certain fedoras with certain kinds of flowers."

He said the government allowed terminals only in licensed drinking places because that meant automatic screening out of anyone under age eighteen. He stuck to oblique comments on what this meant financially. But it was clear that video gambling made a liquor licence more lucrative at a time when people had started drinking less.

"Of these 4,516 machines we know what the average net win is per week," Kowalski said.

Owners of the bars and other locations took a commission of 15 to 19 percent of the weekly net win on each machine. They could have up to ten machines. The return at the best locations could reach thousands of dollars a week on one machine.

"There is actually a fairly healthy return for a fair number of places. . . .

"Very few people take in alcohol when they play VLTs. Liquor sales have gone down like that. There's absolutely no doubt at all about that in any establishment throughout the province of Alberta, but there's been a compensatory upturn in terms of what the local entrepreneur will get." The share for those entrepreneurs translated into about five per cent of the total being bet. They could count on an average take of more than $300 per machine per week.

The move toward privatization reversed the government's relationship with thousands of people. The government was getting rid of employees and replacing them with thousands of other people who seemed independent but owed their livelihood to the government. Sometimes these people needed a government licence to do a particular kind of business. Sometimes they became agents for the gathering and sale of government information.

Steve West led the privatization of the registry offices about the same time he sold the liquor stores. They replaced dozens of motor vehicle licensing offices. They also sold other information and registry services such as birth certificates, land titles, and searches for corporate information.

The privately owned registries made these services more accessible, although prices went up. The government said its rules would keep all information about individuals passing through the registry offices confidential. But they never set out limits on registry functions.

What they did instead was expand the use of registry information for revenue and as a form of social control. From the start, the registries acted as revenue agencies. They collected hundreds of millions of dollars in fees for the province through the sale of items such as driver's licences.

In the spring of 1994 the province passed a law letting the government refuse to renew the licence of any vehicle whose owner had not made child support payments in a divorce. The government would use part of its huge file of personal information in one area to enforce its will in a separate area. The enforcement would work through offices run by the private sector.

At the same time, the government was mailing new personal health insurance cards to everyone in the province. There would be no more family cards. Every individual had a health insurance number, for life. It would be cross-indexed with the federal government's social insurance number.

There had been talk for years about issuing a health insurance card with a magnetic bar allowing access to a person's complete, computerized medical file. Now there was talk of combining the health "smart card" with other identification.

The Klein revolutionaries believed in deregulation and in less government. They snipped red tape. Then they wound computer links around people's bodies.

You know, Steffens, one difference between your time and mine is personal suffocation. Institutions just grew big in your day. Now they spread out tendrils and roots and try to curl around everything alive—everything from trees in a rain forest to newborns who have to be registered with the authorities.

They even control words. Corporations go around trademarking phrases they use in their advertising these days. It's the language equivalent of the attempts to patent certain genes, which are the elements of every life form on earth.

Klein and his ministers tried to reduce some obvious forms of government intervention. They remained blind to the more subtle forms of control saturating our world.

They liked many of those forms of control. They liked others to have them too. After Klein became premier the government kept supporting long periods of patent protection for pharmaceutical manufacturers. Long-running patents meant higher health costs because there would be fewer generic drugs available. That was OK with everyone in the government. They saw the design and manufacture of drugs as one of the industries of the future for Alberta.

In a lot of ways the Klein revolution was a struggle over who had control in Alberta.

Klein functioned as a walking Mr. Happy Face. Behind him worked people who wanted control of their own lives and many other people's lives. You could look around at the landscape of political insiders, bureaucrats, and business executives wielding power, supported by hangers-on looking for crumbs of money and policy decisions, and wonder if something were at work at an even deeper level.

Klein conceived the world in simpler terms. When he heard something he disliked about people he thought were building the province with him he would let an irritated disbelief slide across his face and say something like, "These are good people." That would be the end of that. Silence would follow.

Silence was a distinguishing feature of the Klein revolution too.

The only people who talked were those whose arguments ultimately rested on the statement "I believe," or the communications professionals for whom talk was often camouflage.

I keep thinking of how you went onto the streets of New York City and the police would show you how and tell you why they broke heads on picket lines. You would go into the offices of political bosses. If you had done your spadework they would confirm your information was right. Some even wanted to talk about what their system had cost them and their country.

Things seemed more human then. There are too many experts around now.

Colleen Klein wipes a tear from the eye of husband Ralph the day he resigned as mayor of Calgary, March 1989. Photo: CALGARY HERALD David Lazarowych

*Klein takes part in a PC leadership campaign debate October 14, 1992, with
Elaine McCoy, John Oldring, and Doug Main.*
Photo: THE EDMONTON JOURNAL *Joanne Tymafichuk*

Klein at his desk in the premier's office, February 17, 1993.
Photo: THE EDMONTON JOURNAL *Bruce Edwards*

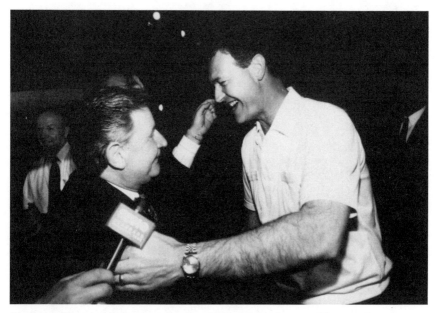

Former economic development minister Peter Elzinga greets Klein on election night, June 15, 1993. Elzinga did not run in the election and became the Conservative party's executive director. Photo: THE EDMONTON JOURNAL *Ed Kaiser*

Klein arrives at a PC caucus meeting during the MLAs' pension controversy, April 1993. Photo: THE EDMONTON JOURNAL *Greg Southam*

Cabinet ministers cutting up during skit show at the PC's annual convention April 3, 1993. Agriculture Minister Walter Paszkowski struts with microphone. Diane Mirosh on far left. Klein, second from right, is flanked by Energy Minister Pat Black and Labour Minister Stockwell Day. Photo: THE EDMONTON JOURNAL *Steve Simon*

Environment Minster Ralph Klein reads to Edmonton schoolchildren during a school read-in week, September 12, 1991. Photo: THE EDMONTON JOURNAL *John Lucas*

Newly-installed Calgary Mayor Ralph Klein is interviewed in his office November 8, 1980. Photo: THE EDMONTON JOURNAL

Klein leads a small gaggle of joggers around an Edmonton track early in the 1993 election campaign, May 22, 1993. Photo: THE EDMONTON JOURNAL *Joanne Tymafichuk*

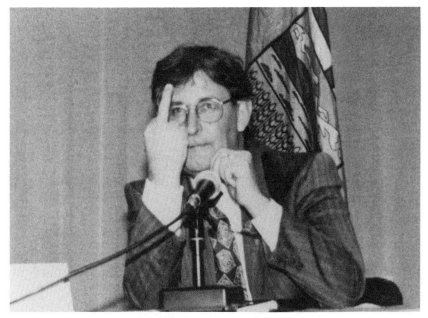

Environment Minister Ralph Klein gives the finger to a particularly rude protester during the news conference announcing the go-ahead on the Alberta Pacific pulp mill. Photo: WEJ PUBLISHING LTD. Mike Griffin

A downtown Edmonton billboard bears the dominant image of the 1993 election campaign, May 1993. Photo: THE EDMONTON JOURNAL Ken Orr

Former premier Don Getty chats with Klein during the swearing-in ceremony for the new cabinet nine days after Klein's election as Conservative party leader, December 1992. Photo: THE EDMONTON JOURNAL *Rick MacWilliam*

Klein dances with Indians in the legislature rotunda in part of the swearing-in celebration for his new government, December 1992. He had years earlier been made an honourary member of the Blackfoot tribe (now Siksika nation) and given the name Bluebird. Photo: THE EDMONTON JOURNAL *Jim Cochrane*

Ralph and Colleen Klein enjoy the announcement of Klein's victory in the PC leadership election December 5, 1992. Photo: THE EDMONTON JOURNAL *Ian Scott*

Environment Minister Ralph Klein takes a doubting look at one of several glasses of water environmentalists dared him to drink as a test of water quality downstream from a pulp mill, Ocbober 8, 1989. Photo: THE EDMONTON JOURNAL *Rick MacWilliam*

Ralph Klein and Nancy Betkowski share a stage during the Conservative leadership race, November 29, 1992. Photo: THE EDMONTON JOURNAL *Ed Kaiser*

9

The Corporate Province

The Edmonton Journal
September 17, 1993

Alberta has a health minister who will not say anything and a health budget with a $122-million blank spot.

The government has a report from a round table on health in Red Deer last month. It is running smaller round tables on health in 10 cities around the province through the next few weeks.

But the public consultation is short, heavily massaged and indifferently informed.

The health project compares badly with other efforts at public consultation—efforts such as the lengthy public hearings on the Constitution or the two years of work that went into Alberta's new environment law.

The government which happily uprooted liquor policy without asking anyone's advice wants to say the public is in charge of future health policy. The public has spotty involvement.

Professionals in the system are wondering what's going on. The legislature has largely been cut out of decisions.

Who is running things here?

That's far more than a rhetorical question.

Someone will end up running things. Who it is will say a lot about what kind of government we have. Health is important enough; the government intends to remake other crucial services the way it is remaking health. They apparently want to reduce the role of the legislature and to shift responsibility, although not necessarily power, from the minister.

The Red Deer round table report makes that point bluntly: "The message to depoliticize the process was received loudly and clearly."

You don't really depoliticize health, however. The government has been trying instead to rechannel the politics of health. It will try the same with education and other service areas.

The round table was an attempt to move public policy matters out of the hands of elected politicians and into the hands of another body largely made up of people directly involved with the industry.

As a general concept that's hardly new. It smacks of a theory pushed in various forms around Europe and North America over the last two centuries; different versions went under names like syndicalism or corporatism. The old United Farmers of Alberta embraced a variant with their theory of group government.

When I look at the way things are going and write about a drift toward a corporate state I mean a different method of government, not just a government influenced by business.

Ralph Klein's government has moved to strengthen the legislature in some ways. The first free vote has been held. Today the first subcommittees will meet to discuss the 1994 budget. These will theoretically allow a far more detailed look at the province's operations and spending plans than was possible before.

The government has also started changes which tend to undermine the legislature.

The new budget system makes it far easier for the government to change its programs without legislature debate.

The new method for making public policy tries on the surface to put the job into the hands of the general public and in particular into the hands of groups directly affected. It actually keeps a controlling power in the hands of the government, a government which relies on the mass appeal of a popular leader.

It tends to stifle criticism on the ground that the people have spoken, although some people may have a stronger voice than others while some may have no say at all. It tends to devalue debate. It separates political decisions from elections.

Whether embraced by unions or by business, in the 1800s or the 1900s, the effect of such ideas has always been the same: to make it easier for part of society to impose its will on another part.

These were dark days in which to be a solitary watcher. Klein and his government were changing democracy in Alberta.

They were building new structures designed to drape a velvet cloak over dissent.

They were setting up a system in which Albertans were presumed to speak with one voice and anyone who said "I protest" was dismissed as a special pleader. People who liked the government complained about "whiners" and said it was time for everyone to join the team or get out of the way.

It was not long before they even turned on their own. Dave King, a Conservative education minister in the mid-1980s and an also-ran candidate in the 1992 leadership campaign, had become executive director of the Alberta Public School Boards Association. He resigned from the party in May 1994 to protest the government's changes to school law. King said the province was taking rights away from school boards.

"Perfect!" Klein said on hearing the news. "Now he can whine and snivel and sob and at least he won't be doing it as a Tory. He's been fighting us every step of the way and I totally disagree with him that what we have done is discriminatory. . . . I don't want to sound pushy or like a bully, but school boards are there at the pleasure of the legislature. They are creatures of the government." A few weeks later he said the government could fire provincial judges too.

The fall of 1993 was a confusing time. These were days when I asked myself if I were watching the creation of a sugar-coated fascism. But I also wondered if I was losing grip on reality. Hardly anyone was asking the same thing. The only person I knew thinking in those terms was former New Democrat MLA Barry Pashak and he thought about it before anyone else. He had spent a day that March watching the budget round table and told me that afternoon it was fascism.

That fall no one much seemed to notice or care. People were decompressing from the election campaign and waiting for the big budget decisions. The New Democrats had disappeared. The Liberals were enjoying the feeling of being accepted into the club in the legislature. They took half a year to figure out that the new open government had a mind to impose its will on everyone.

Klein tipped off the new attitude in a speech to weekly newspaper publishers in the fall. He wanted to push ahead with wage cuts. For the first time since becoming premier he let people see his tough-guy side. The time for debate is over, he said. It was time for the government to act.

But where had the debate taken place? Not in the election campaign, except in the most general of ways. All the campaign had settled was that people wanted to balance the budget and create jobs without adding more taxes.

Alberta has always been different from other provinces when it comes to political debate. The differences did not begin with the Klein era. Since before Alberta's creation in 1905 the people here have tended to form one dominant group, stuck here and there with unhappy splinters.

Some call this the effect of a nearly colonial experience. Albertans were always grouping together to fight eastern politicians and eastern business.

Others point to the effects of living in an economy dominated for long periods by a single commodity. If nearly everyone in the province thinks their prosperity and their future is tied up with wheat, or with petroleum, they tend to group around the policies seen as doing the most for that commodity. I'm partial to this theory. I have a hunch the political realignment of the early 1990s happened partly because there was no more single commodity which people could trust and build a culture around. All the economic rules had changed.

But what happened in 1993 was different. The Klein revolution did not simply revive old traditions.

Klein and the people around him reinvented the structure of public discussion. They were not alone in thinking it was time. The urge to simplify public life extended far beyond Alberta. Institutions everywhere ripen and split open. They change rapidly when they do. People accept disturbances when they get into that mood. When that spirit gathers in a land it often goes hand in hand with the search for a leader.

You saw this many times, Steffens. You saw it when people looked for civic reform leaders. You saw it when you met Benito Mussolini in the 1920s and he refused to tell you his plans for Italy. The way you recalled it in your autobiography, he said, "My people don't want to know my plans. They wouldn't, they couldn't, but they don't want to have to try to, understand a plan that involves difficult economic problems. They want me to do the work, and when I tell them I will, they are satisfied to let me and they go back to work."

You thought a lot about Mussolini's words and the nature of his government, and concluded that democracy, honesty, peace, and liberty all had to be founded on economic arrangements that abolished fear.

There was plenty of economic fear around in the early 1990s. It combined with disgust at decaying political institutions—in all sorts of places. In the summer of 1992, when Klein was at the brink of his leadership bid, something similar was going on in the United States.

Ross Perot was building a presidential campaign on disillusioned people like the ones a *Wall Street Journal* reporter found in a shopping mall just outside Buffalo, New York. They said things like, "I just dislike all politicians so much, and he's saying the things we've been thinking about all these years." They were vague on exactly what Perot would do but liked him and thought he would do right: "He's got class. He's unique. I don't like the politics in politics. We need to do what's best for the people, not what's best for the Republicans or the Democrats. . . . He'd do something about jobs. He'd tackle welfare reform and get some of those people to work."

A lot of Albertans were in the same state of mind. They had not found their Perot yet—their political leader who could convince them he was not a politician.

When they finally found Klein he had no trouble persuading them he was an ordinary guy personally. That came as naturally as bumming a cigarette. He needed a way to persuade them his policies came from the people too.

The answer was the round table.

It was a technique that sounded good but it came with a catch. Only the government knew what was going on.

Officials and cabinet ministers controlled invitation lists. They controlled the agenda. They controlled the information booklets normally sent out to participants. The people at the round tables always split into a dozen or more workshop groups so they never had direct knowledge of what most of the other participants were saying.

People in the workshop groups were always guaranteed anonymity; no one could know who was promoting what. They might or might not have much relevant background information. No votes were ever taken; one statement in one workshop could filter up through the workshop reports and eventually become a statement representing the entire round table session. Anyone was free to speak in workshops but the organizers always picked the people who reported on the small workshop sessions. Control was built in at every level. What this structure did was create a mythic voice of Alberta—a united, one-dimensional Alberta.

Round tables did not debate the way a legislature would. There was no public clash of strong-minded individuals or economic interests.

Worse, there was hardly a private clash either. No one really had to come to terms with anyone else's arguments or their view of reality or even with the fact of their existence. There was only a winnowing of ideas written down on giant sheets of flimsy paper.

The government sometimes turned the results inside out. A notorious example came from the education round tables of 1993. The report suggested little support for cutting kindergarten funding in half or for creating charter schools. Half a year later, the government went ahead with both. They still claimed their reforms were legitimate reflections of the opinions of Alberta as gathered in the round tables.

The round tables of the Klein era refined what had been started earlier. The big ones all took place under Klein—the budget round table of March 1993 and the health and education round tables of later that year.

The first round table had come into being in May 1990, in Klein's own Department of the Environment. It included some figures who would show up repeatedly through the next few years.

The Alberta Round Table on Environment and Economy was not strictly a provincial creation. Nor did it operate like the later round tables. It grew out of suggestions from the Canadian national task force on environment and economy. Klein said it was supposed to offer high-level policy advice but was not intended to replace existing government functions.

It brought potential adversaries into an organized setting with corporate leaders. It created a safe containment area for disputes, one open to outsiders but dominated by people the government could trust. The results could be described as representing a widely based consensus.

Klein and Peter Elzinga had places on this first round table because they ran the environmental and economic development ministries respectively.

The chair was Ken McCready, president of TransAlta Utilities Corporation of Calgary. Virtually no one outside the business community knew much about him although he ran the largest of Alberta's electrical utilities. He showed up in so many places in the next few years that he seemed at times a shadow premier.

Also on board was Klein's old Calgary friend Sherrold Moore. Others among the twenty-two members included ranchers, local government representatives and exactly one environmental activist.

People like McCready and Moore had a place in other, more private policy exercises. They were even brought into the heart of the government process—budget planning.

In the fall of 1993 the government began for the first time to write business plans for every department and major agency. Eight corporate executives joined MLAs and senior civil servants on subcommittees reviewing those plans. Mel Gray, president of Resman Oil and Gas, took part in a review of business plans for energy and environmental protection. A Liberal MLA protested that this created a potential conflict of interest. No one else said anything. Gray told a reporter he had only offered some general planning advice and urged some privatization. He said he had not seen any details of proposed spending for 1994-95.

Gray did not appear frequently in the government's policy exercises. Others did. Together they suggested a corporate directorship acting behind the facade of the government. Some of the members could be tracked.

Ken McCready ran the largest investor-owned utility company in Canada. Trans-Alta provided electricity to about 1.5 million Albertans. In the early 1990s it was starting to branch out to Central Canada and to Argentina. McCready began his career with the company when it was still called Calgary Power. He rose through the ranks in electrical engineering and management consulting. TransAlta had longstanding ties with the Alberta government and had historically been one of the largest contributors to the Progressive Conservative party. McCready had almost no public profile but held one of the most influential positions in Alberta industry and became increasingly prominent in government policy circles. He had been, among other things, a director of the Conference Board of Canada, a member of the Business Council on National Issues, a member of the Business Council on Sustainable Development, a member of the governing council of the Canada West Foundation, a president of the Construction Owners Association of Alberta, and deputy chair of the Southern Alberta Institute of Technology. He was one of the featured speakers at the Toward 2000 conference in Calgary and one of the official advisers for a series of regional round tables leading up to that conference. He acted as a moderator at the March 1993 budget round table.

He sat on the government subcommittee that reviewed the 1994-95 business plans for the Departments of Education and Advanced Education. Several months later the government appointed him chair of the newly created premier's economic forum, a kind of round table established to work on productivity inside the government. Some of his TransAlta colleagues had influence too. The financial review commission was headed by Marshall Williams, recently retired as TransAlta chair. Williams also helped write the final economic strategy report from Toward 2000. A review of postsecondary policy begun in 1994 was led by new TransAlta chair Harry Schaefer.

Eric Newell was president and chief executive officer of Syncrude Canada. Newell, a chemical engineer with a background in management studies, was invited to one of the private group discussions held in advance of the Toward 2000 conference. He took part in the Calgary conference and joined Marshall Williams on the advisory committee which wrote the final Toward 2000 report. He helped review business plans for the Public Works and Treasury Departments while McCready looked at education. At the same time, Newell was taking part in a review of municipal and educational services around Fort McMurray. The city joined with the local boards of education and the oil sands industry in what they called a stakeholders' group, to find ways of amalgamating, privatizing, or otherwise slimming down local government costs. Part of the inspiration came from Syncrude and the neighbouring Suncor plant; they were major contributors of property tax and were looking for a way to reduce that cost. The stakeholders group flew Ted Gaebler of *Reinventing Government* fame to Fort McMurray in February 1994 for what amounted to a public education session and pep talk. Gaebler arrived and left on a Syncrude jet. It was one of more than a dozen trips he made to Alberta to talk to business groups or to civil servants being indoctrinated in the new ways. Newell's influence on education policy began during the Getty era. He was chair of the Alberta Chamber of Resources education committee when the committee sponsored the international study of comparisons in education. The resource firms organized the study in cooperation with the provincial Education Department because they had already been getting worried by signs of a coming shortage in skilled trades; they wanted to beef up science and mathematics training. Newell was also a member of the Conference Board of Canada National Council for Education and of the Corporate Higher Education Forum.

Norm Wagner was chair of Alberta Natural Gas Company and a key manager of policy discussion under Klein. Wagner had been a classics professor. He became president of the University of Calgary and shifted into private business through a directorship with Alberta Natural Gas. He arrived on the ANG board in 1986, a year before ANG succumbed to government persuasion and made its ill-fated investment in a magnesium smelter at High River. By the early 1990s Wagner was also a member of the provincial audit committee. Treasurer Jim Dinning named Wagner and another committee member, Ralph Young, as co-chairs of the budget round table in March 1993. Dinning did not at the time identify their role with the audit committee. Nor did he talk about Wagner's connection with the magnesium plant, which failed at a cost to taxpayers of more than $100 million. Wagner eventually became chair of the audit committee. He proceeded from the budget round table to run the round tables on health policy. Health Minister Shirley McClellan later appointed him to help organize a new system of regional health authorities. He and provincial officials hired a small consulting firm owned by his son, Richard Wagner, to work on the budget and health round tables. He appointed his daughter, Marj Koepke, to handle conference management and secretarial support during the creation of the new health regions. When the family connections became publicly known he argued, "The way I run my office is surely up to me. I have to deliver the goods in a very short time frame."

Art Smith was chair of SNC Partec, the petroleum division of the engineering giant SNC-Lavalin Group, and an active Klein adviser. He had been a Calgary city councillor during Klein's days as mayor, a member of the Alberta legislature, a Conservative member of Parliament and was part of Klein's inner circle. Smith held few official roles during Klein's time in government but was a founding co-chair of the Calgary Economic Development Authority and was apparently instrumental in the province's decision in 1994 to create an Alberta Economic Development Authority. He became Klein's co-chair on the authority in late 1994 at the same time that Klein made himself minister of economic development. The realignment almost certainly ensured Smith a large say over policy decisions related to economic development.

Hal Wyatt was a director of the Royal Bank, former senior manager of the bank and active, with many others in this list, in organizations such as the Calgary Chamber of Commerce, the Ranchmen's Club, and the Petroleum Club. Wyatt served as co-chair of the Calgary Economic Development Authority. More prominent in the Getty era, he chaired the Toward 2000 Together project and steered it to its final report. Klein rarely referred to the report but it set out the intellectual groundwork for the government's economic and social policies.

Gordon Barefoot was a chartered accountant and a partner in Ernst and Young management consultants in Edmonton. Barefoot sat as a member of the financial review commission. Fred Snell, an Ernst and Young partner from Calgary, sat on the provincial audit committee with Wagner and Young. Accounting firms became increasingly aggressive about policy advice during the Getty and Klein years despite their questionable role in financial disasters such as the collapse of Principal Group and NovAtel. No one figure dominated. Other prominent names included Bill Stephen, a partner in Stephen Johnson in Calgary, Bill Grace, a partner in Price Waterhouse in Edmonton. and Brian McCook, vice-president for finance at Nelson Lumber Company in Lloydminster. The profession as a whole wielded more influence than it had during the 1980s. The Institute of Chartered Accountants of Alberta began issuing annual commentaries on the province's fiscal situation and ways to mend it. Five of the nine members of the financial review commission were executives of accounting-management firms, and four of those came from Calgary. The commission unabashedly recommended the government draw upon "external expertise" to develop an effective management control structure. At a time when most professional organizations in the province were taking their turns at the guillotine of public opinion and being dismissed as "special interests," accountants led a charmed life. They enjoyed a certain invisibility despite their increasingly prominent role.

Sherrold Moore was a vice-president of Amoco Canada Petroleum, a key figure in Klein's leadership campaign, and one of Klein's private advisers for years. He was appointed one of the moderators at the budget round table and became chair of the government's Sport, Recreation, Parks and Wildlife Foundation, continuing a role he had held before. Besides joining the round table on environment and economy, Moore had served on advisory committees for Alberta ministers of energy and consumer and corporate affairs. He too sat on the advisory committee which wrote the final report for Toward 2000.

Jack Donald was chair of Parkland Industries, an independent refining company and gasoline retailer based in Red Deer. Donald took part in Toward 2000 and became chair of the tax reform commission. He also joined the board of directors of TransAlta.

Ric Forest was president and owner of Forest Construction of Edmonton. He took part in Toward 2000 and the health policy round tables. Forest acted as chair of the Caritas hospital group in Edmonton until 1993 and took a lead role in the construction industry. He was involved in, among other things, creating construction management firms in the early 1980s to operate with nonunion labour. He took part in the province's official review of labour law in the mid-1980s and was for a while chair of the Merit Contractors' Association. He sat on the tax reform commission too.

George Cornish was a Calgary city commissioner during Klein's days as mayor. Cornish acted as executive director for the financial review commission, the body which recommended that the provincial government develop management goals and performance measures. He sat as the private-sector representative in the subcommittee reviewing the first business plan for the departments of municipal affairs and transportation. He was later appointed to the province's Local Authorities Board.

John Ballheim was president of DeVry Institute in Calgary, a private vocational college. He played an aggressive role at the Toward 2000 conference and in various forums dedicated to education. He took part in the advisory committee which wrote the workbook used by participants in the education round tables. Ballheim was perhaps the most aggressive and well-connected member of a strong but largely unnoticed lobby for private, postsecondary education. He also lobbied for charter schools run by parents and financed with public money. An Iowa native, he held dual Canadian-American citizenship. He held several teaching jobs before becoming international operations manager in 1983 for Bell & Howell, which ran the DeVry operations in the U.S. and Canada. He moved to Calgary in 1984. In late 1993, as president-elect of the Alberta Chamber of Commerce, he warned the government was getting off track with its educational reforms, allowing the public focus to settle too much on budget cuts instead of on ideas such as replacing some certified teachers with less expensive aides and computers.

Rob Peters was president of Peters and Company investment dealers in Calgary. Another Klein insider, Peters did not play formal roles but maintained ties with Klein. When Klein went to Asia in the fall of 1993 he delivered greetings to dozens of investors who had poured several hundred million dollars into junior oil and gas firms in the preceding year, much of it through Peters and Company's operations in Hong Kong. Peters accompanied Klein on his trip to Ontario in early 1994 to sell Alberta's fiscal strategy and the province's attractions as a home for investment.

Dee Parkinson was a vice-president at the Suncor oil sands plant. She acted as a moderator at the main health policy round table in Red Deer, was a member of the tax reform commission, and took part in the "stakeholders" group reviewing local government at Fort McMurray.

These names cropped up repeatedly and in influential corners. There were others. Stephen Murgatroyd, a management professor at Athabasca University, advocated a system of total quality management in education. He had influenced Dinning and had served with Ballheim on a secret committee which developed alternatives for advanced education in 1992. That committee's work helped lead to a proposal in the 1994 budget to create a $47-million "access fund," some of which would end up financing private colleges. George Pheasey was former manager of corporate relations for Delta Catalytic Corporation, one of the engineering firms the government had helped flourish. He was appointed an assistant deputy minister of labour in September 1991 as part of a two-year exchange program involving government and business managers. Three years later he was still a Labour Department bureaucrat, in charge of the client services division, one of the hot spots for privatization efforts. Stan Schellenberger, the former Conservative MP whom Peter Elzinga had hired to run the policy shop in Economic Development, was named in 1994 to a committee appointed by cabinet to look into ways of using the advanced education access fund.

Other executives brought in to help review the first departmental business plans included John Simpson, president of CANA, a major construction firm, and Gwyn Morgan, at the time senior vice-president with Alberta Energy Company.

The directorship of the new Alberta included a few highly influential civil servants such as deputy ministers Doug Radke in Agriculture and Al Craig in Economic Development. Deputy education minister Reno Bosetti in particular appeared to direct many of the policy changes in his department. The government's eventual decision to take over collection of $1.2 billion in property taxes for the school system had not been proposed by anyone else in the system. It seemed to be an idea from the bureaucracy itself.

These were people who led the movement to shrink the size of government and the cost of labour. They were part of a plan to start trimming government with symbolic cuts at the top. They worked at a level where inhabitants usually enjoyed privacy and freedom from cuts. A new securities law was throwing a light on some of them for the first time in 1994.

Among the revelations to any interested stockholders was the news that McCready had taken a 10 percent increase in salary and bonus from 1991 to 1993 and racked up options to buy thousands of TransAlta shares. Wagner's pay and bonus climbed 45 percent in the same two years. He also racked up thousands of share options. The pay for chief executives of typical, large private firms in Alberta was running about $345,000 a year. They often received not only stock options but cars and paid insurance packages. They were different from everyone else. One reason was that hardly anyone paid any attention to them.

These were the most prominent of the people telling Albertans how things would be.

Some of what happened reflected a plan. Much of the plan was set out most clearly before Klein was even elected.

Even at that, Klein ran a government which often seemed to make things up on the fly.

But he clearly ran a government in partnership with business—government as a joint venture.

The new partnership grew out of powerful forces at work in Alberta, forces out of the province's history, out of policy work dating back to Getty's time. For Klein it was also an elaboration of an old way of doing things. Klein seemed to need business friends. He leaned on their judgement. He had no independent grounding in economics and no inclination or training to look for it elsewhere. He told a reporter during his first mayoralty campaign that he had felt intimidated during an early venture into "Chamber of Commerce territory." A few days after he won, an interviewer asked what he saw as his major weakness. He replied, "Certainly, my lack of business experience, my inability probably to read financial statements. I taught accounting for two years so I have some understanding of very basic accounting."

He was a fast learner who had been running a city for nearly a decade but he had also gravitated toward business leaders early on and stayed close to them. His friendships sometimes caused embarrassment. Hal Walker, for a time the president of his Conservative constituency association in central Calgary, was involved in a golf course resort development at Canmore, just outside the gates of Banff National Park during Klein's time as environment minister. Walker's project cleared environmental hurdles quickly. He got through before the rules were toughened, and Klein was often hard put to explain his friend's easy progress.

An early list of Klein insiders at city hall included the head of a building firm, at least four developers, an oil company accountant and the accountant's wife, and a recreational therapist. One of his administrative assistants was the son of the provincial minister of economic development.

In early 1982, a banker friend helped persuade Klein to lobby Ottawa to make Calgary a tax-free zone for international finance. Klein said he wanted to see Calgary become the "Zurich of the West." He explained the dream in classic Alberta fashion, in words which could have come from any Conservative cabinet minister of the day: "When the oil runs dry we have to have a sound economic base and finance is going to be that base."

All the brightest business people were saying things like that in 1982 and Klein listened. He had grown out of a disorderly past. He had been at home with bikers and in beer parlours. But when it came to official business he seemed to crave order and stick to established authority. The pattern stuck with him right into the premier's office.

A lot of other things were happening that fall. The round tables on the most sensitive social policy areas were going ahead.

Health came first. The government had organized a general round table on health policy in Red Deer in August. One look at the crowd said everything you would need to know about the story that decisions were being made by "the people of Alberta."

The official list of participants had 206 names. Of those, 46 were connected with hospital management; 38 were MLAs, provincial officials or, in a handful of cases, people occasionally hired by the province; 17 came from local government or health units, primarily from management; 7 were nurses; 3 came from unions representing other workers. There were also 14 business executives or lawyers. Most of the remainder were physicians, university leaders, or other health professionals. Eighteen people might have been called representatives of the general public but as a group they were heavily weighted toward Health Minister Shirley McClellan's political home in central Alberta; it appeared the average Albertan ran a farm somewhere southeast of Red Deer and voted Conservative.

This was a stacked deck. The invited met behind closed doors in small groups and threw out statements, hoping their words would survive the winnowing process and make it to the final report. They worked with a discussion guide which limited what they could recommend. Even at that, some of them strayed. The conference report said some had talked about new revenue sources. The report also warned that no one really knew what spending to cut in health: "We do not have enough information on the effectiveness of certain medical interventions. We have little in the way of assessment of the value for dollars spent and the resulting benefits to Albertans. Our measures of outcomes are crude."

The health conference spawned ten regional round tables, a reversal of the Toward 2000 process, which had held regional meetings first. The reversal helped create exactly the sense of stage management which public consultation was supposed to prevent.

Norm Wagner ran these shows. He worked under the general direction of Dianne Mirosh, a Conservative MLA from Calgary who had been given a job as minister without portfolio in charge of health planning. Lyle Oberg, a physician and newly elected member from the town of Brooks, helped run the planning secretariat.

The regional meetings came in two parts—a public meeting one night followed by private workshops for invited guests the next day. Wagner said the public and private meetings always seemed different. The difference was hardly a surprise. The private workshop sessions were dominated by the same class of administrators, professionals, and public officials who had been invited to the general round table in Red Deer. Some of the workshop leaders had attended Red Deer.

The show hit Edmonton September 26 and Wagner was its star.

About five hundred people showed up that night, filling seats in a west Edmonton hotel's tradeshow hall. People had ninety minutes to tell the government what they thought. By then their thoughts had been heavily massaged; Wagner lectured them for nearly an hour first.

He began with a comment about bringing the road show to the provincial capital: "People in Edmonton have an advantage because the bureaucrats are nearby and you can go and beat them up or whatever you have to do to them." Scapegoating had become so commonplace that a supposedly impartial moderator could make jokes like this.

He also said, "The future of our country is going to be determined by communities. It's not going to be done by the big guys and it's not going to be done by government."

Within eighteen hours it looked as if the big guys and the government were still running things, whether they claimed otherwise or not.

Wagner was one of the big guys himself but he never explained his status. No one else did either. He looked and sounded like a tougher and more intellectual version of Klein. He was literally big—a muscular and spread-out mound of a man who favoured Hawaiian-style shirts, stared out bluntly from a knobby face and told the crowd, "I'm just a chicken farmer." No mention of his success as an academic and university leader, of his chairing of a major pipeline firm, of his place on the provincial audit committee.

He told them the government had run into billions of dollars of debt because resource revenue got cut in half in 1986. No mention of provincial budgeting failures. No mention of more than $2 billion blown on business failures, including the magnesium plant disaster in High River, which had also cost Alberta Natural Gas $50 million.

He said that while he was "just a chicken farmer" he had seen a model of the economy which made sense to him. It had three boxes. Box A contained wealth production. Box B included wealth-supporting sectors such as transportation. Box C contained health, education, culture, and all the other things which made a pleasant quality of life. He said most governments were dealing with debt by making cuts in Box C. He did not mention any alternative views. He did not venture that health and education might support wealth production and prevent costly social problems.

He told the crowd the Red Deer round table had produced a five-point strategy on health. He said he thought everyone might like to know the "general overall view from your fellow Albertans, a point of view I may add that has been echoed and re-echoed at other round tables."

It turned out this crowd did not want to be echoes. Several people put themselves on the line. They gave their names and they talked about life in hospitals where nurses were being run ragged—having to hire a private nurse; being left alone in an X-ray lab for half an hour wondering if chest pains were actually a heart attack; seeing a cleaning lady come to help a patient in distress. One seventy-seven-year-old woman said she had watched her husband left more and more alone in a long-term care bed. She said she knew that when her turn came she would not have a spouse to come visit three or four hours a day. They kept asking why the budget cuts were coming first and the plans later.

Some of them were special pleaders. They made pitches for chelation therapy, for chiropractic treatment, for transcendental meditation.

Health-care union leaders made statements.

One man in the audience asked why the government did not set out its ideas in a discussion paper and go to the public for response and for improvements. "You're just being ridiculous," he added. Mirosh, who was on the dais with Wagner, replied that the government was under new management. She had begun the evening by telling people, "Tonight you are here to help us . . . you are here to help us build that new health system."

Three hours later she told reporters, "I've found in both Edmonton and Calgary that the unions are well organized to come forward and put forward their opinions." It seemed the people of Alberta were not among the five hundred or so people in the hall. This meeting had not been the genuine voice of Alberta. That voice would be heard outside the major cities and in the private workshops the next morning.

The workshops were closed. No one outside the small groups could know exactly who said what. Moderators summarized the workshop discussions at an open meeting later in the day. The invited participants had much the same backgrounds as the participants at Red Deer and they produced many of the same recommendations: a move to regional health authorities; a definition of publicly insured medical services; less emphasis on hospitals as part of the health system. There were conflicts too: people for and against user fees, for and against immediate wage cuts throughout the health system.

All these comments would end up in Wagner's hands, along with comments from all the other round tables. He would decide in a summary report what the people of Alberta had said about health. He did not explain how he would decide what the main themes were or how to weigh conflicting views.

It was even a touch-and-go proposition to find out who the "people of Alberta" were at this Edmonton meeting. A media aide to Mirosh initially refused to give reporters a list of participants.

A few hours later the Opposition asked Klein in the legislature about some of the stories people had told the night before. Klein accused the Opposition of playing up "little horror stories." He said, "This is melodrama at its absolute worst."

Mirosh sounded ready to write off the public sessions in Calgary and Edmonton. Klein did write off parts of them. In the round tables you had to listen carefully to pick out the whiners and special interests. The voice of Alberta was a lot like crude oil. Before it could be used, it had to be purified.

That's what happened, Steffens. That's why I was writing about a corporate state that autumn, and wondering whether I was dwelling on it too much or not enough. A year later the government would try to pass a law apparently giving itself a free hand to turn government functions over to private businesses and non-profit societies. They eventually withdrew it but said they would bring it back in revised form. The bill brought a distinctive red-market approach to the restructuring of government. It was privatization, but not complete free-market privatization. It was was instead a privatization with continuing political control.

Whatever responsibilities the government intended to hand over would go to agencies which lawyers who commented on the bill had difficulty describing as either public or private. The agencies would apparently have a free hand in many ways but would be answerable to individual ministers and could be stripped of their powers on two days' notice. At the same time, there were no controls on how corporations would receive contracts to take over government responsibilities. The opportunities for patronage were huge. The bill confused public and private business in many ways. One of the few certainties seemed to be that cabinet ministers would not answer in the legislature for anything done by corporations to whom they had delegated responsibility, although the ministers would retain significant control over those corporations. And the province's auditor general would not have free access to review any of the agencies. By then, however, greater power with less accountability was a theme Albertans were getting used to.

There was a progressive blurring of the lines between government administration, private groups or businesses, and the Progressive Conservative party. The blurring had been a feature of Alberta politics for many years. But it was spreading. it was accompanied by a new insistence that people not part of the system shut up about what they saw. More and more, when I had call to write about "the Conservative party," it felt instead that I should be writing about "the Party."

I wonder what you would have said. You liked what you thought was the first step toward an open political-commercial relationship in the United States—a conference which brought Henry Ford to the White House to talk with Herbert Hoover.

Corporate states come in many colours. Their essence is some political arrangement involving direct relationships between players in an economy. Some political scientists describe some social democratic countries such as

Denmark and Austria as corporate states. Japan has been run for forty years by a combination of civil servants, politicians, and business leaders. Quebec leans in that direction with its negotiations between business, government, and labour. Mussolini's Italy was a kind of corporate state too.

Was Alberta turning into a home for some kind of benign version of fascism? I ended up not thinking so. There was no deliberate and conspiratorial malice, no measure of belief in violence as a political tool.

And I do not want to exaggerate the newness of everything that was happening.

The urge to create a united provincial voice—one political party or leader communicating directly with the people—was a habit as old as Alberta. People had noted that urge with William Aberhart in the 1930s and with Peter Lougheed, and some had commented caustically on its potential.

Harold Innis was writing back in the 1930s about Canada being run by an "economic dictatorship." He also said the country was threatened by "the new internationalism." That internationalism even had its own identifying communications technology—radio.

Still, something new was happening.

Klein had gone a long way toward opening the premier's office. In some ways he lived out the ideals of common sense and communication described by Havel. He kept up a hard pace of public speaking appearances. When controversies blew up, like a stiff reaction over cuts to seniors' financial benefits in early 1994, he sent ministers out to hold public meetings.

It was not enough. To many people, these measures looked like flimsy camouflage for more vital decisions. By the time of the Conservative party convention in April 1994 Klein knew about the skepticism. He responded with his patented irritation. He told convention delegates, "And it should not go unnoticed that those critics insult every Albertan who took some time out of the present to help plan the future."

Some of those critics may have been on the convention floor listening to him. A party questionnaire a few months earlier had turned up solid support for the government's actions from the more than four thousand PC members who answered it. Nearly half of them said they were not convinced the government was adequately consulting the public on its decisions.

It was tough trying to create a partnership while making sure that some of the partners had a controlling vote.

They made it up on the run. They may have surprised themselves with how they scraped the boundaries of a kind of fascism. The political science books cite characteristics like a focus on a strong leader, the creation of a popular and all-encompassing political myth, scapegoating, the denigration of rational debate, the undermining of liberal democratic structures of government, insistence on discipline, an emphasis on subordinating individual rights to a national will, the defence of a dominant group's social and political position.

The name tends to be controversial and confuses things. It distracts people from the reality at hand. The problem with the reality is not the name. The problem is that it tends to create inequities and absurdities. It is simply bad politics. The name also reflects an older reality from a time when political leader were able to infuse almost supernatural elements into different nationalisms, and to control more easily the flow of information across their borders.

You could use more modern descriptions such as "programmed society" or an "opaque and mystified form of oligarchy."

Klein and his friends had something modern in mind. You could call it a sugar-coated globalism. The Global Village was were they fully intended to go, even if it lay in a jungle where the vines always seemed ready to curl around just about anyone's neck.

10

Asia

The Edmonton Journal
October 30, 1993
Vancouver

Asia starts at about Granville Street these days.

The Pacific Rim culture in Vancouver—part Asian, part Canadian, a little bit American—explains why Premier Ralph Klein takes off here today for a three-week trade mission to Korea, Japan, China, Taiwan and Hong Kong.

On Granville Street you can peek up a steep driveway toward what looks like a wealthy family's secluded home. It is really the Chinese consulate. West of Granville, amid the terraced pastel condominiums and rounded glass office towers, sushi and noodle shops are normal and the odd pizza stand is what looks exotic.

More than one-third of British Columbia's exports go to Asia these days. Alberta sells about one-eighth of its exports to Asian countries. It would like to sell more. The province also wants to attract more tourists like the Japa-nese who flood into the Rockies each summer, and more investors like Li Ka-Shing of Hong Kong, who put some of his fortune in Husky Oil.

Alberta tends to follow others' slip-streams in this market.

What counts is Asia's massive scale.

Harbin, Edmonton's official "twin" city in northern China, has a metropolitan population of about five million—one city with twice as many people as Alberta. China wants its national economy to grow by about 10 percent a year.

Alberta sells tens of millions of dollars worth of pork to Japan each year. The only barrier to selling more is the lack of pigs.

A southern Chinese economic triangle has been forming. Local business leaders envision a partnership of Hong Kong money and management skill, Taiwanese manufacturing, and Chinese labour and markets. East Asia's economy has been growing fast enough to match the European and American economies by 1997.

Hong Kong wants to become the financial centre for the Pearl River Delta in the next few years. Local business leaders see the area of 45 million people emerging as one of the world's leading economies.

Even the lighter side of business looks huge. North Americans tend to think of Disney and Universal Studios when they think of massive theme parks. A Hong Kong developer wants to build a "world wonders" theme park at the nearby Chinese city of Guangzhou—58 attractions including replicas of the Sphinx and the mountain in the movie *Close Encounters of the Third Kind,* price about $75 million.

The numbers can't fail to impress. Is seeing the reality behind them worth three weeks in Klein's schedule at a time when his government faces the first shocked reaction to its plan for 20 percent spending cuts?

It's an old question. Going to China (and other Asian stops) has become almost a requirement of office since Richard Nixon finally said it was OK two decades ago.

Results of these trips tend to be vague—an official signing of an agreement here, rumours of large investment potential there.

Klein will at least have company when he meets the local politicians. They, too, often have an easier time with foreign trade than with domestic affairs.

Japan has been in an economic slowdown, is trying to clean up widespread corruption and is trying to reduce agricultural protectionism despite protests from rural areas which have a disproportionately large share of seats in the national legislature.

China started an austerity drive early in the summer; fortunately for Alberta, energy investment is one of the few sectors spared. Hong Kong worries about its future under Chinese rule, has criminal gangs with memberships as big as the population of Red Deer and has found it can no longer depend on the tides to wash raw sewage out of its main harbor.

Politicians around the world know one another's problems.

People mostly remember you for one thing, Steffens. It is not for your muck-raking. It is for going to Russia just after the Revolution and coming back to say, "I have seen the future and it works."

I guarantee you no one remembers why you wrote that — that you thought Russia was the future because polititians and economic power had openly been fused.

Asia looks like the future too. It looks like a giant but it is an unstable giant, a skyscraper missing half its foundation. Perhaps it will work anyway. If it does, I hope the way it looks now is not Alberta's or Canada's future.

Klein left for his tour a couple of weeks after a supplementary budget came out with plans for spending cuts of 20 percent accross the board. Drastic cuts had looked like an option but few people had wanted to think they would happen.

It seemed a strange time for a premier to leave the province. Klein acted as if it were a good time for him. He never reacted well to anger. One of his favourite phrases beginning with his time as environment minister was "Stop yelling."

As reports crossed the Pacific about high school students pounding on the legislature doors and Liberal MLAs forcing an all-night sitting of the legislature he looked bemused. At one point he had to deal with a difference of opinion back home between Dinning and Kowalski over the amount of flexibility in the 20 percent target. He gave me his version and then he walked away joking with one of the officials on the trip: "I wonder what the boys are up to back there." He did not rattle easily. That was one of his strengths.

A few days into the trip the timing seemed not so strange at all. Asia and the budget plan were linked.

Klein travelled with his wife Colleen, a security man, aide Gordon Olsen, and two officials from the Department of Federal and Intergovernmental Affairs. They flew first to Seoul, South Korea.

Everything about the city suggested the bigness of Asia. The world's largest cities had outgrown everything around them now. They sucked up people from the countryside faster and more powerfully than ever. They belonged not to the nation-state of their origins, but to an international network of airports, shipping, computers, brand names, joint ventures, and pools of cheap labour.

Seoul was one of the biggest. In the fall of 1993 it was a concrete-grey megalopolis laid into the folds between arid Korean hills. The Kimpo airfield had a khaki look about it as if it had not changed much since the Korean War forty years earlier. Most everything else must have changed.

A bus travelled from the airport into the city, across a river as dusty looking as the hills and as broad as the twelve-storey apartment buildings being constructed in ranges all up the valley. Cranes hung across new apartment shells. It looked as if the builders here could have poured as much concrete in one day as Alberta had poured all summer.

The bus followed a crooked route to the midcity, past side streets which served as paths to an older world, onto a multilaned boulevard wider than a Los Angeles freeway, and past the domed main railway station where thousands of commuters disembarked every morning. It whined up into the driveway of the Seoul Hilton Hotel.

The hotel lobby had a marble and rosewood look. Japanese businessmen and wives sat on plush chairs underneath abstract paintings the size of movie screens. Underneath a bank of lights at the far end, inexorably drawing the gaze of everyone passing through, lay the lobby's central feature, a sculpture the size of a car. It was a reclining woman by Henry Moore.

One of the officials told me later the party was staying here because this was a reasonable international hotel by Seoul standards. There was a grander and more expensive German-owned place a few blocks away.

Asia was clearly going to require a recalibration of a person's measure of what is big.

None of this seemed to matter to Klein. He had dealt with hugeness before. He was mayor when the Winter Olympics came to Calgary. He seemed able to shut out the surroundings and concentrate on what mattered. He measured everything by some personal scale and in the end he measured what counted in Asia as well as back home—the people.

But what he had come here to sell them was nothing related to people at all. It was a budget policy apparently written to fit the requirements of whatever anonymous force had created a megalopolis in the dusty Korean hills.

Back home people were starting to get worried about what huge spending cuts would mean to schools and the health system. Some people were not worried. They liked the idea of cutting spending enough to get the deficit under control without paying a sales tax.

In Asia everything got reversed. The deficit was a secondary issue. The point of the new policy was low taxation. The point of low taxation was not to keep voters happy but to make Alberta a pleasant place for international firms to do business.

In Seoul these firms were the Hanjin Group, with interests in transportation; the Hyundai group, best known in Canada as a car maker; Pohang Iron and Steel, the third-largest steel producer in the world and a firm which came to Alberta for about one-quarter of its coal requirements; the Daewoo Group, which dabbled in just about anything, building an auto plant in Turkestan, trying out forestry in Brazil, expressing interest in getting into the oil sands in Alberta or possibly even organizing a way of shipping Alberta natural gas to Korea in liquefied form.

These were not just big companies. They were dominant in their sectors of the economy and they worked hand in hand with the government.

Klein had an uncanny ability to bridge the chasm between world-size scale and the highly personal. He could translate the needs of one into the wishes of the other. He had done that during the election and now he was doing it in Asia.

When he spoke he looked as if he were campaigning. He even had a slogan—the Alberta Advantage. The "advantage" basically came down to the lowest tax rates of any province in Canada. He said so. He told the Koreans that business taxes would go even lower than they already were.

When he talked, you could close your eyes and swear you were in Ponoka or Lethbridge. Alberta voters, Korean business leaders, they were all the same to Ralph Klein. They were all just plain folks.

And here was the most surprising thing of all—they responded to him much like a crowd in Lethbridge or Ponoka. About one hundred and fifty Seoul businessmen came out to an Alberta government reception during Klein's first night in Seoul. He gave them the full-bore pitch on the Alberta Advantage. They soaked it up and, when told the premier was turning fifty-one that night, they sang "Happy Birthday."

Whether they were impressed by the promise of "the lowest tax regime of any province in the country" was another matter. The purpose of a low-spending, low-tax policy was to carve a spot for Alberta in the wildly competitive wilderness of the new world economy.

The Asians seemed to take it less as a critical factor than as an advertisement, a sign of interest. The heads of the industrial conglomerates focused on a much bigger game than taxation. They wanted control of resources.

Pohang Iron and Steel wanted a secure supply of coal and were considering an investment in Alberta. Daewoo wanted a secure supply of petroleum and that's why it was thinking about putting money into the oil sands. It was interested in liquefied natural gas because Korea needed a cleaner source of fuel. The millions of people who had moved into Seoul in the past twenty years still burned coal and cooked over charcoal briquets. The smoke put a choking quality into the air, as if all the exhaust from all the cars and furnaces and ovens in Seoul had turned into an oily, sulphurous talcum that settled over the city and would not wash or blow away.

The choking air never came into the hotel. Inside the hotel were air conditioning, international visitors, extravagant art, business managers coming to see the first Canadian politician to show up since the Canadian federal election. Outside the hotel lay the everyday Korea. Workers, men and women, slowly raked a layer of leaves as thick as winter's snow in a hillside park. Traffic boomed down streets so wide they could be crossed only by going through subway tunnels. People lined every tunnel selling trinkets, gadgets, watches, pocket knives, shoes, shirts. Up top, alleys wound back from the main streets. The alleys were lined with enterprise too. You could walk through them and see small offices, machinery shops, hole-in-the-wall printing plants with bundles of posters or flyers stacked outside their doors, restaurants, food stands with corn and chestnuts roasting over charcoal or bushels of peanuts lying on a counter.

Masses of people moved up and down the alleys and streets. Everyone seemed to have something to do. This was one Alberta dream come to life—a society where all people worked hard and made their own way, finding a small enterprise for themselves if they did not have a big job. They worked, they laughed, they got by in a rugged geography. They reminded me of Canadians.

The "Alberta advantage" had nothing directly to do with them. Unless they were living in the kind of society Alberta's leaders wanted to build.

At night you could go wandering down the safe streets and into crowded markets filled with the smells of frying and boiling delicacies—filled with people. The darkness seemed comforting. In the dusk before it came, the fume-laden sky would turn a ghastly pink, bathing the whole city in an apocalyptic glow.

At that time of day, in that light, the mind wandered to the North Koreans and their baby atomic bomb program just beyond the hills where the sickening light drizzled down. You could go outside to marvel at the light or you could stay in the hotel to read or to look at the paintings and the Henry Moore. But even there you could not escape the feeling of something big breathing beneath the surface. Something big lay behind everything here. The hotel was named Hilton. It was owned by Daewoo.

Klein went to Japan next. He talked about the "Alberta advantage" there too. By then it was obvious that most Asians had other things on their minds. He spent much of his time explaining the results of the Canadian election. He explained the puzzling collapse of the Progressive Conservative party which had run the country for eight years and described the new opposition parties which had formed in Quebec and the West. Mostly he talked about North American free trade. The Japanese, like others, were looking for reassurance that free trade between Canada, the U.S., and Mexico did not amount to a regional trade bloc aimed at freezing out Asian countries.

If the Japanese cared deeply about Alberta's tax policies they kept their opinions behind closed doors. What they and the Canadians who knew them talked about was the importance of building long-term relationships, and of securely meeting Japan's needs. Commerce in Japan is double-edged. When Japanese spend money abroad they act as if they are doing someone a favour. Yet there is always an edge of desperation in the transaction. At some level the purchase fills a crucial need. The trick for the Japanese is to keep enough safe sources of supply open that they can maintain some bargaining power.

So when Japanese firms think about looking in Alberta for building components such as doors and windows their arrival becomes a huge marketing opportunity for Alberta. On the Japanese side, the Alberta products fill a need more cheaply than similar Japanese goods. They also fill a need for distinctiveness; they offer variety and a touch of the exotic in a country where a tradition of orderliness and a population of 170 million forces many people into living exactly like their neighbours.

An official of Sumitomo Forestry. came to a Canadian Embassy reception for Klein in Tokyo. He said his firm wanted to start an oriented-strand board plant or similar operation soon in Alberta. Sumitomo was not being drawn by the province's fiscal policies. He said the firm was being drawn by the prospect of a secure supply of building material: "We need it. We need it urgently."

You could get the idea sometimes that Japanese firms do not so much get lured into investing in Alberta as driven to it.

The highest official levels in Japan did not show a clear interest in Alberta policy either. The situation left Klein with little to do but cement relations with Alberta's sister province of Hokkaido, and sell. He always said he planned to be an international salesman for Alberta and he filled that role in Japan. He visited a furniture store selling Edmonton-made products in Sapporo. He presided at the launch of an Alberta-brewed beer. He visited a Tokyo grocery store to help sell its first shipment of Alberta-grown carrots and other vegetables. But then he went to Osaka and visited a place that finally revealed the bigness of the network Alberta was trying to join.

Osaka was huge to start with. A city sprawled for kilometres around a park dominated by a seventeenth-century castle. The bullet train line stretched northeast to Tokyo through endless suburbs, villages, and cities. The waterfront looked like a city itself, with a container port where the cranes stretched on for more than a kilometre. Even here there was room for one more step up in scale.

Klein went down to the bay to visit the nearly completed Asia and Pacific Trade Centre. It was supposed to house an Alberta-produced dinosaur show the following spring. The show would fit indoors. That was appropriate, because what Klein and his delegation saw was a sight that would have made dinosaurs look about as impressive as toy poodles.

The trade centre occupied a spot on the docks where you could look across the bay and faintly see the towers of the city of Kobe. The building itself was designed with glass fronts, fanciful parapets made to look as if they belonged on the bridge of an ocean liner, and monstrous indoor caverns of concrete meant to create the biggest meeting place anywhere in Japan for joint congregations of exporters, retailers, and distributors.

As big as these caverns were, they were dominated by the 252-metre World Trade Centre building taking shape behind them. The trade and office buildings were part of Cosmosquare, a business centre which would dominate the south end of Osaka Bay. And Cosmosquare was not the end. It was only the heart of a $20-billion, twenty-year development called Technoport Osaka. The concept included the new Kansai Airport being finished on reclaimed land out in the harbour. The integrated development would take until 2010 to build. It would comprise a technical and trade centre with roads, rail lines, and fibre-optic cables tying the parts of Technoport together and tying Technoport to downtown Osaka. The airport would link the whole development to the rest of the world. Bruce Davis, Klein's Saskatchewan-born security man, looked around and said, "This sure isn't Wakaw."

It wasn't even Toronto. Osaka held six million people. The immediate area around it was home to 20 million people and an economy as big as Canada's. This part of Japan had long felt overshadowed by Tokyo. Now they were staking their own place. Yoshihide Ishikawa, managing director of JTB World Vacations, the region's largest tourism operator, described the intent later at an Alberta government reception: "We were off-line. Now we are going to be on-line."

Going on-line meant being plugged in. It meant flipping a switch in some computer which organized the world and becoming part of the central network. It meant transforming what had been merely a thriving economy into a place where the economy grows so dynamically and with such organizing purpose it becomes almost a living thing. That was a concept as stunningly big as the building plans which supported it. That was the twenty-first century.

But there always seemed to be something more behind any structure. We found it in China.

In a continent where jumbo jets were used as commuter planes and where city populations seemed to start at a million, China dwarfed everything. It had the biggest land mass and the most people. It had the most catching up to do. Those two factors combined made it the biggest market—a place where more than a billion people were trying to build a replica of the developed world, seemingly in a few months.

The Americans were here, the Germans, the British, and all the other Asians. Klein, just as all his supporters had claimed, was absolutely right to bring Alberta here too. China was the place where overproduction and overinvestment seemed impossible. If there was money in the world it could go to China and find a use. The only question was whether China was big enough to absorb all the world's excess and remain unchanged.

The road from Beijing Airport into Beijing passed two worlds. At first the road led past barracks-like buildings, donkey carts, sheep grazing in openings between cedar and pine, bicyclists carrying wicker baskets full of green vegetables on their rear fenders. Then the scenery changed. A billboard announced A New China Is Waiting. Another billboard depicted a golf course. What looked like a strip mall emerged on the right and a sign over one of the shops read Welcome to the Fashion World. A Matsushita-Panasonic plant stretched for what would have been the length of an Edmonton city block.

And then the city proper came into view and new names began appearing on the signs, some of the best-known names in the world: XO Cognac, Ford, Sheraton Hotel. In the middle of the city lay Tienanmen Square. The army had torn down the replica Statue of Liberty which dissenters had raised there in 1989. Police still roamed the site. At one corner of the square, a few hundred metres from where the statue had been erected and opposite the end where Mao had proclaimed the People's Republic of China in 1949, stood a Kentucky Fried Chicken. Something was happening here.

Klein reacted to Beijing much as he had to Japan. He toured a factory, took part in a couple of contract signings, and went to an official dinner. The dislocations behind this game became apparent when the president of one of the firms at the contract ceremonies, Bob Bow from Canasia Development Corporation of Calgary, explained what had drawn him to China.

Until a few months earlier he had been manager of commercial petroleum marketing for the UFA agricultural co-op back home. He had first gone to Beijing on a dare from a trade agent who had told him of great trade opportunities. He said he helped form Canasia when the economy made some choices for him: "Everywhere in Alberta is layoff, layoff, layoff, and here it's go, go, go. . . . I took the leap, frankly, when they cut out all the middle-aged middle management."

One way or another, most of the foreign firms coming to China were coming for the same reason.

They were looking for and found remarkable growth. Growth was the right word. New forms of economic life were taking shape in a city of bicycles and one-storey brick housing compounds. They seemed to develop organically beside and in the streets where pedestrians, bicycles and cars all pushed their way through one another in a chaos that organized itself.

Some of the growth was based on traditional market skills which forty years of revolution had not been enough to wear away. Shops and food stands opened all over the side streets of downtown Beijing as soon as officials began allowing some free enterprise in the late 1980s.

Other developments seemed to spring from an almost organic information transfer. That was what appeared to be happening at the China World Hotel, a 1,000-room hotel and trade centre developed jointly by Shangri-La International of Hong Kong and the City of Beijing. City officials started the project because they saw a major trade and convention centre as a necessary part of their infrastructure, as necessary as roads and telecommunications. Shangri-La provided management expertise. The firm also spent two years training twenty-five hundred staff in the ways of running an international hotel. Shortly after the opening it was still sending selected employees overseas for advanced training. Brian Harries, the hotel manager, found other firms or government agencies quickly began to poach his people.

In Beijing this had consequences far different than would have been the case in North American or European cities. In the body of a growing new economy those employees acted like genetic messengers, carrying crucial information to their new jobs.

Klein knew the vast opportunities here but he saw them through a telescope vision of his own. He always looked for people. Beijing was too big for that.

The delegation took a night flight north to Harbin, to a frozen terminal not much bigger than a number of prairie bus depots. Harbin had about five million people in its metropolitan area. It was manageable. For Klein, it somehow seemed like a second home.

Harbin was the centre of government in the northeastern province of Heilongjiang, the part of China that bulges between Korea and Siberia. It lay off the beaten track for many international investors. The relative isolation and absence of competition made it more attractive for Alberta firms. Harbin also specialized in producing the kinds of products Albertans know about— chemicals, industrial equipment, milk, beef. The Alberta government took the farsighted step during the oil boom of twinning Alberta with Heilongjiang. Harbin was also twinned with Edmonton and the nearby oil centre of Daqing with Calgary. The twinning relationships had led to visits through the 1980s and Klein had been here before in the mid-1980s.

By 1993 the place had changed. Canadian officials with the tour said it had changed remarkably in the last three years. At the turn of the century it had been a Russian railway centre and it still bore the signs in the Moscow-like domes decorating the local architecture. Much of the city consisted of drab buildings and low, brick housing compounds like those in Beijing. But many of these were being torn down.

Harbin had money. A century earlier it had existed on the edge of the Russian Empire. Now it lived on the frontier of the anonymous, global, postindustrial empire. Money was seeping in and so was an international culture.

The new hall of the Heilongjiang People's Congress, the imposing railway station, the telecommunications centre all said something had changed. Farmers brought goods in from the countryside. You could see chickens squashed into three-metre-square racks on the back of pony carts. The chickens looked resigned. The farmers wore flap-eared hats against the first freezing winds of fall, a reminder that Mongolia was only about four hundred kilometres away. But they came into a changing city. A wholesale merchandise mart and department store which looked as if it could belong on any Edmonton or Calgary street corner had just opened. The once-lordly Russians flew in to visit such places and buy the goods they could not buy at home.

One of the biggest changes was hidden. It lay throbbing in a former air-raid shelter which stretched on two levels for several blocks under the main part of town. The shelter had been maintained for protection against Soviet bombs. About three years earlier, city officials decided it could be turned over to small businesses. Hundreds applied almost overnight to open stores. Within weeks they created one of the world's largest strip malls—a crowded, neon-lit, garish underworld where people could buy things, mostly clothing and electronics. Up on the street you could pass buses and bicycles and people with umbrellas and a man roasting potatoes over charcoal in a beat-up metal drum. Down a few flights of steps you found thousands of people shuffling past the long string of shops.

And the whole enclosed mall seemed like a thing alive—a cell transplanted from a body that lived in places like Hong Kong and Tokyo and growing here on the edge of the world of cities.

The new economic forms seem more like life forms. They exist for themselves, not for the purpose of an Andrew Carnegie or Frederick Weyerhaeuser or J. P. Morgan. They transfer information into new locations like the China World Hotel. Then they reproduce. Some people clearly benefit from this more than others. It is not clear who or what is in charge—maybe nothing. That is part of what makes the global economy formidable.

In the underground mall at Harbin, you could see the filaments of this life probing forward. Many of the shops carried clothing made in or near the areas of the southern cities of Guangzhou and Shenzhen, where Hong Kong investors were helping create a new industrial structure on their own doorstep. They furnished money and designs. China furnished cheap labour and a land surprisingly free of regulations, although not of complications. The

171

clothing factories were just starting to feed production north to places like Harbin, which had the money to buy. The long-term goal was to build on the potentially huge domestic market and start exporting.

The government wanted Alberta to become a welcoming place for these filaments, to take a secure place in this network. Klein never put his impressions quite this way. It's hard to say what he thought, or would have thought if his official duties had been lighter and let him roam for a few hours. He had different interests. For the first time in the tour he looked as if he happily found himself in the company of old friends.

Companionship had both hazards and surprising moments of emotion. Northern China developed into a never-ending round of visits and banquets. It was tea in the morning, rice wine and mao-tai (more or less a drinkable diesel fuel) at lunch, tea in the afternoon, rice wine and mao-tai and an endless variety of foods in the evening. Hospitality came in plentiful supply in Harbin. Klein soaked it up.

He had something to offer in return, however. At the official lunch in Harbin he had the Chinese hosts, including most of the top-ranking provincial and municipal officials, hanging on his every word during one of the several obligatory toasts.

He declared his fondness for Heilongjiang, and finished with a plain and eloquent call for international harmony and friendship. He was selling Alberta here while Albertans were just realizing the enormity of planned provincial spending cuts. He was doing it because the selling and the cuts were linked. In Harbin another reason became clear. He liked this part of his job and he genuinely liked the people here. They seemed to know it.

Another banquet followed that evening, and more rice wine and mao-tai all around. Then the Albertans and their escorts piled into a convoy of two cars and two small buses and set out for a two-hour drive down a fog-ridden highway toward the petroleum centre of Daqing (pronounced Dah-Ching).

And here arose one of the hazards. Klein's aide, Gordon Olsen, joined the premier and his wife in one of the lead cars. That meant displacing a Chinese escort, which turned out to be a mediocre idea. The switch left no one to translate for the unilingual Chinese driver.

An hour down the highway the increasingly worried bus passengers, still coping with the effects of the evening banquet, sighed in relief as they turned in to use what appeared to be the only highway rest stop on the trip. Klein's car sped on.

Olsen later described what happened. He and the premier, both edging toward frenzy, waved their arms and banged on the windows of their car until the driver finally understood they wanted him to stop. They stepped out into the darkness and walked toward the ditch, unzipping their pants and relieving themselves in what turned out to be a patch of mud as sticky as any prairie gumbo back home.

Relief lasted only a second or two. The bus carrying the Alberta officials pulled up behind the premier's car. The headlights caught Klein and Olsen like a pair of deer nailed by jacklighting hunters. Olsen, incredulous and irritated, said, "Why don't they turn the damn lights off?" Laughter filled the bus. It finally ended. Klein and Olsen clumped back to their car dragging several centimetres of mud on their shoes. Here was final proof, if any more had been needed. Klein was an ordinary guy with ordinary weaknesses, a man of the people.

He put his talents to use again in Daqing.

About two hundred kilometres from the Mongolian frontier, Daqing lay at the farthest outskirts of the global village. About two million people lived here in the middle of an oilfield supplying about 40 percent of China's petroleum needs. Thirty years earlier the population had been a little over ten thousand. They were evidently proud of what they had accomplished here on a flat, waterlogged plain which, except for the thousands of creeks and ponds and rivulets and sloughs, looked like parts of southern Alberta. They said they had built the local petrochemical complex, a virtual city of more than thirty thousand employees, on their own, without Soviet engineers.

Cities did not exist any further away from the centres of the global economy than this. The remoteness stripped off the usual trappings and left the realities in the open. The connections between economic and political life were put on display. In Daqing, some of Alberta's political and economic relations came into the open too.

Klein charmed the Chinese hosts as he had in Harbin. But here he showed his executive side, and he showed, too, the links between business and government in a world of global competition. He looked the civic officials of Daqing in the eye at a formal trade session and told them he personally supported the efforts of specific engineering and building companies hoping to land contracts there. Business leaders had helped get him elected in part to go abroad and sell Alberta. Now he delivered their sales pitch. This was the way things were done. About the same time, Chancellor Helmut Kohl visited Beijing to sign several huge construction contracts for German firms.

There was one more revelation. The local officials spent a day taking the visitors to see the sights. They showed the new water treatment plant built with Calgary expertise and equipment. They showed the house-size model of the petrochemical complex with blinking lights to demonstrate the materials flow. They took the delegation to a dance hall where the officials signed a contract for a chemical plant to be built with Canadian help. At the end of the day, with the light fading and all the Albertans eager to get back to the hotel and prepare for the evening gala, they insisted on finishing the schedule with a trip around the high-technology development park.

The bus drove into a flat, muddy field with lots staked out and a building sitting here and there in the middle of nowhere.

All around, they said, was the development zone. It stretched for twelve square kilometres. They had set aside an area big enough to swallow downtown Edmonton and expected it to be full of cutting-edge international technology production in about three years.

They pointed to one building three or four storeys high and nearly the length of a city block and said their workers had built it in eight months. They handed out pamphlets describing the tax breaks for investors here. They insisted everyone go inside one of the buildings already in use. The delegation tramped in and up a flight of stairs to an area where a handful of workers were producing sterile, special-purpose bandage materials in a sealed laboratory.

We left the building and stood on the steps a minute before boarding the bus again. In front of us lay dirt fields, an occasional anonymous building, a stack of pipes and valves.

Through the disorganization and emptiness the underlying structure became clear.

It was possible to make money and produce sophisticated technical products for the global market in the middle of a barren place.

This was the meaning of Asia—an economy apparently cut off from anything human; a sterile lab funded by investors from overseas, employing only a handful of people, attracted by cheap labour and land and tax costs, sitting in a desolate field where the mud did not matter because none of it would ever get inside the sealed production room.

This was the global economy. It was different from anything that had come before, even in Daqing, one of the wealthiest cities in China.

It had come to the frontiers of Asia but it had come as a matter of convenience. For the international investors behind the bandage lab this was a relatively cheap experiment. If it did not work out they could move somewhere else, just as they could find markets elsewhere to replace the withering middle class in North America.

The Chinese were building fast now and dreaming on a huge scale, but everything they built could collapse easily. Even the winners in this game could lose overnight.

We slept in the Daqing hotel, on a segregated floor where military security kept watch near the central elevator and took custody of all the room keys. The bus left next morning for Harbin and the flight out. We waited four hours in the freezing terminal. Klein wrapped himself in an extra layer of coat and slumped into a lounge chair. He could snatch short naps in the middle of travelling. That was one way he survived long nights and a long work schedule.

The rest should have been an anticlimax. A day in Taipei came down to another several hours of Klein meeting potential investors. He broke ground here because Taiwan had been off limits for years in deference to Canada's attempts to build relations with the Chinese mainland. Alberta was keen to make friends here. The island republic had developed a powerful manufacturing economy and held what officials thought were the largest currency reserves of any country in the world—$90 billion or so straining to find a safe and productive home. Klein dropped in to bring greetings to an immigration and investment seminar organized by the Calgary law firm Bennett Jones Verchere.

The end came in Hong Kong. Everything about the city said this was the Manhattan of the Pacific Rim, the one place that even more than Tokyo and Taipei combined money with style.

Klein was relaxing now. His emotions were running more loosely. He toured the military cemetery for Canadians killed during the defence of Hong Kong in 1941. He broke into choking breaths, appearing to fight off sobs, as he told his wife the grave markers of the youthful dead reminded him of the veterans he had shared Remembrance Day ceremonies with in Calgary.

It had taken three weeks of touring to get to Hong Kong. He looked comfortable. His life had been entwined with Chinese in Calgary. He would tell a story of one of his first jobs: "A very dear family friend was a Chinese

175

fellow and I started selling popcorn at a concession for him when I was ten."

During his time as a television reporter in Calgary he covered the long-running story of an attempt to cut a major road through the city's central Chinese business district. He admitted after going into politics that he may not have been 100 percent neutral in his work on that one, his sympathies going to the Chinese community.

Toward the end of the visit, Klein spoke at a banquet in a waterfront hotel. He told the mixed crowd of Hong Kong business people and Canadian expatriates in the ballroom of the Grand Hyatt Hotel that Alberta would try "to create a unique, pro-business regime in Canada."

He said the privatization of liquor stores and government registry offices had borrowed from the Hong Kong way of doing business. He sounded eager to build a Hong Kong by the Rockies.

He said, "There is a magic here found nowhere else on earth—an energy, a drive, an excitement that I find invigorating. It's a place I can go back to recharge my batteries and reconfirm my faith in free enterprise and entrepreneurship."

Hong Kong did have a magical air. The magic made it easy to forget a few things. The people worked hard but they also could find homes to rent at a guaranteed maximum of 10 percent of their income. Builders contended with environment officials who tried to contain development, transport officials who tried to avoid new strains on the road system, a government levy amounting to 80 percent on the forecast profit made between the purchase and sale of any property. Half a year after Klein's visit, sharply rising housing prices would lead the government to consider a tax on land speculation. Hong Kong had a magical air but it was no free-enterprise fairy garden. It did not even have a secure future, which was the main reason the residents liked to invest in Canada.

Money makes it easy for people to forget.

The crowd in the Grand Hyatt ballroom sat under a rhinestone chandelier as big as a hot tub. Hands reached out for the Belgian-style chocolates laid on the tables as Klein began his speech. Many laughed at the premier's description of people on welfare leaving Alberta to shop for a better deal in British Columbia after Alberta's welfare payments were cut.

The hotel lay in Hong Kong Central, a place where you could look into windows and see glittering Rolex watches or look up and see some of the tallest office towers in Asia. Canadians who had been living here for awhile liked to inform visitors that in Hong Kong there were more Mercedes Benz cars on the street than in any other country outside Germany. The streets did have an efficient comfort about them.

You had to travel to the end of the subway line to see the terraced lines of public housing carved into the hillsides. You had to read carefully or be told before you could know about the colony's unusually high rate of construction deaths, or about the suicides of children as young as eight or nine years, already feeling the intense pressure of having to do well in school or fall by the wayside, into an emptiness like a muddy field at Daqing.

11

The Budget

The Edmonton Journal
January 22, 1994

The Alberta government pays more attention to communication than it used to. One paradoxical result is that some of the communication has become meaningless.

That's a general impression so you can take it with a grain of salt. For me, the hollowing out of communication exists. It will affect the discussion over the province's budget plans.

If Premier Ralph Klein has drummed anything into his MLAs' heads it is his personal theories about news and information.

In the Klein model the government does something and the reaction becomes the story. Then comes the reaction to the reaction. He has said this often.

Cabinet ministers have also steeped themselves to varying degrees in the literature of change—theories of how people react to sharp change in organizations and in society.

They want to answer every reaction and limit its effects.

Finding ways to keep your head in a hail of criticism amounts to good planning. So does understanding the systems in which you work. In this case it can come at a cost. The cost is a tendency to write off every response as just part of the predictable "reaction."

The more a government immerses itself in the technology of communications the less it will tend to hear the substance of what is being communicated.

The give and take between the public and the government stands in danger of becoming as stereotyped and discredited as much of the give and take in question period.

Some MLAs already describe question period as "the show" or as "just cannons firing back and forth." What happens if a similar devaluation saps meaning from telephone calls, letters to the editor, public statements by heads of organizations, questions at public meetings?

Does a government listen to what is being said at that point? Or does it merely hear the trigger for a particular evasion or canned answer?

We are close to that territory if not already in it.

Klein's government can offer some genuine information instead.

They could do more to report what our social programs achieve, then show what those programs achieve after being reworked. They could compare overall social costs of public services before and after the cuts, including the cost of user fees and services which have been sloughed off to the private market.

Some parts of what they are doing look good (the financial management and search for better ways to deliver services) and some look bad (the tendency to shift some costs rather than reduce them, the tendency to cut before reasonable ways to cut have been identified). Some have yet to be revealed.

There has been one outright failure: the government has not created a sense of community for its budget cuts.

Maybe it never really intended to. But some Conservative MLAs had been talking hopefully last year about all Albertans working together for a common purpose.

A comparison suggests how we arrived instead at divisiveness and imposed decisions.

Hand-picked business executives helped write the three-year business plans for government departments. The Agriculture Department used questionnaires to find out what hundreds in the farm community thought of various programs; part of this community designed its own cuts.

Health and education went through a much fuzzier round table exercise more open to manipulation. And the welfare cuts? They were imposed. More are coming. When was the last time anyone in the Alberta government asked welfare recipients what they think, even though they may have some valuable advice?

This sliding scale of influence tells the state of Alberta as a community.

The Klein revolution damaged Alberta as a place of equality, a place where most people had a chance to enjoy more or less the same opportunities and the same prospects.

It damaged language too.

People know words can be filled with whatever meaning powerful governments or political movements stuff into them.

Now the words themselves seem irrelevant. The powerful do not hear them and do not even listen for them. They listen mostly for signs of support or rejection. They assign aides to write letters without meaning. In Alberta, some politicians do not even watch television or read newspapers first-hand. They rely on summaries prepared by media services. The services often provide only a scoreboard—who and what got good play, which outlets seemed friendly and which did not.

When words become meaningless public communication does not exist. Language stops transmitting meaning and starts transmitting power. One hundred years ago political bosses merely hid things from the public. Now they hide things from themselves as well.

If you looked at the words flying back and forth at the start of the Klein revolution you would see a pattern.

The remaking of Alberta appeared to rest on certain principles. It was getting difficult to sort out principles from clichés—living within our means; balancing the budget to avoid hitting the wall; deregulation; realizing that we have a spending problem rather than a revenue problem; reforming public life by streamlining government and trimming administration; competitive taxation; getting government out of the business of business; cutting out layers of fat. These were the catch phrases and ideals.

If you looked at actual events a far different pattern would emerge—centralized control; privatization; flat taxes.

The catch phrases themselves could have surprising meanings.

The "administration" to be trimmed in the school system turned out to include kindergarten.

The "layers of fat" included the jobs or wages of anyone paid directly or indirectly by the provincial government. This took in provincial government workers, doctors, nurses, non-professional staff in hospitals, teachers, academic and non-academic staff at colleges and universities, all municipal employees, court workers, the police. About one-eighth of the entire Alberta work force was now being identified as a roll of fat, as an unhealthy drag on the province.

The attack on public-sector wages surprised no one. A lot of people wanted it. It may even have been the inevitable end of a long cycle of public-sector wage expansion which began in the 1960s and was intensified in Alberta by the oil boom. It was not unique. The Ontario government had just imposed wage rollbacks on its employees to help keep control of budget deficits as bad as Alberta's. Other provinces were headed in the same direction. Dozens of U.S. states had been cutting welfare payments since the late 1980s.

Emphasizing low taxes to prime the economy was not unique either. Klein had gone around Asia telling investors the "Alberta advantage" was the lowest taxation in Canada, if not in North America. In December 1993, Newfoundland Premier Clyde Wells spoke to the Metropolitan Club in New York City and said his own province was aiming at that goal. He gave a speech Klein could have delivered.

Many of the details of the program were not unique. Every organization handing out pay cheques in North America wanted less regulation, lower wages, fewer employees.

Alberta had something else. It had a plan to fit itself into a globalized world. The global economy, for that matter, had plans for Alberta.

Everything that happened in the first half of 1994—the crucial development phase when the new Alberta would begin to take definite shape—furthered that strategy.

Eliminating the deficit was only the excuse.

The government lived up to the sprawling, half-finished, wide-open style of its swearing-in celebration at the Legislature Building.

They wanted to do everything at once. They wanted to remake the way every public service was planned, organized, evaluated, and paid for. They planned for a year.

The caravan finally hit the road January 17, 1994, with the only starting signal that made sense: a provincewide television speech by Klein.

He was made for this kind of event. He brought to it all the sincerity of a cadging patron at the St. Louis Hotel tavern and all the skills of a former public relations man and television personality.

The show did have some rough edges. No one adequately explained why the government paid $50,000 to have the premier appear on CFCN in Calgary and CFRN in Edmonton, two stations long associated with the Conservative government and with Klein himself. The Alberta government's own radio and TV network had been available free. But the rest went as smoothly as skilled professionals could hope.

The speech began a five-week buildup to the provincial budget. It also had a more immediate purpose. It cushioned announcements later in the week outlining how much the province intended to take away from schools, hospitals, colleges, universities, and municipalities.

Its hallmark was simplicity. A folksy Klein stuck to easily grasped generalities. He reinforced the image of bureaucratic fat causing chronic overspending. The insistence on overspending showed how quickly and effectively governments could twist perceptions. Only two years earlier, ministers in Getty's government had tried to explain the growing public debt by introducing the phrase "revenue-loss deficit."

The speech did not leave space for differences. It assumed there was one genuine Alberta speaking with one voice.

Other leaders had staged similar events in single-minded societies. Fidel Castro had made a similar call in his great 1970 speech to the Cuban people. Castro had told them that developing the economy was a battle, one which could be won only "by the people's will aimed at a given goal, marching down a single road, united in a single spirit."

Castro spoke to half a million Cubans packed into a Havana square. Klein spoke to his people in a fuzzier, almost deliberately unmemorable way, on television. The technology kept all the listeners isolated in their own homes.

The grant announcements followed. The government cut more than 12 percent for education, more than 17 percent for colleges and universities, 20 percent for municipalities. The numbers looked shocking but by themselves meant little. Characteristically, there were many holes to be plugged later. Albertans were getting used to having to wait to figure out what was going on.

The five weeks from Klein's speech to Treasurer Jim Dinning's budget speech marked the first hint of longer-range plans.

On February 3, Dinning released the report from his tax reform commission.

The government had provided heavy guidance. The report was supposed to answer eight questions. All were tied to Alberta's global "competitiveness."

One asked how a competitive Alberta tax system would stack up for efficiency, simplicity, accountability, and fairness. That was the one question the commission chose not to answer.

The report amounted to a statement of intentions for the period after 1997, when the budget would presumably be balanced.

It defined competitiveness as a global issue. It said low taxes alone would not be critical to economic development but could "help to offset some of our natural disadvantages of remote location, cold climate and small markets."

It said that once the provincial budget was balanced Alberta should strive for the lowest personal and corporate income tax possible.

Pressure on income taxes could be eased by debating the possibility of a sales tax harmonized with the federal goods and services tax. Property taxes could support education and local services. Specific user fees could cover the cost of some services.

The February 24 budget would begin to take Alberta down some of these roads.

The most politically sensitive change would be to start a provincial sales tax in the only province which did not collect one. How a sales tax got onto the agenda was not clear although Klein's letter to the Canadian Manufacturers had clearly contemplated the prospect. Economists could make a case for one. A shift toward consumption taxes had been a feature of Roger Douglas's New Zealand and Margaret Thatcher's Britain.

A brief passage in the report said all the commissioners had started out being opposed to a sales tax. In less than four months they had been persuaded to consider a sales tax because it offered a way to reduce income taxes, and lower income taxes seemed the best way to stimulate long-term economic growth. The report said a sales tax could shift some of the total tax load to middle-class Albertans and to older taxpayers. It said no more.

The sales tax proposal effectively diverted attention from other huge changes the commission wanted to see—elimination of a specific type of industrial property tax; other property tax changes which could shift the tax burden; education funding designed to let parents take public tax money to pay for private schools; a shift toward flat-rate income tax.

A flat-rate income tax would see everyone paying income tax at the same rate no matter how much they earned.

As with the sales tax, the flat tax left potential problems unaddressed. It would require a new tax administration agreement with Ottawa. It also had obvious quirks: "Some people's taxes would go up and others would go down."

The commission wanted personal income taxes reduced as much as possible. It wanted corporate income tax reduced both as much as possible but also as soon as possible, a distinction not made for personal income tax.

Public reaction to the report virtually ignored the recommendations for a flat tax and for what amounted to a voucher system for schools—a system that would assign a certain amount of money to parents and let them spend that money in either public or private schools.

Letting significant statements go by was part of the disappearance of public debate.

The commissioners had been handpicked and shared the government's new view of the world. Some had helped create that view. They included Jack Donald, Ric Forest, Dee Parkinson, and Peace River Mayor Michael Procter, a longtime local power in the Conservative party. They had government help. The executive director was Al Kalke, recently retired as assistant deputy treasurer.

They explicitly worked from a global perspective. They wrote, "Alberta must be able to compete in national and international markets, markets where people and corporations are willing to move their talent and money readily to places where they can get the best return for the investment and risks. It is no longer good enough for Alberta to be able to compete with Saskatchewan, British Columbia, Ontario or the Rocky Mountain corridor."

Alberta had to create a tax system attractive to the investors Klein had met in Hong Kong and Taiwan, and the multinational conglomerates and trading firms whose leaders he had met in Korea and Japan.

The report said the commission's guidepost was "economic prosperity and security for Albertans.

"To meet this goal, the focus of Alberta's tax system must be on wealth creation.

"For many Albertans, wealth creation sounds like putting more money into the hands of the wealthy. In fact, wealth creation is what keeps our economy moving and is a benefit to all Albertans."

But this all started with more money in the hands of the wealthy. The commissioners admitted as much.

Exactly three weeks later, individual Albertans saw a provincial budget designed to shift money between pockets in ways they had never dreamed.

Reading the budget was like standing in an avalanche.

Everything the new government wanted to accomplish was tied in somehow.

The budget moved Alberta a long step toward ending the government's chronic deficits by 1997. It chopped nearly $1 billion from spending in one year, with unprecedented whacks taken out of the most sensitive social policy areas—an overall $252-million cut in education, $138 million in social services, $287 million in health. Other departments lost even more. Some began what would amount to a 30 percent cut over three years.

The departments refashioned the way they planned and accounted for spending. They all submitted three-year business plans.

The business plans opened vast areas of policy to change. It would take months or years to clarify intentions. The plans apparently opened the door to a system of private schools and private hospitals. No one would admit as much but the potential suddenly came into sight.

Cabinet ministers followed up immediately with legislation for the radical restructuring of health and education. These reforms would sharply reduce the number of school and hospital boards in the province. They would also create the legal groundwork for a much wider system of private education and health care.

The government was trying to recast the character of the province.

Some of their aims involved turning around the legacy of nearly twenty-three years of Progressive Conservative government. The Conservatives had come to power under Peter Lougheed believing that government could force and nurture economic growth.

Hugh Horner had presided over a doubling of staff in the Agriculture Department between 1971 and 1975. The government was seen as the tool to lead and guide economic growth. A generation of bright young Albertans had headed from universities into public service. The Lougheed Conservatives had spread provincial offices and employees around rural Alberta to pump up local economies.

Now the Klein Conservatives wanted to shrink the official government structure. But they still wanted to keep control. They had discovered they could exert influence despite a shrinking formal organization.

Other aims were less clear. The spring of 1994 opened possibilities but committed the government to none. The government greased the way for the most sensitive changes by handling them in the most quiet and gradual way.

In the end you could only point to some common features. Anything which held promise for replacing public employees, especially unionized employees, with private firms would be tried.

Anything which promised to replace government funding with fees paid by individuals also tended to receive support. This had far-reaching implications. For one thing, large portions of tax money came from a progressive system of income tax—a system in which the rate of tax increased the more income a taxpayer had. Replacing this revenue with user fees amounted to a kind of flat tax. A flat tax was even more regressive than a flat-rate income tax. A flat-rate income tax would extract more money from people who earned more; a straight flat tax would extract the same amount of money from everyone.

These were the kinds of changes which had remade the United States during the 1980s. The evidence was coming in now on the results. Research found a sharp new concentration of wealth in the hands of the richest one percent of the U.S. population, a shrinking middle class, a growing poor class, and a pronounced drift away from corporate taxation. The individual states had shifted markedly toward a reliance on sales taxes and lotteries.

The speed and size of the changes caused confusion. The departmental business plans all had a rushed look. Relevant information lay scattered through the business plans, the budget book, and the accompanying news release. Sometimes you had to check all three to find out where a department was headed.

The government as a whole said it was headed toward "a prosperous Alberta."

The road could apparently lead in any direction. The first goal listed in the comprehensive new budget plan was this: "To provide the best possible education for all Alberta students, giving them the skills, knowledge and positive attitudes they need to achieve and succeed." One of the first ways of getting there was to cut kindergarten funding in half at a time when most industrialized countries were expanding their kindergarten programs.

The numbers were more clear, more comprehensive, more in line with reality than they had been during the Getty years.

But the words—they tended to pull one way while the numbers pulled another.

Dinning said his budget offered "no tax increases for Albertans." He committed the government to reform and renewal rather than to more taxation.

In the narrowest sense this was true. Yet the business plans showed a 20 percent increase in medicare premiums over the coming three years. User fees would go up for more than eighty government services. Some government services would be hived off to private firms, where costs which had once been covered by taxes now would be covered by individual payments— and the overall price of some services might go up because the price might have to cover both service costs and a government rake-off.

Tuition fees were expected to go up and the government expected the amount of student loans outstanding in Alberta to rise by $200 million over the coming three years. There were even unforeseen secondary effects. By summer, campers at Cypress Hills Provincial Park were being asked to pay a private hauler six dollars for one-and-a-half cubic feet of firewood; most started picking up deadwood from around the campsites instead, a small but real change in the park ecology.

Dinning cut grants to towns and cities by 20 percent. He promised to cut the remaining grants in half in the next two years. He planned to charge municipalities for services such as planning and property assessment. And he said he was not transferring his problems to local authorities. He said they could work things out with less money. If they could not, they would suffer "a form of self-imposed downloading."

He said his budget provided "jobs for Albertans." The fine print said there would be fewer jobs for certain people such as nurses and therapists: "Some will work in other industries. Others may continue to be unemployed."

There were snippets of near-satire. An explanation of government financing said, "Governments must take decisive action early on to eliminate the deficit, otherwise unexpected events can and usually do derail their intentions." You could have taken this as the voice of chastened experience. The Getty government had begun a four-year plan to balance the budget by 1990. Instead it had dived deeper into debt every year.

There were evasions. You could only accept that taxes were being held down if you did not count items like the increase in medicare premiums or the $80 million in new user fees, or if you left out the fact that the new video lottery terminals had tripled the province's lottery revenues to $162 million from $51 million in just two years, and that the number of video lottery terminals was going to double.

There were reckonings put off. The three-year plan said revenues were going to increase by about $400 million. But investment income from the Heritage Fund was dropping steadily. And the federal government, with much bigger debt problems, was certainly going to stop pouring $1.7 billion a year into the Alberta treasury. Cuts in federal transfers at least had a political advantage. In a pinch, Klein could even use this as an excuse for missing the balanced budget target in 1996-97, although a blind man in a blizzard could see the cuts coming.

There were spectacular warnings about Alberta's continued dependence on resources, for anyone who wanted to see them. Everyone talked about oil. They had been talking about oil in Alberta since the Leduc No. 1 well blew one February morning in 1947. But the stronger long-term bet had always been natural gas.

The two years from 1992 to 1994 had finally seen Alberta reach its destiny as a natural gas province. Oil and gas royalties collected by the province had been just over $1 billion each in 1992-93. In 1994-95, gas royalties climbed to $1.5 billion while oil royalties shrank to less than $700 million. The remarkable reversal stemmed partly from Rick Orman's royalty reductions, and very much from a hard push on natural gas exports to the United States.

Gas exports rose by one-third in two years—to 1.9 trillion cubic feet in 1993 from 1.46 trillion cubic feet in 1991. The modest economic revival in 1993 and 1994 had depended on the extra sales and the drilling of thousands of gas wells. The budget's economic outlook said manufacturing looked good for 1994 but "exports of oil and gas are again expected to lead economic activity."

The only politician who thought the pillaging of natural gas reserves worth worrying about was Nick Taylor. He had lost the Liberal leadership in 1988 but still sat on the Liberals' front bench in the legislature. Taylor had been the most successful, and later the most broke, international oilman ever to sit in the legislature. But he had talked about the importance of environmentalism a decade before the government got the message. Now he was worried about how long the natural gas would last and what it would cost in five years if ever-increasing streams of it were pipelined south. This was an individualist attitude. Albertans only liked orneriness if they could be ornery with a crowd.

The deficit numbers mattered most. The overall provincial budget deficit had reached $3.4 billion in 1992-93. Two years later the government planned to chop it to $1.5 billion. The plan was to keep cutting spending and run a small surplus two years further down the road—all without overt tax increases. A good economy could even push the balanced budget a year ahead of schedule.

In a lot of ways Klein and his government had produced the right relevant realities.

They visibly got halfway to a balanced budget in only two years by relying on spending cuts. Most Albertans liked the idea, although Saskatchewan was proving next door that it was possible to work toward the same goal with a mix of taxes and more modest and focused cuts.

Alberta's consolidated deficit had stood at $3.4 billion in 1992-93. This starting point had been inflated by stuffing about $400 million in business losses and an expiring municipal works program into that year's accounts.

Dinning said the deficit had dropped to $2.5 billion in 1993-94 and to $1.55 billion in the budget he was tabling for 1994-95. He got off to a fast start. Rising gas revenues and income taxes made the final 1993-94 deficit only $1.6 billion. They brought the 1994-95 deficit to about $650 million. That apparently put a balanced budget within reach a year early.

Once the province was running a surplus again it could start paying off debt. This was important. Debt payments were expected to level off at about $1.5 billion a year. They were going to account for about 10 percent of total provincial spending—a horrible waste and a number dangerously certain to expand if interest rates started to rise.

Acting years earlier could have eliminated the need for about $1 billion a year in debt payments—the largest and simplest spending cut available.

The Conservative establishment chose to act in 1994 instead. They did it, in part, this way:

Advanced Education: A $135-million cut, part of a planned four-year cut reducing the budget by 15.8 percent. The cut did not tell the whole story. The department planned to set up a $47-million "access fund." The fund was supposed to create an extra 10,000 student places in colleges. It would also become a groundbreaking effort to funnel public money directly into the operation of privately owned colleges. Tuition fee policy was going to be reviewed. Inevitably, students would pay a bigger share of the cost of their education. Eight months later Ady announced he wanted to let tuition fees gradually rise to the point where they could cover 30 percent of the cost of university education by the year 2000. Putting a date on the target created the impression of a stop, a goal where change would end. But the government was really proposing a rapid and continuing increase. Tuition fees had covered only 12 percent of costs in 1989. There was no reason to think the shift to private payment of education costs would stop in 2000. The tuition fee announcement was accompanied by a call to universities to change tenure policies which traditionally protected professors from being fired for saying unpopular things. The changes were supposed to make it easier for universities to lay off academics when entire programs were shut down. But the University of Calgary already had such a provision written into its staff agreement. The board chair at the University of Alberta said his institution wanted the flexibility to keep the best staff in other jobs when it ended a program while pruning others. Tenure as it affected academic freedom seemed in doubt after all.

Agriculture: An $85-million cut, part of a four-year cut amounting to 22.4 percent of the department's budget. The department planned to end 109 jobs in one year. An amalgamation of lending corporations would save $11.7 million. The government planned to save $28.1 million in one year by lopping a two-cents-a-litre rebate on farm fuels. It would also save $36 million by ending a subsidy on grains fed to livestock. This subsidy was called the Crow benefit offset. The program had eaten up about $500 million in ten years, during part of which feed grain prices had been at extremely low levels and livestock prices had been unusually high. Sometimes it seemed that the financial side of the Klein revolution had a particular rationale: the government's closest supporters would let their handouts be cut if they could see cuts to areas like welfare and public-sector wages. The agriculture cut was supposed to be one of the signs of solidarity, an indication that the cuts would hit everyone. The particulars of these cuts had been worked out by consulting farmers. A few weeks later, Agriculture Minister Walter Paszkowski said a program like the Crow benefit offset had to be cut because it would not be acceptable under new international trade rules anyway.

Economic Development: A $47-million cut, part of a planned four-year cut of 30.7 percent. One of the big savings came from the $8.2-million elimination of a Crown corporation's venture funding program for small business; there was no explanation why. Other savings looked odd given the government's economic strategies. The department planned to cut $5 million, or about 20 percent over four years, from the Alberta Research Council. It also cut millions from Westaim, a federal-provincial-industry program to develop advanced materials at the Sherritt Gordon plant near Edmonton.

Education: A \$252-million cut, part of a 12.4 percent cut over four years. Some of the money would come from reducing the number of Alberta school boards to 57 from 141. Some would come from suggested 5 percent pay cuts for teachers and other school workers. Some would come from chopping the provincial grant for kindergarten in half.

Education Minister Halvar Jonson claimed the department had over one thousand studies showing results all over the map on the benefits of kindergarten. Parent groups formed to challenge the decision. They pointed out that most studies looked at the potential benefits of going to full-time kindergarten from the half-day system then in use in Alberta. Most industrialized countries were also tending toward more kindergarten.

Jonson tabled a list of more than one thousand studies in the legislature later in the spring. His critics quickly discovered education officials had simply photocopied some long bibliographies, and that many of the titles seemed irrelevant. Jonson soft-pedalled the research after that. He continued to insist it was anyone's guess whether kindergarten accomplished much, although he conceded it had benefits for various kinds of disadvantaged children. He never explained how this fit with the department's newly adopted mission statement: "the best possible education for all Alberta students."

The education plan went much further. The department decided to end a problem of funding for poorer school boards by taking control of more than \$1 billion in education property taxes away from local school boards. Full control opened the way to new tax shifts, away from corporations and onto homeowners and small businesses. Any shift would be intensified for some homeowners because the province wanted to change the assessment procedure for property taxes by 1997.

The education business plan proposed to achieve new efficiencies with experiments such as the creation of charter schools and mandatory parent councils at every school in the province. These unexplained changes, like some of the key tax changes, had not been widely recommended in the education round tables and had nothing directly to do with efficiency. They left the door open for an eventual manipulation of the school system away from public education and toward private schools.

Family and Social Services: A \$122-million cut, part of \$290-million or more than 20 percent cut over four years. Social services had been cut before anything else, starting in 1993. Hacking at welfare proved to be one of the government's most popular decisions. It was also one of the murkiest in terms of actual decisions being made, and least-explained in terms of what happened to people as a result.

The broad picture was clear. Welfare cases had shot up by the tens of thousands as a recession took hold between 1990 and 1992. The economy clearly played a role. There was also some evidence from internal studies that anywhere from 4 to 20 percent of the welfare case load could involve wrong calculations or plain fraud. Endless stories circulated about people choosing to stay on welfare rather than work. The stories reflected the usual blaming of the poor for their poverty, but they had substance as well: many of the working poor would be better off financially staying on welfare than taking jobs which paid poorly and did not offer welfare benefits such as dental care.

The cuts covered a remarkably broad swath—from a drop of more than one hundred dollars a month in shelter and food allowances for single recipients in 1993 to new limits in 1994 on what welfare would pay for items such as school fees, although the government increased the amount allowed for fees a few months later. The department decided that sixteen- and seventeen-year-olds would no longer qualify for welfare if they had parents able to look after them.

Files of the handicapped were combed to see who could be classed as employable. Thousands of other people were transferred into the student loan program. They were told to borrow money to take courses rather than receive money for living expenses. One of the nastier decisions affected people over age sixty. They were told to apply for reduced Canada Pension Plan benefits. People could take the federal pension up to five years before the usual age of sixty-five. If they did, their pensions were reduced for the rest of their lives. The government refused months later to say how many people had been shifted to a reduced federal pension; a department spokesman said the information was confidential.

The welfare numbers began shrinking rapidly, an apparently real policy success as well as a political plum. But no one really knew what had happened. Food banks reported business nearly doubling in one year. Some of the poor got shifted to the federal government as unemployment insurance recipients, or as applicants for early retirement or disability benefits under the Canada Pension Plan. Their pension income too would be lower for the rest of their lives.

Numbers were hard to track. At least three thousand people may have simply moved, with the help of free bus tickets. Later it seemed the major effect had been to persuade the migrating poor not to stop in Alberta in the first place; if they were heading west they could head straight for B.C. No one could know for years what the experiment in giving people student loans rather than welfare payments was going to produce. Several weeks after the budget, Opposition members asked Social Services Minister Mike Cardinal what had happened to the thousands apparently leaving welfare. He formally replied the government had no way of knowing. Nor did it intend to find out.

Health: A $287-million cut, part of a planned 18-percent cut over four years. The budget lacked significant detail but much of the savings were clearly going to come out of hospitals. The three-year business plan called for cutting the number of acute-care hospital beds nearly in half. In 1991 there were 4.3 acute-care hospital beds for every 1,000 Albertans. The department wanted that down to 2.4 beds per 1,000 Albertans by 1996.

This formed the most ambitious plan to scale down health institutions in the country but was not in itself a radical departure. Health care was moving out of expensive—and occasionally unhelpful or even unhealthy—institutions across the country. Alberta had already cut its ratio of acute-care hospital beds nearly in half during the 1980s.

The emptying of institutions had political implications, however. The boom of the late 1970s had been accompanied by a boom in hospital building. Now the Klein government was turning Progressive Conservative practises inside out. The same party that had won votes by building hospitals was thinning out hospitals. Many rural communities wanted to hang on to as much of a health establishment as they could. They did not trust anyone but Conservatives to do the thinning out. They had not even trusted an urban Conservative like Nancy Betkowski to oversee the job. They certainly counted on escaping the trend as much as they could. Months later, it became clear that health budget cuts would be deepest in Calgary and Edmonton.

Physician payments would be cut. Provincial officials struck a deal with the Alberta Medical Association in June 1994 for a more than 6-percent cut in total physician billings. Doctors had already accepted a cap on medicare billings in the early 1990s.

The hospital spending cuts implied bed closings, layoffs, wage cuts, and a further move toward day surgery and other ways to shorten hospital stays.

Klein's rhetoric of sharing the pain with 5-percent pay cuts all around fell apart within months. Mental health workers at Alberta Hospital Edmonton were hit with demands for cuts of nearly 20 percent. Nurses in Calgary accepted 5 percent in the winter and were asked for another 5 percent in the spring.

Health was the largest area of provincial spending. It was also one of the areas ripest for reform.

But no one knew where the government wanted to end up. As with education, health policy mixed sudden spending cuts and long-term reform with ideology. There were signs of a possible attempt to take apart public health care and spend the next decade handing it over piece by piece to private business. In a globalized world, those businesses would not even necessarily be Albertan or Canadian.

There were proposals for new user fees, for greater "individual responsibility," for trimming the range of health care offered by the public system, for shifting care "to the community," for fund-raising foundations, and for alternative care—so many of these proposals that you could also see the outline of a future in which health increasingly became a private industry. The province had already let private clinics flourish for eye surgery, migraine care, and certain diagnostic techniques such as magnetic resonance imaging.

By May the legislature was hearing a pitch to let Calgary eye surgeon Howard Gimbel transform his eye clinic into a nonprofit foundation with legal authority to run hospitals, do research, teach, and operate outside Alberta. Donations would have been tax-deductible. Some of the fees would have been paid by the government. The proposal amounted to an effort to start a privately owned research hospital earning its money in part through a funnel lined up on the provincial treasury. Dr. Dennis Modry said the province should sell its flagship research hospital at the University of Alberta to private buyers.

Klein said two weeks after the budget that the government had received informal proposals from a number of Canadian investors interested in buying an unused Alberta hospital and running it as a business: "There are people out there who say they can do it more efficiently, more effectively, and offer the same service, if not better. . . . I've basically said, 'Give us a proposal, we're willing to listen to anything reasonable.'"

The department's business plan spoke in jelly-like evasions. It laid out principles but some of the principles were conditional. One said health services "will be publicly funded, subject to what society can afford." Another said decisions "should be as consistent as possible with the national policy framework and legislation."

The government had not simply trimmed administration and begun the layoffs of thousands of workers and forced a wage cut on nurses and janitors. The budget formally began a wide-front battle over the principles of public health care. The health business plan even threw in some old-fashioned political number juggling.

Some of the apparent spending cuts actually reflected plans for increased revenue. Medicare premium collections would go up in four years to $666 million from $431 million. The government insisted this was not a tax increase.

The increase had hidden implications. It would put medicare—the health insurance plan covering physicians' bills—on a virtual pay-as-you go footing. For everyone above the poverty line, premiums would cover the full cost of medicare—another flat tax.

Only the lowest-income Albertans would have their premiums paid by the province. By 1997, working families getting by on incomes of $30,000 or $40,000 would pay about $860 a year for medical insurance. So would families earning $150,000 a year and more. The growing burden seemed likely to erode public insurance, and certain to increase administrative costs. The government had already been hiring private bill collectors to go after people late with their premiums. A sharp increase in fees could end up persuading some people to gamble on formally opting out of medicare; by March 1993, 209 Albertans had already done that, without explanation.

Justice: A $40-million cut, part of a four-year cut amounting to 16.6 percent. Aside from making the standard wage cut throughout the system, the province planned to close two correctional centres, deplete policing grants to municipalities, and reduce spending on Legal Aid and the Law Reform Institute.

Among the department's primary business goals were providing "cost-effective and efficient correctional programs" and "appropriate levels of custody and supervision for incarcerated persons." Within weeks, these phrases translated into surprising realities. The government wanted to try a privately operated jail. Its more radical proposal would avoid jails completely. Some convicted criminals were supposed to be kept in their own homes, with occasional telephone calls or visits from probation officers to make sure they did not leave. At the same time, the government was trying to present a law-and-order front by whipping up public interest in bringing back the death penalty. It also reacted to public concern about crime by holding hearings on the law governing criminals under age eighteen, the Young Offenders Act.

There was room for changes. Alberta habitually had one of the highest per-person jail populations in the country. Indians and Métis generally made up about 40 percent of the prisoners. The budget plan committed the Justice Department to lowering the aboriginal numbers.

The business plan promised an evaluation of recommendations from a commission which had reported on aboriginal justice three years earlier. A public inquiry in the early 1990s had made it plain that many aboriginals who ended up in jail, particularly youth, came from a fractured social background and tended to commit property crimes which they saw as crimes against authority. In other words, a large measure of aboriginal crime amounted to a rudimentary form of rebellion against a dominant Alberta society. Nothing in the budget tied justice matters to social affairs. Broken links lay all over the place.

Despite the sharpening law-and-order rhetoric of the government, the tighter budgeting resulted within months in some inmates going home from jail after only a few hours in custody.

Municipal Affairs: A $59-million cut which was only a prelude to bigger cuts. The province rolled significant programs into one overall municipal assistance grant. It cut that grant by about 10 percent to $169 million. But the budget outlined plans to cut this grant in half again, to $88 million by 1996-97. No one knew whether any grants would survive by 2001.

Dinning argued that provincial grants covered only 3 to 5 percent of the budget for major cities and they should be able to cope. The argument ignored recent history. Cities had cut spending sharply in the early and mid-1980s while the province had made only minor corrections. It also ignored long-term complications for the province. One of the grants went to a popular and effective program called Family and Community Support Services. This helped pay for services such as Meals on Wheels for housebound seniors. Cities would be forced to juggle social such spending with regular road and sewer maintenance, with increasing business calls for lower taxes, and with provincially inspired changes to the property tax system.

The Municipal Affairs budget documents were blunt: "With deficit elimination being the major priority of the government, subsidizing solvent municipalities by borrowing is no longer feasible."

Dinning did something he was explicitly telling Ottawa not to do. A few years earlier, the federal government had capped its share of social assistance for the three richest provinces, Alberta, Ontario, and British Columbia. Dinning now said he wanted no repeat of such a decision: "That would be wrong."

His budget made exactly that kind of distinction between large and small municipalities. The larger cities saw the core of the old municipal assistance grant eliminated. Small towns and villages would still receive $25 million a year.

The cuts also forced deficit pressure onto municipalities in a way Alberta did not want Ottawa forcing federal deficit pressures to provinces. The shifting echoed the downward transfer of deficit pressures to U.S. states and cities in the late 1980s. It also guaranteed more pressure to raise property taxes or municipal fees.

Senior Citizens: Every Alberta resident aged sixty-five and over had enjoyed financial benefits for many years—property tax rebates, rent subsidies for those not in their own homes, some of Canada's lowest rental rates for long-term care, automatic payment of medicare premiums, other extended health benefits such as eyeglass coverage. The golden age suddenly ended. Many seniors, the same people who had kept the Progressive Conservatives in power since 1971, rebelled. Others said they had enough money to help get Alberta out of a financial crisis and thought Ralph Klein was doing the right thing.

Seniors' policy was so complex that no one could put a final figure on the changes.

The government planned to save tens of millions of dollars by ending some programs and making others income-tested. By and large, any senior earning more than $19,000 a year or any older couple earning more than $28,000 a year suddenly had to pay their own way in areas such as medicare premiums. Rents would go up in long-term care homes. Seniors would also be subject to subtle but often costly effects from the various shifts in property taxation.

The trimming of seniors' benefits reflected changes taking place on a scale of decades. Seniors had been one of the pillars of Conservative support since the Lougheed days. The new income-testing ranked as part of the revolution in terms of a grand reversal of Conservative policy. Yet spending on seniors would still total nearly $1 billion a year and Alberta would still do well by its seniors compared with most other provinces.

The other point was that seniors' policy was heading almost inevitably for change. A government study sent to cabinet ministers in December 1990 and leaked to New Democrats shortly afterward found Albertans over sixty-five had been the only age group in the province to increase their disposable income during the 1980s. In 1970, about 36 percent of Alberta seniors had incomes below the Statistics Canada poverty line. By 1985 that figure had dropped to 6.2 percent. About two-thirds of Alberta families headed by seniors were living in mortgage-free homes.

Most striking of all, the retired share of the population was increasing, would keep increasing, and was cutting sharply into the spending pie. The 1990 study said, "Growth in expenditures for seniors' programs over the past five years has been 30 percent, as compared to nine percent for all Alberta government programs." If everything else held steady, that fact alone would prompt the government to review what it could afford to spend on seniors.

This outline hardly conveys the enormity of change. No one could keep track of all the decisions flying down the slope. There were too many of them. Some were camouflaged. Some were held back for release later.

Elaine McCoy's experiment with business-style budgeting was suddenly taken up by every department. That turned the budget into a collection of individual policy statements. In the spring of 1994 the government changed more of its beliefs and operations than at any time since the Conservatives had won their first election in 1971.

Small and large decisions lay buried in the seventeen departmental business plans. You could read through them and come across virtually anything.

The government wrote off $54.8 million of its loan guarantee on the High River magnesium plant. That was a lot of money to go up in smoke. In other years it would have been noticed.

There would be no more funding for mosquito control spraying; greater self-regulation of the insurance industry and of industrial pollution; a provincial fee on sales of lightning rods; an Environment Department fee on large-scale water use (quietly ruled out half a year later); closer provincial supervision of schools through the use of more standard tests of student abilities in writing and mathematics; quasi-independent agencies taking over the regulation of real estate, funeral services, and home rental.

Seventeen departments had been asked to reinvent everything they did at once. The departmental planners and the cabinet ministers and the businessmen acting as unelected advisers had produced too many proposals to track.

They had not linked any of their plans. Each department looked from the inside like an independent business. They were not independent and isolated islands. A human bridge spanned them. The budget chopped that bridge in many places. It cut the population into bits so that the government could manage and measure.

The human bridge particularly spanned education, health, social services, and justice. What happened to individuals as they came into contact with each of these departments affected what happened to them in the other areas. The Health Department for a time considered handing hundreds of millions of dollars to Social Services on the theory that this would provide some of the most effective long-range preventive health, especially for children. In the end, no one attempted such a connection between any department. The business plans ended up with narrow targets.

The Department of Family and Social Services said it would measure how its programs were doing by counting such things as the number of months an average person spent on social assistance or the number of welfare cases as a percentage of the population. Its "program outputs" would be measured by looking at items such as the percentage of error-free files. None of this spoke, for example, to alleviating child poverty as a way of reducing barriers to infant development or to a good education.

The education business would focus on student test results. Other issues were ignored. Edmonton police chief Doug McNally did not welcome the kindergarten cuts. He said publicly that helping the youngest children adapt to education and society was one of the most effective and efficient crime prevention measures anyone could devise.

The Health Department recognized that Albertans' well-being was affected by social issues such as unemployment, underemployment, unsafe neighbourhoods, and drug and alcohol abuse. Its mission statement explicitly recognized a relationship between health, prosperity, and the environment. But its principles for reform comprised fifteen points reading like this: "Funding mechanisms will reward desired behaviour of providers and discourage inappropriate, inefficient and ineffective practises ."

The Justice Department said it had a primary goal for policing: "To provide high-quality, cost-effective programs to prevent and control crime." It was going to do that by reducing staff and police grants to municipalities. Its business plan did not mention social factors behind crime.

Alberta recorded the highest or one of the highest rates of teenage pregnancy every year. Aboriginals accounted for 30 to 40 percent of the jail population but only about 10 percent or less of the provincial population at any one time. The high school dropout rate ran about 30 percent. The Family and Social Services Department had custody of thousands of children. Natives made up about 9 percent of the child population but about 37 percent of the children in custody.

There was plenty of reason to see Alberta as a whole and its government as a whole. The rush to turn government inside out had made planners work in separate compartments.

The budget had still other subtle but large-scale effects. The landscape of change seemed endless.

The government introduced net budgeting. From then on, some departments would have certain sources of revenues tied to their own specific use. Transportation got all the fees from drivers' and vehicle licences, plus fuel taxes. Other departments had rights to scores of new fees for permits, licences, and ordinary services. If the dedicated revenue flowing to any department fell short of expectations, it would have to cut spending. This seemed likely to make government more efficient. It was a system designed for American government and for the city administrations which served as models in Osborne and Gaebler's *Reinventing Government*. The Alberta legislature was a parliamentary form of government. The financial system used by parliaments grew out of reforms made in Britain in the 1780s. The reforms had been designed to end abuses spawned precisely by practises such as special-use taxes. Revenues were brought into one pot. The legislature then approved all spending. The new net budgeting system tended to undercut those principles. Political scientists such as Roger Gibbins at the University of Calgary and C. E. S. Franks at Queen's said change was creeping unnoticed into the foundations of government. Bills brought into the legislature later in the year would extend this principle. They were written to create a system in which ministers would be free to create whatever programs they thought necessary to their departments, and pay for them with user fees rather than by asking the legislature to authorize spending. The programs could also be contracted out to business firms or non-profit societies.

The business plans sometimes included huge policy assumptions no one had discussed with voters, not even in round tables. Transportation's plan committed the province to developing highways for the trucking industry and to a vision of cities built on a grid of roads and car traffic. If Calgary and Edmonton had any thoughts about public transit, no one in the provincial Transportation Department shared them.

Backing out of payments for regional planning would likely end such planning. Planning inside the larger cities could slacken too as budget pressure shifted to municipalities. Alberta stood to begin looking more like the casino-studded, weed-infested strip developments in parts of the U.S.

New grant policies shoved academics and industrial scientists firmly toward applied rather than basic research. No one explained why the government was doing this or whether anyone had considered the long-term effects for Alberta's universities, not to mention the government's own economic development plans.

There were only two justifications for the government's financial course. Dinning's budget documents laid them out plainly:

Alberta has a structural deficit: we cannot grow our way out of the deficit. We must attack the root cause of our problem and re-structure spending to reduce its level and rate of growth.

There are also reasons beyond deficit reduction that make it necessary for us to restructure our spending. The world is changing too rapidly for governments to keep on as they have in the past. Albertans require their government to provide quality, essential services at the lowest possible cost.

In today's highly competitive global marketplace, businesses pay special attention to taxes when making investment decisions. We must keep our taxes low to attract new investment and create jobs for Albertans.

Albertans wanted to believe they could get by without paying taxes at the same level as most other Canadians. That was at the core of provincial politics.

But plenty of evidence of another inescapable demand lay scattered through everything the government had done for the preceding three years. Low spending was required by low taxes; low taxes were required by economic globalization.

The government's own tax reform commission and independent studies were finding that Alberta already had competitive taxes. That did not matter. No tax was low enough. Taxes always had to be driven down, no matter what their level.

The energy powering Alberta politics in the 1990s surged down two circuits—one local and one international. Ralph Klein became the transformer joining them.

Some of this change reflected real attempt at reform. The business plans were not a fad. The government had been trying since 1983 to control its own growth. It had achieved haphazard success. Klein's cabinet finally found both technique and political will.

Spending really was a problem in Alberta. During the boom, provincial spending had leapt up as much as 17 percent per year. The Conservative governments of the Lougheed era had built their style and their philosophy around more spending and a bigger government presence in most areas of economic life. The Getty governments had not found a way to reverse that.

Governments all over were trying to hold down or cut public-sector wages. The New Democrats in Ontario did that more forcefully than the Alberta Conservatives. Dozens of U.S. states had been trying to hold down taxes, cutting welfare, searching for ways to reform government operations, experimenting with initiatives like charter schools or funnelling public money into private colleges.

Klein liked to say the government was more open and its finances more transparent. In many ways that was true. During 1993 and 1994, the government published more financial information more clearly than it ever had. The changes all conformed with recommendations from the auditor general.

The government pushed ahead with a freedom of information and protection of privacy bill. Alberta was years behind the federal government and eight other provinces there, but the final form of the law was fairly strong, although there were immediate hints that cabinet ministers who begrudged having to pass it might try to pervert its intent—hints that they might start to hold back much of the information routinely available in the past, releasing it only after a formal and precisely worded official request, which would have to be accompanied by a fee.

The sprawling reforms in health and education and the trend toward privatization in other departments sprang from many sources. A broad movement had begun across Canada to focus the health system more on keeping people well than on inventing new ways to treat them in intensive-care hospital rooms. Community health centres had been operating on a large scale in Quebec for more than twenty years. Saskatchewan and British Columbia had moved earlier on regionalization. Much of the government's new initiatives reflected these currents.

The provincial reforms came at a time when it seemed as though everyone was finding better ways to do things. Similar reforms had already begun in the postal service. The grain transport system operated with fewer and fewer prairie grain elevators every year. Alberta politicians and civil servants knew about such changes, and about events like General Motors' decision that the only way to build its new Saturn was to create a separate company designed from the ground up to do things differently than Detroit car makers had always done things.

The budget which served as the centrepiece statement of the Klein revolution contained endless fine print.

It drained money out of public life and it drained meaning out of words. When the budget talked of "flexibility" that meant universities and municipalities would receive far less money but would be left free to decide what they could no longer afford. The "simplification" of seniors' programs meant less money.

Klein worked through this period with a foggy grasp of details and a clear grasp of his job. His job was selling the big picture in simple words.

The legislature began sitting in mid-February and there were days when he proved a juicy target for the Opposition.

After weeks of public concern about the proposal for charter schools, and three weeks after someone at a public meeting had asked Klein what charter schools would do, Liberal education critic Duco Van Binsbergen asked the premier to define a charter school. Klein floundered. He passed off the question to the education minister. Later in the day he dutifully explained the concept with the help of a note from an aide. One of his most important skills was an ability to absorb and remember briefing notes. That could not hide his not knowing much about the fundamental changes his government was bringing about.

He seemed not himself. He had come out of China in November with a raging cold. Ever since then his voice had frequently sounded strained and he lacked his customary energy. He looked physically worn but he may have been emotionally fatigued by the job of getting the ambitious plan through its most dangerous time. At one point later in the spring he cancelled an appearance because of what was described as a bad reaction to a sleep medication.

He got out of the legislature more and more. He spent most of the last two weeks of the spring legislature session speaking and resting in Manitoba and British Columbia.

The travelling fit in with his concept of the job. He was there to sell. The weekend after the budget speech he flew to Ottawa and Toronto to talk about Alberta's vision of a balanced budget, a responsible spending plan, and "the Alberta advantage."

He took some business help. One fellow traveller was Gary Campbell, longtime key Conservative fund raiser and chief executive at North West Trust, a firm the Alberta government had taken over during the financial failures of the late 1980s. and finally arranged to sell in October 1994. Also along for the ride was Rob Peters. This budget of losses and shrinkage and cuts held advantages for some.

Klein's official script during his eastern swing took up the theme of going after the comfortable, the special interests. In mid-1992 the people seen as privileged had included the entire Conservative government. Now, for many people, Klein had extricated himself and the people immediately around him. There were still dangerous exceptions but he was making ground.

One of his admirers put it plainly when Klein visited the town of Beiseker later in the spring. W. A. Schmaltz, a senior citizen, told a reporter he did not think Klein should have allowed income-testing for old-age payments: "But I sure like to see those fat cats run for their lives. He's on the right track there."

Klein worded it this way during his postbudget swing through the power centres of Central Canada: "And about our critics, let me just say this: they are easily identifiable as being those most comfortable with the status quo."

He was warmly received. The speech was prepared for delivery to audiences gathered by the Canadian Chamber of Commerce, the Canadian Imperial Bank of Commerce, Peters and Company, and Coopers and Lybrand management consultants.

12

The Jubilee

The Edmonton Journal
April 10, 1994
Banff

Was there ever a happier time to be a Progressive Conservative in Alberta? Not since the early 1980s.

But there is no happiness in politics as alluring and poisonous as the happiness of being able to ignore what you dislike. The Conservative convention this weekend featured delegates by the hundreds drinking from that particular cup.

They love their leader, who happens to be a remarkable and effective person in a number of ways. They are convinced they will have power for the rest of the 1990s. They feel they are part of history; while Ralph Klein was fending off reporters' questions about becoming prime minister someday, federal party leader Jean Charest was telling delegates, "Alberta, through your recent initiatives, has set the national agenda for Canada."

All this was not enough.

Everywhere at this curious celebration, people were looking for ways to take things away from others.

A group from Edmonton even led a successful call to reduce the number of seats Edmonton has in the legislature. The Edmonton-Gold Bar PCs want fewer constituencies the next time Alberta's electoral map is redrawn.

Gold Bar president Mike Hodgins explained the idea was to merge "some of the very small urban ridings that have large populations." He told delegates the fact that Edmonton did not elect any Conservatives in 1993 helped the argument. The 100 or 150 people at the sparsely attended resolutions session voted for the motion by about a two-to-one margin. Acting on this would be difficult legally. Still, it was an indicative moment.

One delegate told a session on social services that people on welfare should receive vouchers rather than money because the current system makes them "three-day millionaires" and they spend the money unwisely. Someone else wanted better birth control to avoid young women having babies to qualify for more social assistance. Someone else wanted higher tobacco taxes to persuade welfare recipients not to spend their money on cigarettes.

Another discussion group voted overwhelmingly to split the Alberta Teachers' Association into a professional body and a bargaining group, despite pleas from a teacher and despite advice from Medicine Hat MLA Rob Renner that splitting the ATA could create a more aggressive teachers' union. Delegates at this session talked about "the iron grip of the ATA" and the ATA leaving its members "little room for dissent" and the ATA representing "nothing less than totalitarianism under another guise."

There have been more happy and confident faces at this convention than at any PC convention in years. There have also been fewer dissenters. The ones who did show up were dismissed easily.

Russel Lacusta of Wandering River complained about oil companies' "greed" and asked why a royalty cut put into effect several months ago was not rolled back despite a rise in natural gas prices and in company profits. He said Syncrude and Suncor are trying to cut their local property taxes in the Athabasca-Wabasca area as well, all in the name of shipping more shareholder dividends out of the country. Treasurer Jim Dinning usually takes things under consideration but this time he gave a clear answer: "I don't know about Athabasca but I'm with some of these oil and gas companies when it comes to heavy taxation."

A handful of oil and gas companies and a few dozen other firms were in turn onside with the party this weekend. Delegates got a break on convention fees because the party lined up 65 corporate sponsors, including the Alberta School for the Deaf and some firms, such as Canadian Airlines, Cargill and the Calgary Flames, which have received help from taxpayers. Peter Elzinga, the party's executive director, said he did not know how much money the sponsors had contributed.

Membership in the club has its privileges. Most of the people here are pretty nice when you talk to them. They seem to have not a clue of what it's like not to be a member of the club. They seem to believe that most reasonable and deserving people are members.

They said they had a plan. As the spring wore on it looked like all they had was a mood of celebration.

I kept seeing new things. Oh, how I kept learning, looking for the hard forms underneath the pliable surfaces.

The revolution had started as a sharp financial turn toward a balanced budget.

Then it began to look like a desperate political rebirth.

Then it looked like an attempt to reform the internal workings of government for the information age. Some of the people around Klein wanted to rethink everything about the delivery of public services, including whether they should be public.

Then the revolution began to look more like a political and economic upheaval with two goals—grind Alberta under powerful economic forces while allowing groups attached to the government to protect themselves against change.

After a while it took on a different character. It began to look more like a calmer version of the tribalism racking Eastern Europe and Africa. The rallying cry was a balanced budget. Often enough the goal looked like a sort of political cleansing.

Rage and numbness settled over Alberta. The loudest voice came from what the government liked to call "the silent majority." They vented their rage. The rage had been building since the days of NovAtel and the Charlottetown Accord and had been made worse by economic fears. Everyone else stood caught, without leadership, without any real response. Much of the government's argument lay in simple statements followed by silence. How could anyone respond to silence? How could anyone know what to respond to? Change was everywhere but it was uncertain. Klein kept opening many doors to the future while committing himself to none.

They brought Roger Douglas in from New Zealand to talk to all the Conservative MLAs. They bought scores of copies of his book *Unfinished Business* to hand out to senior civil service managers. They even videotaped one of his talks to show around the government. They stopped talking about New Zealand only after word spread about that country's disastrously rising rates of crime, teenage suicide,, and poverty.

Douglas ran an international consulting firm. He peddled advice for revolutionaries. Among his key principles were the importance of standing firm and the importance of launching every change so quickly that no opposition had time to organize.

Steffens, you would have laughed. You had seen it before, in a place where politicians could figure out tactics for themselves—in Philadelphia in 1903, one of the most graft-ridden cities in your country.

Philadelphia's political machine had started a vast campaign of new corruption. Instead of proceeding carefully it had granted its friends private monopolies over five municipal services, all at once. You met Israel Durham, the unelected political boss of the city, and asked him why the grafters had moved so publicly and boldly. And he told you in words you set down later in your autobiography:

> "If we did any one of these things alone the papers and the public could concentrate on it, get the facts, and fight. But we reasoned that if we poured them all out fast and furious, one, two, three—one after the other—the papers couldn't handle them all and the public would be stunned and—give up. Too much."

We sat there, he amused, I as stunned as his public. "Well, you Pennsylvania politicians know something even Tammany doesn't know."

He nodded. "Yes," he said. "we know a lot they don't know. We know that public despair is possible and that that is good politics."

However stunned you were on hearing the straight goods from Durham at the beginning of the century that's how stunned I was reading those words nearly at the century's end. Israel Durham could have been talking about Alberta.

Of course, the Alberta government was not merely relearning the lessons Durham and his gang knew intuitively. It apparently had to pay money to learn what Bill Bennett's government had done in British Columbia only eleven years earlier. But then, maybe they did not want to remind anyone of that experiment. Bennett had failed to balance his budget.

Public despair might be a strong word to apply to Alberta. Many did not feel that way. Many were merely concerned or confused. Many in fact liked what they saw.

Something strange emerged. The strongest supporters of the government should have been happy to be getting their way but they remained angry. They wanted more. They wanted silence.

The reaction began immediately after Klein's televised speech January 17. After that evening, the calls for silence began. They flowed into the radio open-line shows and the pages of the conservative press and letters to the editor everywhere. The "silent majority" wanted the talk to end. Everywhere you could see criticism of "the whiners."

They wrote letters to editors and said things like: "We can only hold in shame and contempt all those whiners, bitchers and moaners who are singing the universal song—'Everybody, anybody but me.' Seniors, students, educators, civil servants, health care workers, the information industrialists, the judiciary, the unionists, the rich, the middle class—all join the chorus: 'I am too important, my work is too important, for government to expect me to bear my share of the cost of the social goodies to which I have been, or would like to be accustomed.' "

Or: "Premier Klein is attempting to bring our debt and out-of-control spending in line with present revenues. Present revenues, meaning not to increase taxes, but live within present tax revenue by reducing our bloated, inefficient and bureaucratic government agencies, both provincial and municipal along with related health care and school boards. We know many of these bureaucrats, who care primarily for their own interest, will purposely create much difficulty and stress for the public as Klein implements the programs necessary to reduce the wastage in the school systems, health care, provincial bodies and provincial/municipal governments."

Wherever you looked that spring you could see accusation. Sourness and distrust had settled in deeply. The backbiting mood helped explain why no political coalition formed to oppose the government effectively. Many people in groups opposed to specific decisions disliked one another more than they disliked the government.

Klein himself sporadically tried for reconciliation and consensus. He announced a Premier's Forum where fifty representatives of public workers could meet to suggest ways to improve public service. He declared he was "solidly on side" with the Alberta Union of Provincial Employees in its protest against attempts to negotiate pay cuts of as much as 20 percent at some hospitals; he said demanding anything more than a 5-percent pay cut was "reprehensible."

Few of his own people were listening. Some were ready to turn on him. They thought the government could cut twice as much as it planned to. Some of them still talked about politicians' salaries. Klein announced a long-promised review of MLAs' pay and benefits during a swing through south-central Alberta in early June.

People in the towns he visited thought that was good news. Cabinet ministers were making about $100,000 a year and driving government cars. The basic MLA salary was a bit over $57,000 a year but a third of that was a tax-free "allowance." Olive Thompson in Beiseker told a reporter it was time for MLAs to come down to earth: "If they're cut by even $20,000, they're still well paid." Kelly A. Lang, a journeyman welder in Linden said, "I would like to see people in Ralph's position or lower take a cut. I don't think they're worth $100,000 a year. Thirty thousand net should be good for an MLA or MP and $50,000 for somebody like Ralph." The Conservative party's own newsletter had printed such sentiments. A senior from Ryley had written in saying there was plenty of room for more wage cuts everywhere: "Start cutting management of big companies, hospitals, teachers, lawyers. Nobody should be earning more than $60,000. I am living on $9,000."

Like other revolutions, this one had a potential for devouring its leaders.

But Klein still represented what many Albertans had been looking for. If the 1993 election had been a search for a politician who was like themselves they had found him. That was what counted. It was all that counted. A certain irrationality had entered Alberta's public life—irrationality in the sense that facts, arguments, and political debate itself no longer counted.

Taxes offered a clear example. Everything pointed to more money coming out of the average Albertan's pocket. Fees were being introduced on services. Existing fees were going up. Many costs were being transferred from public accounts to household accounts. Hundreds of millions of dollars in taxes were likely to be transferred from large corporations to individuals and to small business. None of this mattered to Klein's supporters. They said they did not want taxes and said Klein had not raised their taxes.

They even jumped at the chance to pay some taxes. One of the few Conservatives to speak publicly against video lottery terminals was Roy Brassard, MLA from Olds-Didsbury. He made the moral case against video lotteries in the legislature chamber one day. Then he walked out and conceded to reporters that many of his own constituents were pressing him for more video lottery terminals at their summer exhibition.

There was no discussion of much broader elements like the long-term effect of business strategies the government was adapting with the help of unelected business executives.

Dinning, Klein, and other cabinet ministers talked from time to time about the government having to trim itself the way the oil and gas companies had done. Yet doubts had been cropping up about the effects of business cuts. In early September 1993, the Gallup Organization reported the results of a survey of 400 top U.S. executives for Proudfoot Change Management of Winter Park, Florita. The survey found half the firms involved saw their business changing, but half were cutting staff as a short-term measure to cut costs and raise profits. Robert Gilbreath, president of Proudfoot, said, "Cost control—any fool can do that. But what is much harder to do is making a company robust enough so that you don't have to cut workers every six months." The executives told Gallup they cut despite their own perception that the biggest pressures facing them were customer demand, competition, government regulation, and changing markets.

In April 1993, Right Associates, a consulting firm in Toronto, released a survey of 505 Canadian executives in twenty-one major industries, including some government institutions. Nearly 80 percent said they had laid people off. Only 26 percent said their remaining employees felt secure about the future. Terry Szwec, a senior vice-president with Right Associates, said companies had to work on the survivors' morale: "Like a sick patient, if you don't . . . work on strategies to revitalize, the consequences could be severe."

The oilpatch, a major inspiration for the government, had started to take a closer look at long-term employment effects by early 1993. As the Klein government began gearing up for cuts, a study for Employment and Immigration Canada found that a five-year cut of 11,500 staff from the oil and gas industry's exploration and production side had achieved remarkable efficiencies. It had also cut morale among surviving workers, eliminated many older employees with prized experience, and persuaded hundreds of students to stay away from industry-related disciplines.

By 1991, seven large Canadian universities were graduating less than half the number of geologists they had turned out in 1987. A related exodus from engineering, petroleum engineering, and land management had led to an overall drop of 35 percent in graduates from disciplines needed by the industry. Paul Ziff, a Calgary investment analyst who helped write the report, said a two-thirds enrolment drop in some university programs put their future in doubt. If the industry started expanding again in the mid-1990s it might find itself short of talent.

Information like this might have cast doubt on what the government was doing. Then again it might simply have reinforced the plan—serving as another indication that anybody earning a pay cheque directly or indirectly from government should take the same medicine being served up to private-sector workers.

There were also indications from some business studies that significant spending cuts had to start big to ensure they would work; if you wanted to spend a lot less money, nibbling would end up accomplishing virtually nothing.

Such details hardly mattered. No one was arguing.

This revolution proceeded on the theory that no one should argue about anything at all. The round tables had put the theory into practice. Municipal Affairs Minister Steve West put it into words in the legislature.

At one point that spring, he grudgingly supported the government's freedom of information and protection of privacy bill. He said no one had been calling for such legislation among "the silent majority that I've talked to." He also opposed a Liberal bill aimed at forcing the government to release a full review of any proposed privatization. West argued that governments should not release that kind of information and he said the sale of the province's liquor stores showed why.

Blind faith was enough: "I'll make this boldest of statements: there isn't a government operation, a government business, a Crown corporation that is as efficient as the private sector, and indeed they're 20- to 40-percent less efficient. You don't have to do a study. You can guarantee it because of the structure in the way they run their economics. Therefore, you don't have to do a study to save the first 20 to 40 percent."

That was a remarkable judgement considering what the sale of the government liquor stores had produced—more stores, lower-paid employees, less choice of product, generally higher prices, and a system which still did not offer real free enterprise.

West said political tactics ruled out such studies anyway: "If you were to lay out prematurely a business plan, you would of course have every individual on the face of the earth that is doing well by the status quo immediately raise their heads and stop you. . . . When you put your plan out and tell everybody and block it into blocks, politically then the process starts." He said the privatization of liquor sales would have been opposed by store employees, brewers, distillers, and any firm with shelf space in government liquor stores.

He was in effect arguing the case for privatization of the political process itself. Political debate would have to take place somewhere outside the political system.

They wanted government by a silent population speaking to political leaders who had no need to hear. Things had come a long way from the campaign slogan He Listens, He Cares.

Israel Durham would have nodded in approval. But his machine and others sometimes beat the reformers fair and square at the ballot box—as long as they answered people's needs or spoke the people's language. Most people said in polls they liked the liquor store privatization. Polls said most people liked what the government was doing generally.

But most people does not mean everyone. The new policies were polarizing the province. The government could count on support from 50- or 60-percent of the voters. The same surveys which made those findings found opposition from the rest was hardening.

The dissent had no political focus. The New Democrats remained off the political map. They elected a new leader, former Edmonton East MP Ross Harvey, but he was reduced to watching the legislature from the Speaker's gallery and walking down the steps to the rotunda later, wondering if each day might be the day when reporters would talk to him.

The Liberals had trouble settling on what they represented. Their caucus had obvious left-right tensions. They had no program partly because there was no obvious "liberal" program anywhere, inside or outside Alberta. The Conservatives had soaked up most of the intellectual currents.

Early in 1994, one of the Liberals' few rural members in the legislature left to sit as an independent. Paul Langevin had been the mayor of St. Paul. He said he had felt unable to speak his mind because of the group around Decore. He also said the party was complaining too much and was drifting out of touch with his constituents, many of whom liked the government's general trend. When the Liberals did do a good job on a specific issue, people like Langevin's constituents were just as likely to call them complainers. It was tough being an opposition party in a province where the idea of dedicated opposition was widely seen as unsavoury.

Liberal Leader Laurence Decore saw politics as a contract. There were a lot of obligations on the public. If he said something and people did not respond, he would wonder why they didn't get it. Late that spring he climbed into a four-wheel drive vehicle with one of his aides, who wanted to show him her new plaything. They climbed up the side of a steep hill on the legislature grounds, tore up some grass, slipped back down the snowy slope, and bumped into a truck owned by Nick Taylor, the man from whom Decore had taken the party leadership. Decore turned more heads being funny than he did being serious. That summer he quit. He was succeeded by his former leadership rival Grant Mitchell, who won the job in a phone-in election which turned into a technological and political fiasco.

It was a strange time. New ideas were flowing everywhere but the province's politics had been paralysed.

For one thing, the public had paralysed itself. Hardly anyone was willing to tolerate the idea of a tax increase, even after seeing the budget cuts. That meant if they wanted to end the deficits, they had to support Klein. They only wanted to reserve the right to complain.

They did not show much faith in the usual political process. Politicians and legislatures had been damaged.

Other groups had no power. Alberta unions covered only about one-quarter of the work force and their membership was concentrated in public service. The Alberta Union of Provincial Employees was notorious for internal bickering. Most people just laughed when they heard an AUPE executive blurt out a suggestion of a general strike. Teachers, nurses, doctors, professors—the professionals who were best organized and most likely to say something had been shoved off to the sides as "special interest groups" out for their own members' welfare.

Some grassroots groups formed to protest actions like the kindergarten cut. None had a great impact on the government. The largest protest saw fifteen thousand people march in south Edmonton to demand their neighbourhood hospital be left unchanged. It was called the largest demonstration in Alberta history but the hospital was still downgraded.

Without leadership, without a program, without a comprehensive alternative to offer, none of the protest mattered much.

The most eloquent objection came from a University of Alberta English professor named Gary Kelly. He received the university's J. Gordin Kaplan prize for excellence in research that spring. With Advanced Education Minister Jack Ady looking on, Kelly delivered an ironic, passionate speech outlining his own rise from poverty thanks to the existence of a good system of public education. Not many people paid attention. Kelly seemed to be just another voice in the tumult. Ady simply said the government would not let the college and university system close out young people because too many politicians had children of their own needing an education. A few weeks later, Kelly said he was leaving for a permanent post in England. He had used his brains and access to a university education to work his way out of poverty and become an asset to the province. He should have been an example of what the government wanted to see. Instead he became another "fat cat."

You could not help thinking that his story meant kids growing up in poverty should know their limits. They should not be too successful; if they were then maybe they had received one scholarship too many. They should not end up writing about the relationship between literature and women's history. What rang out loudest about Kelly's departure was that only some people around the university noticed it. Everything was muffled in silence.

Silence also fell over the peculiar relationship between the budget and women. It was broken only for a few hours when the legislature sat during International Women's Day.

The Liberals had a number of women MLAs experienced in community organizing. They asked about the effects of the budget on women. Cabinet ministers exchanged incredulous looks. Klein bunched up his mouth and stared off at a wall in his well-used "I can't believe this" expression. He stood up and pointed around the assembly to what he said were some "mighty fine" women in the government.

He did not believe this kind of talk any more than Jack Ady believed that squeezing university budgets, allowing tuition fees to go up, and making more room for private vocational colleges in the postsecondary system would affect advanced education.

Yet the budget forced reflection.

Cuts to health and education would translate into lower pay and lower status for women in two of the major areas where women had achieved a middle-class income and professional standing. About 98 percent of Alberta's ten thousand nurses were women. About 60 percent of teachers were women.

Changing the health system tended to affect women on the receiving end too. Women used the health system more than men. Health reforms might do their job and leave women better off physically. No one had any way of knowing. The only sure point was that women would probably feel the cuts first.

Cuts to seniors tended to affect women more. Women made up 56 percent of the seniors' population and 60 percent of the population aged seventy-five and over.

Cuts in social services affected women in particular ways. Women were usually the ones trying to raise families on their own. At any given time through the 1980s and early 1990s, more than twenty thousand single-parent families were on welfare.

Part of the urge to reform everything at once—to reinvent the government and, to some extent, the society surrounding it—involved steps to break down professional barriers. Nurses could do some things physicians had done, licensed practical nurses could do some things registered nurses had done, teacher aides could do some things teachers had done. The reform movement took hold as more and more women were entering the top ranks of many professions.

The restructuring of both private industry and government aimed at trimming out managerial and professional workers. Managers and professionals were the people a lot of Albertans had in mind when they talked about "fat cats" or the "layers of fat in the bureaucracy." Darned if women weren't the majority in this overall job category—206,000 women compared with 190,000 men in Statistics Canada's labour force survey for Alberta in December 1993.

Part-time work was an issue primarily for women as the government pursued a job creation strategy built partly around the idea of a flexible work force. Government MLAs liked to say that many women preferred part-time work. The December 1993 labour force survey had found 49,000 women and 6,000 men working part-time because they said they wanted to. But other part-time workers were not volunteers. They were working part-time for other reasons: 31,000 women, and so few men that the number showed up on the survey as zero, did so because of personal or family responsibilities (both bound to grow as a result of budget decisions); 43,000 women and 37,000 men were going to school; 46,000 women, 16,000 men could find only part-time work.

It would take years for the differing effect of the cuts on men and women to become clear but a preliminary study late in 1994 suggested the trend. Men and women shared the job loss among members of the Alberta Union of Provincial Employees about equally in percentage terms. But there were more women members to start with, which meant more women were losing jobs. The job loss from 1993 to 1994 amounted to 1,707 men and 2,939 women.

There were times when it seemed the whole Klein revolution could be analysed in terms of male-female politics. Anything associated with gathering wealth became the social priority. Anything associated with looking after people was a frill and was being put clearly at the bottom—way down in Box C, to use Norman Wagner's analysis. It did not take much of a leap to see this as a large-scale application of the thinking used by divorced fathers who saw no need to make support payments for their children, or married fathers who wanted all the fun but none of the diaper changes.

But then, the budget had trouble in store for males too. Boys had the most trouble adjusting to school. They had even more trouble if they received less than adequate nurturing in the first few years of life. They tended to drop out of school earlier than girls. The new education and social service policies arguably left them worse off than before. You could call that a balancing mechanism.

No one was asking questions about such matters. No one had answered as tough and basic a question as whether abused and neglected children were better off staying with their families or being taken into government care. Both ways had been tried and had fallen short. At any one time, thousands of children were wards of the government. Early in 1994 a study in Calgary found most of the under-eighteen runaways living on the streets had left either foster homes or provincial institutions. The government often simply closed the files of these children once they left. They disappeared. The department did not know what happened to them and made no particular effort to find out.

There was a broader issue here. What if the real social problem in Alberta was the growth of an international economy which simply did not need a large part of the population? What if that economy increasingly demanded skills which not all people had or could even be trained to develop?

The issue then would be what to do with surplus people. That was in part the problem the Alberta government and all others had with seniors.

How would a society share wealth with people not in the workforce and with no hope of joining it? How would that society decide who was legitimately not working and who was simply lazy? What about people who did not want to be part of mainstream society—people for whom living on the margin was not so much tragedy or bad luck as freedom or rebellion?

The government assumed that if the economy grew fast enough, everyone would be happy. Either that, or some people would always be poor no matter what the social and economic arrangements around them.

The budget needed new laws to back it up. They were introduced in the spring session of the legislature.

The Municipal Government Act had a relatively easy passage. It stemmed from years of consultation and set municipalities free in many ways from provincial rules. There were only two catches. The province still retained complete authority, starting with its setting down of rules for municipal governments in an act more than two hundred pages long. And the municipalities were largely being cast adrift with less money.

There would likely be more pressure on property taxes. The property tax system itself was about to go through fundamental change virtually guaranteed to increase the tax load on older homes and on inner-city neighbourhoods—with largely unexamined effects on home-owning seniors and on city planning and development.

The new foundations for health and education were laid in two pieces of legislation. The government put these bills through in small chunks of time, sometimes an hour or less, often late at night. The scattering effect made the debate virtually disappear. After several weeks the government simply brought the debates to an end using the parliamentary device of closure. Before the spring was over, the Conservatives had used closure fifteen times in sixteen months. A once-rare parliamentary device was turning into a frequently used weapon to enforce the politics of silence.

The bills themselves contained dozens of empty sections to be filled in later by ministerial or cabinet regulation. It looked like another spectacular step toward stripping the legislature of power by having it preauthorize decisions made by cabinet ministers. In fact, the government had forced its key proposals into law so fast that it had simply had not had time for the usual thorough drafting. Ministers filled in with several pages of amendments as they went along.

But they knew more or less where they wanted to go. More or less. The undefined parts of their plan were the unsettling parts.

The health regions bill allowed for the consolidation of dozens of hospital boards into seventeen new health regions. Regional authorities would govern the hospitals. They would also oversee and coordinate a reformed health system built around the idea of more prevention, more simplicity, and more flexibility.

Still, there were blank spots. The health bill did not guarantee regional health boards would ever be elected. Even if they were, the minister would have the power to fire them. Connections between regions were left unclear. Thousands of patients would have to cross regional borders. No one knew whether they would run into administrative barriers. Nor had the Health Department straightened out what the province would do and what the regions would do.

The province left the door wide open for entirely new arrangements between health regions, charities, and private enterprise. The Health Department had quietly squeezed hospitals' equipment budgets since the late 1980s and encouraged community fund-raising to make up the difference. Now fund-raising might become even more important. The regions could also coordinate care with private health providers.

Private clinics were already flourishing in certain specialized areas—migraine headaches, eye surgery, a radiological procedure called magnetic resonance imaging. Now even grander schemes were hatching—the public ones being Dr. Modry's for the sale of hospitals and Dr. Gimbel's for the transformation of his Calgary eye clinic into a charitable foundation controlled by himself and a handpicked board. Gimbel said he wanted merely to establish a permanent life for his clinic after he retired, a kind of institutional cloning. A coalition of health organizations and the health ethics centre at the University of Alberta swarmed into the legislature to fight the bill and managed to have it put off for several months. It was one of the few cases of even partially successful resistance during this year of the revolution.

When Gimbel and his lawyer came to the legislature to make their pitch, they were flanked by unmistakable symbols of access to power. Sitting behind them were Thompson MacDonald, Klein's old television boss, and Bruce Green, one of Klein's development friends from Calgary City Hall days. Conservative MLAs put the bid on hold for several months.

All the signals said Klein and his ministers were interested in expanding private health care and private health insurance. Private health care management and private insurance could be offered by foreign-owned corporations. Its costs would fall most heavily on low-income workers—precisely the group already losing in Alberta's tax changes, and a group likely to expand as the global economy demolished middle-class jobs.

Among the remaining mysteries was the future of rural hospitals. Alberta began the Klein years with 127 hospitals. Rural authorities had blocked moves toward regionalization in the late 1980s. They did not want to lose their hospitals. By 1994, many rural political leaders saw a regional plan as either desirable or inevitable. For them, the Klein revolution was a way of ensuring they still had the most control possible over the results.

The new school bill and its implications followed the same pattern. The government used closure to pass it. Then it sent five committees of Conservative MLAs around the province to hold meetings on how the new system would work. Among the undecided items was how to split more than $2 billion in provincial grants and local property taxes between about sixty new school boards. Rural areas were looking for protection here too.

There were many more similarities with health. One was centralized control. The school bill set up a confusing system in which the education minister, school boards, school superintendents, school principals, and parent councils all had overlapping powers. For the first time, every school would have to have a parent council. But the main line of authority seemed to run from the minister's office through the superintendents into the classrooms.

The government took control of more than $1 billion a year in local property taxes away from school boards. A few other provinces had already moved in that direction. The rationale was that the province had to even out the tax loads and educational opportunities. Some school boards were scraping by with high local tax levels and some were relatively rich from taxes on large industrial plants. School boards had not been able to agree on a plan for "fiscal equity." The government said it would take over property taxes and share the money fairly. This imposed a $1-billion solution on a problem which could have been solved by giving $30 million a year to the poorer boards.

In the long run the tax takeover looked more like a way of increasing control over the entire system. It would simplify provincial attempts to restructure property taxation. It would also obscure the continuing shift in education financing: now almost all the money for education would appear to be coming from the province, but more of the money would be coming from property taxes and less from provincial taxes than ever before.

The school bill aimed to open the system up to more innovation. The system already contained a significant alternative in the form of separate schools. Catholic school boards saw their tax power being taken away. Some threatened a legal fight based on the Constitution. Several thousand Catholic parents turned out for a protest organized in five cities. The most active protest came from Catholics in Calgary, the linchpin of provincial politics for the foreseeable future. Catholic boards won the right to keep their own property taxes and about half of them took up that right. Public boards then said Catholic schools were being granted privileges denied to others. The public boards went to court. The government had arbitrarily jumped into a situation and landed in a mess.

The school bill also authorized the creation of charter schools. No one knew why, aside from talk about how these autonomous schools would allow a forum for innovation. Charters did not necessarily have to be governed by the local school boards, but then again they might be. They might or might not be governed by standard employment rules. The Alberta Teachers' Association suspected the new schools would be an experiment in letting school principals fire teachers more easily. One obvious possibility was to carve out part of a school system unconnected either to local school boards or to the Alberta Teachers' Association. Another was that the first experiments with charter schools would begin a privatization of education. Charter schools had sprung up in other countries in the 1980s. In Britain, they were called locally managed schools. There they formed an explicit half-step toward privatization—the furthest that Margaret Thatcher's government had been able to go toward ending public education. The idea was that if they did a good job, parents could be led toward finishing the step.

You could not pin the government down on these issues. They were proceeding gradually.

Besides, a lot of ordinary people had other things in mind and liked the idea of reforming the schools. They wanted better discipline. They wanted children who learned how to spell. They wanted better use of class time and less indulgence in experiments like the circular curriculum, which saw the same subjects covered in more and more detail in several different years. They knew they had as little influence over local school boards as over the provincial education ministry. They wanted an end to the seemingly endless growth of highly paid school board jobs and to projects like the construction of an Edmonton school board office known locally as the Blue Palace. They looked at high math and science scores in other countries and thought their own children might be swamped by the international competition. All this provided a lot of fuel for change.

The elements in health and education were the same—sharp cuts in spending; political protection for Conservative clients; vague but real opportunities for privatization in a province where a number of government members openly supported the privatization of what had once been public services.

Control was being centralized and responsibility was being decentralized. Cabinet ministers would control policy and overall budgets. Regional officials would answer to the ministers. The ministers would answer to far less than ever in the legislature. They could argue regional boards were running the system, with public participation.

The business plans fragmented the government. The new operating structures drained out accountability.

Accountability had for centuries been the fundamental link between the executive and legislative sides of government—between the executive council (generally known as cabinet) and the full legislature. Such changes took the Klein government a long way past a simple 5 percent pay cut for public workers and a streamlining of administration. Klein stuck to the simpler story. It was selling well.

You could tell the believers that the government appeared to be opening cans of worms. They would argue back that no one had any guarantees in life. One purpose of the Klein revolution was to offer as much security as possible for its supporters. Having security also meant taking it away from anyone else who seemed to have some.

The politics of social revenge crept into the legislature that spring too. Liberal finance critic Mike Percy, an economics professor from Edmonton, got into a verbal scrap with Conservative MLA Lorne Taylor, who represented the rural area south of Medicine Hat. Taylor responded to a comment on school budgets by calling Percy an "urban member" who knew nothing about rural Alberta. Percy said, "That type of redneck garbage really puts me off. We know as much about the rural sector as he knows about the urban." Taylor said, "He certainly knows nothing about rednecks, coming from the campus of the University of Alberta, and knows less about rural Alberta. He knows the area a little bit up here, just over here. That's the only area university professors live in, a very protected, rarefied atmosphere. I was one for ten years, and I was smart enough to get out. He wasn't smart enough to get out."

A number of MLAs did not play that game. Among those who did was Treasurer Jim Dinning, who had led a more privileged life than most or all of the other eighty-two members. One day a lawyer on the Opposition side said the reduction of seniors' benefits could make it profitable for some seniors to live apart. "And you'll charge them a fortune to do a divorce," Dinning commented. Later that evening he talked about having listened to "the barrister from Fort McMurray and . . . the professor on the hill, both two very fine and honourable gentlemen but who come from the hallowed halls of cloistered life and have no understanding of what real life is really like out there."

Public life in Alberta had not turned vicious but it had become meaner. There were still examples of courtesy and thoughtfulness around, people like Advanced Education Minister Jack Ady or Olds-Didsbury MLA Roy Brassard. Yet there was a much wider scope for taking swipes at people.

You could see the casual sweeping aside of the inconvenient or unwelcome even at high official levels. The provincial ombudsman released a report saying the province's day-care licensing inspectors had no training in investigation. He said the investigation of hundreds of complaints against Alberta day cares had essentially failed. Social Services Minister Mike Cardinal said he had not asked for the report. Various cabinet ministers and backbenchers said the Alberta Foundation for the Arts would lose its government grants if it gave money to theatres and art festivals putting on shows deemed to offend family taste.

Lorne Taylor and a handful of other MLAs proudly proclaimed themselves to be "rednecks"—a term of varying definition according to who used it.

Klein himself backed off using it, although he had called himself "a bit of a redneck" back in 1982 when he told "creeps" and "bums" from eastern provinces they were not welcome in Calgary. But he had always moved carefully when people's emotions were at stake. A few months after becoming mayor, he spoke at a banquet held by the Gay Information Resources Centre in Calgary. The speech was unpublicized but word got out. Reaction seemed bad. Klein quickly said homosexuals should not hold demonstrations in the city because that would offend many people. He said they should not apply for city parade permits and "should neither ask for, nor expect any special rights or privileges." He said all he had meant to do with his comments on rights was commend the Information Centre for taking a "sensitive approach" to these issues. He did not mean to support rights for homosexuals "if those rights are to be any different than the rights we all enjoy."

It was exactly the rights that others enjoyed—the right to keep a job or to rent a place to live—which Alberta would not put into its rights protection act for homosexuals. A public inquiry recommended in 1994 the rights act be amended. Community Development Minister Gary Mar rejected the idea out of hand.

There was a whiff of the personal in some of the government's stances. The education cuts were led by a premier and an advanced education minister who had not been to university. The liquor stores were sold by a minister who had kept his cabinet job years earlier by standing up in the legislature and pledging that he would not drink alcohol as long as he served in government. The social services minister who cut welfare payments and emphasized the responsibility of fathers to their families was revealed to have fathered a child many years earlier by a woman who ended up on welfare.

The legislature itself seemed to be losing relevance. Some of the members themselves thought the legislature was a joke and said so with their behaviour. One government member stuck a paper hat from a fast-food restaurant on his head and had to be told by the Speaker to take it off. Another stuck paper cups over his ears during a debate. The Liberals contributed. They had decided they had been too polite to make a public impact during the preceding fall. They heckled constantly and often without apparent purpose. For several weeks they marched into the chamber wearing symbols such as ribbons or, on one occasion, arm bandages. It was mild behaviour by some standards but it was unprecedented in Alberta, and it all reflected the private opinion of a number of government members that much of the legislature session was a waste of time. This opinion was one reason behind their eager use of closure. For a political movement which liked silence, a casual denigration of the primary arena for political debate was no loss.

Opposition to the changes was not growing but it was hardening. Some voters disliked what they saw. One wrote, "Who says Alberta's deficit is out of control? It is the Klein government's call of 'wolf, wolf' that has everyone so upset that they are willing to throw out bath water, baby and all; it is brainwashed Albertans' acceptance of the right-wing ideological view that there is a major financial problem that can only be solved by Klein's slash and burn policies. . . . Kleinism in all its negative, uncaring, finger pointing, right-wing doublespeak is not about the deficit; it is about moving Alberta into the space vacated by bankrupt politicians such as Margaret Thatcher, Ronald Reagan, and their advisers."

By the middle of 1994 Alberta was a society splitting nearly in half.

The myth of a united voice on the province—a silent majority talking to members of the government in the privacy of round tables—could not stand up to close examination. The only way it could be made to stand up was to tell dissenters they did not count: they were whiners, they were out of touch with reality, they were defenders of stale privilege, they were selfish special interests. They were not real Albertans.

In large measure the moral browbeating seemed to work, or maybe it was just that no one offered a comprehensive and believable alternative. The "silent majority" was only a fanciful notion. The real silence came increasingly from anyone who thought the revolution was headed in the wrong direction. Yet silence did not mean acceptance. The population really was splitting—coming apart in some measure because the lack of debate over specifics meant there could be only two options for anyone who cared. The only subject left for debate was the idea of the revolution as a whole and the only arguments were Yes and No.

The fracturing went on all the late winter and spring and into the summer of 1994.

It reached a zenith at the Conservative convention in early April. People argued singly or in handfuls most of the time. The convention gave party members the conviction they could get only when they jammed into a room with about fifteen hundred like-minded people.

They gathered at the Banff Springs Hotel—the destination of many of the Asian tourists Klein had been luring in his overseas trip the preceding fall.

When they walked across the courtyard between the hotel and the convention centre they passed by a statue of corporate visionary William Cornelius Van Horne, one of the builders of the Canadian Pacific Railway. He gazed steadily at the hotel. The line of sight passed over a historical plaque saying the Banff Springs had "appealed to a wealthy clientele seeking a wilderness experience in an opulent setting."

Conservative conventions never used to start with a speech from the premier. They did now. Everything the Conservatives did started with Klein. He began by playing down the notion that a revolution had been going in on Alberta. A few minutes later he told the delegates that many tough and crucial decisions had been made in the five weeks from January 17 to February 24, and that those weeks would go down as the time "when Alberta was changed forever, and for the better."

He seemed to want to believe the tough part of the revolution was done. Or he wanted to get people thinking that way.

For the next two days the party members poured out adulation for Klein, and urged the government to act on much tougher ideas. They had won the election with 45 percent of the popular vote but it had turned into a revolution and now they were ready for anything.

Avril Allen, a University of Calgary student, told a panel of cabinet ministers the government should make students pay the full cost of the postsecondary education instead of just 20 percent. She said students could take loans and pay them back according to their later income.

Alex Groot, a Calgary consultant, told Advanced Education Minister Jack Ady the government wasted "an awful lot of money by providing philosophy and psychology" at universities.

Ezra Levant, a law student at the University of Alberta, suggested selling law faculties to legal firms.

One delegate from Three Hills wanted privately owned universities with no tenure for professors.

The Alberta Teachers' Association and cities and people on welfare all took hard licks. A feeble outdoor protest by figures from the beaten Alberta labour movement—a movement defeated as much by its own failure to generate new ideas as by any government action—drew curious stares and gloating smiles.

Young delegates took hard-line stands. They took seriously the notion of a Generation X seeing its rightful inheritance stripped away by comfort and greed somewhere up ahead; none of them looked particularly poor.

Organizers set up a new procedure putting elected members more tightly in control of policy panels. The "firing line" sessions began with MLAs and cabinet ministers making opening statements which generally stretched out to thirty or forty-five minutes. Every panel had an MLA designated to offer the official perspective on every policy resolution.

The party's preconvention newsletter had stoked the leadership cult with an editorial finishing, "Ralph is thinking about our future! Ralph Cares!"

Souvenir keepers snapped up bottles of Kleineken beer, a specially labelled convention item supplied by a Calgary brewery.

Energy Minister Pat Black started talking about Klein with a former minister out in the courtyard and said, "I'd follow that man anywhere."

The Klein karma kept humming. Klein had won a pygmy billy goat at a school raffle about a month before the convention. At the convention, the party hierarchy took time out Saturday night to drink a little beer and do a little gambling. Colleen Klein hit a video slot machine for $700.

Ruben Nelson, one of Klein's rivals for the leadership a year and a half earlier, showed up to repent. He had dismissed Klein during the leadership fight as an "Albertan Brian Mulroney." Now he stood up in Klein's closing bearpit session with delegates and said, "I see things in you now I did not see then."

The bearpit turned into a love nest, except for the occasional moment when it snarled at outsiders.

Olive Stickney was there. She was a diminutive older lady from the northern Alberta town of Hythe. She stood straight and wore a hat at events like this. She had been one of the firmest and most colourful voices among the two hundred delegates who founded the Reform party at a convention in Winnipeg in 1987. Now she was telling Klein she hoped the new regional health councils would be formed the right way. If they were set up properly back home in Hythe "then we can kill the union." Hundreds of delegates broke into applause.

Klein was asked about this at his news conference later. He said the applause had not been general: "I don't know where you were standing but I heard sporadic applause."

Things seemed to be moving a little fast even for the leaders of the revolution.

Ady wrote to the *Calgary Herald* claiming opinions at the session on postsecondary education policy had been more balanced than they appeared.

Klein conceded that many delegates had wanted to cut spending faster and deeper than the government planned. He said, "That's sort of scary too."

The most popular political leader in Alberta since the heyday of Peter Lougheed stood balanced on a very high wire with nothing underneath except a crowd of gleaming-eyed people measuring short on sympathy.

A lot of what was happening now had little to do with Klein. That was the point. This was a revolution. It had been building before Klein became its leader. The revolution was unfolding in ways he sometimes seemed not to notice. It was not something as simple as cutting spending and bureaucracy to adapt to tough times.

Klein really seemed to believe in the idea of a community. But it was a smaller and more restricted community than the one Alberta had become.

The day he announced he wanted to become mayor of Calgary he said, "I've lived here all my life, and it just seems to me a lot of people are paying very little attention to the quality of life in this city. There's not enough attention to the heritage of the city and the community spirit has been lost. Just because we're a young and growing city, we shouldn't forget our roots."

A few months later he travelled to Newfoundland and told an audience in St. John's an economic boom had its costs. As thousands of new people moved into Calgary "our sense of civic belonging and pride are diminishing."

He had been uprooted from his family as a child. He could look for roots around him.

Many people in Alberta were in the same boat. Alberta was and is a place of immigration and turmoil and growth and defeat, all coming too rapidly to handle.

The Alberta government and business leaders had been looking for a kind of community spirit for years. They seemed to have in mind something like the Japanese system—everyone working together on the same team, no one making trouble, the common effort devoted to success in the international economy.

They dreamed a community. They tried to get there by force and they broke it, with a lot of willing help from ordinary people.

Klein felt the results almost before anyone else. He finished the spring legislature session in 1994 saying the government had accomplished a lot but his rear end felt a bit burnt.

His security staff were shaken in the spring when an Edmonton high school kid walked up to Klein after an appearance at a school in nearby Sherwood Park and squirted a water pistol at him.

By late June, when Klein called a Premier's Forum to get fifty public worker representatives talking about ways to improve public service in Alberta, he thought it best to stay away most of the day. The organizers worried that the beaten labour and professional leaders at the forum—who would only have lost more public support with any kind of action—might stage a demonstration or worse. The Edmonton Convention Centre supplied muscular young men in blue blazers to stand at the back of the room in case anything happened.

In early July, the Calgary Stampede began with its usual flamboyant parade. This was Calgary's history and community spirit rolled up and strung out across the city's streets for the world to see. Klein had ridden in many Stampede parades since being elected mayor. He skipped this one.

A reporter found him at his home. Klein said security staff had advised him a month earlier to stay away.

He looked smoother these days. He was sleek from a combination of partying and working out. He had picked up a blow-dried hairstyle during a short trip to the West Coast for a little fishing that spring. He was beginning to travel around the country making speeches to promote Alberta and the federal Conservatives under Jean Charest.

He smiled and said it had been an "interesting" morning. He had ridden his exercise bike and watched the parade on television.

13

Past and Future

You have probably guessed that part of this story is as old as Alberta and has been lived before, since the very beginnings.

It goes all the way back to the muckraking days. Wall Street and its master, J. P. Morgan, even played a small role in the first telling.

Alberta was legally founded in 1905. In 1910 the government's credibility collapsed in a scandal over loan guarantees for an economic development project. The premier resigned and was replaced. The new premier had a forceful character. Many believed he personally saved the government from defeat at the hands of an opposition led by an aggressive big-city lawyer.

The parallel with events eighty years later is not perfect. But the lines of the story are similar and they are bent by the same forces. These look very much like the forces described by Harold Innis. He described the structure—a region dependent on a few primary exports tries to develop its economy during a boom and ends up in a financial trap, usually when export prices inevitably collapse.

In the 1980s the Alberta government tried to nurture the finance industry, transportation, forestry, and assorted ventures in advanced technology. They ran into failures. The losses culminated in the NovAtel fiasco—a fireball streaking across the political sky, a failure so huge that it defied belief and held a population in awe.

In 1910 the government was Liberal and the dreams were simpler. What everyone wanted was a railway. Premier Alex Rutherford and his ministers were interested in many potential projects. They settled on backing one called the Alberta and Great Waterways Railway.

The railway was to run from Edmonton to Fort McMurray, a road opening the north. The province guaranteed more than $7 million in bonds. Within months, Rutherford faced hard questions. One of the chief promoters came from Kansas. No one seemed to know much about him. The technical specifications for the line were weak. They called for as poor quality track as had ever been laid in Western Canada. The government had promised to pay an unusually large sum per mile built. The bonds yielded interest at 5 percent when they should have been going at 4 percent. They were sold to the Morgan bank in New York, which resold them at a 10-percent higher price in Britain. One of the backers could have pocketed a considerable commission on the side. The railway shareholders had risked almost nothing of their own. They virtually manufactured their $50,000 cash deposit out of thin air: the chief promoter received a $50,000 line of credit, wrote a cheque for deposit by the railway on condition it would not be cashed, then received a cheque from the railway to pay off his line of credit.

Mysterious investors moved in and out of Edmonton hotel rooms. Far more government money was at stake than private money. The government kept parts of the deal secret. The rationale was that building something had to be right and worrying about details was bothersome, if not naive.

The Alberta and Great Waterways disaster even produced a richly explanatory report which embarrassed many but put no one in jail. As with the auditor general's report on NovAtel, it was incomplete because the head of the company chose not to give evidence.

A royal commission said there was no evidence to suggest that Rutherford or his attorney general had personal interests in the project. The chilly finding of no evidence capped a report filled with findings of poor business decisions and failure to protect the province's interests. By the time the report became public in November 1910, Rutherford had stepped down.

He was replaced by Arthur Sifton, chief justice of the province and brother of powerful federal cabinet minister Clifford Sifton. One thing was different in those days. It was still possible for party establishments to pick a premier without consulting anyone else.

Sifton governed the province for the next seven years. He tidied up the Alberta and Great Waterways project in a drawn-out process and soon plunged the government into the backing of more railway construction than Rutherford had ever imagined. Charles Stewart replaced him as premier. The railways never developed as planned. They created heavy financial pressure. In 1920, the postwar economy soured and wheat prices collapsed. A non-partisan movement, the United Farmers of Alberta, defeated the Liberals in 1921.

Old stories, if they are strong, tend to get played out again and again with new characters.

I can see now that this has been a story of the West.

You would know about that, Steffens, having come from an Ontario family that migrated to Illinois and then to California. You must have become a lifelong, free-spirited inquirer during the boyhood you spent riding a pony through the country around Sacramento.

Ralph Klein grew up in Calgary. He embodied a rough-edged society— a place of broken family ties and dreams and threats. He made his own success and it was spectacular. He always seemed decent. His succeeded so well he finally reached a plateau where careless people lived. They lived in a world where it was more and more possible to act as if much of the population was unnecessary. They were people who broke things. They broke them often without meaning to or without even thinking. They lived in many parts of the world and they broke communities. If Klein ever broke they would let him go as carelessly as a damaged car or workers they no longer needed.

Alberta had always struggled with the carelessness of outsiders and of economic forces. It was always a place where people reached for prosperity and some sure idea of who they were.

All they ever really achieved was impermanence. They seemed to grasp prosperity, and have it wrenched away by luck or ill will or negligence. They seemed to join the club whose members made economic forces, only to be told they did not really belong. The disappointments made them believe in contradictory political ideas they never managed to reconcile.

They tried to live by their understanding of self-reliance and free enterprise. But the province had been founded on the privilege of the Hudson's Bay Company and on the federal subsidies to the Canadian Pacific Railway.

They believed in individual effort and built that way. They also called the provincial government to step in when the market failed—a pragmatic response which led to the creation of the Treasury Branch, the Energy Resources Conservation Board, the Heritage Savings Trust Fund, and endless government aid for economic projects, each of which promised the end of economic fear.

Harold Innis wrote a long time ago about the pattern of Canadian economic history—resource-based expansion and public debt leading to periodic crisis. Alberta reached one of those crises in the early 1990s.

The Klein revolution looked like an attempt to remove the government from the debt trap forever. But for all the effort, Alberta remained very much a resource economy on the margins of a commercial and industrial empire. The economy and the province's revenues started growing again early in the Klein era because of a sharp rise in natural gas exports to California and the New England states. Subsidies and infrastructure investments were not so much ended as replaced by attempts to cut or eliminate taxes.

The new economy seemed to promise that any place could become part of the centre—where decisions were made and people could control their lives, where you could find prosperity and try to keep it forever.

If that was so, it would hold only for some of the people. Alberta could be plugged in to the global economy. There would be a price: there was apparently not room for everyone.

Even the Albertans who succeeded often lost something. I telephoned Hugh Horner a couple of years ago. He had worked in the centre of the Lougheed government. He had been instrumental in building up the provincial government to the point where it was big enough for a later generation to start tearing down.

In the 1980s, he retired to his farm near Barrhead and, with his sons, began building a grain milling business. The family eventually had to sell a majority interest to ConAgra, an American food conglomerate second in size only to Kraft. Horner explained it was simply a matter of financial backing: ConAgra was more patient than any Canadian lender because ConAgra knew the business. His sons were running different parts of the business. The new owners left the family a free hand, requiring only a regular report on how things were going. The joint venture won nearly $2 million from governments, half in a federal grant and half in an interest-free federal-provincial loan. Business opportunities seemed particularly strong in Mexico. Every week, a number of people from the office took a Spanish lesson.

If you were in a brooding mood you could find something to cry over in that. Horner sounded cheerful enough, although he could not have been dreaming about building a future like this back in the 1970s. Alberta was always a place where people had to adapt.

That's one of the things Klein was good at. Sometimes you could look at the history of his life and see *The Great Gatsby*. That comparison catches his intelligence and ambition but it seems awfully tragic and American for a man like Klein.

His spirit? Maybe it was closer to the hero of a Canadian novel called

Turvey. *Turvey* is a comedy about an ordinary, down-to-earth guy who scuffled through the Second World War and confounded officialdom and got out in one piece because he was lucky; it was written by Earle Birney, who grew up just outside Calgary, in Banff. The book has been largely forgotten but Turvey was a real Canadian type—an adapter and survivor. Klien had that mixture of innocent luck and calculated toughness.

You had to know how to adapt and survive in Alberta. You had to know that more than ever in a time of a global economy.

This economy did not need many people to keep it running. Some people talked about the Global Village but really there seemed to be two parts to the new world. There was a global metropolis forming where people had power and money. Most people would find themselves in the surrounding global village. They would have only life, labour, and the right to buy some of the cheaper products and culture of the metropolis. The political and business leaders of Alberta were scrambling to gain admission to the global metropolis, to plug in to the international circuit of power and never mind if many other Albertans might be left behind.

It took me about three years to figure out, piece by piece, that this had a lot to do with what was happening in Alberta politics. Who knows what else there is to figure out? You never stopped trying.

The Klein revolution came when Alberta was beginning to break apart. The forced changes made the break spread faster.

The revolution was many things—not least a fear-filled scramble by people who could sense the division starting in Alberta and all around the world. They wanted to join the winners. If they could not, they wanted to drag back others who seemed to be enjoying undeserved protection and in some cases maybe even were.

An economist might describe this as part of a natural clearing away of inefficient and artificial structures. That explanation might work, but it would not account for the bitterness in people's words.

Alberta could be a harsh place. It could be an extraordinary place.

In its youth and empty spaces you could see lines of history which would be hidden in an older and more crowded land.

I remember travelling during the spring of 1982 to see how far an earlier anxiety and anger had gone toward causing the growth of the Western Canada Concept party. Klein once called it a party of "bigotry and fear."

The WCC conventions sounded at times like transcriptions from populist meetings in the western United States a century earlier. If you went out and talked to people you could see why.

In Hanna I met a grizzled old man who talked about coming across the prairie with his family in 1910. They had set out from North Dakota in a wagon. It was still possible then.

In Cremona an aging couple pulled out their scrapbook to show their memories of the old days around Dogpound Creek. Wildfires swept through the area regularly until the 1920s. The man remembered a nurse who had been a family friend. She had come from Missouri. When he was a boy she would tell him about going to a dance with Jesse James.

These were some of the people who had helped build a new province. There were others too still around to talk to—children of Ukrainian farmers who remembered clearing the bush to create farms, survivors of the Depression and of underground coal mining. The people and their stories were as varied as the landscape.

It was a beautiful land where disasters sometimes struck. Then, people had no one to rely on but themselves and Providence.

All across southern Alberta that spring of 1982 I found signs in small shop windows advertising religious meetings. The remnants of the 1930s Bible Belt clung to these places. Newcomers said they were amazed at how much religion affected life and politics in these towns.

There and in northern Alberta people had voted Social Credit within easy memory. They were not sure Peter Lougheed was independent-minded enough for them.

An unemployed builder in Taber pulled out his last bank receipt and showed me he had nine cents left in his account.

A plumbing contractor in Grande Prairie said, "I'm scared to death, because we don't live in the same Canada we used to live in. . . . What we're looking for . . . are people who know what it's like at the grassroots level and know what it's like to hurt."

They did what they thought was right. Often it was. Sometimes they went astray. During the Western Canada Concept days some people were pretty much convinced that old Trudeau was set to turn the Bowden medium-security penitentiary just south of Red Deer into a civilian internment camp. They figured people like themselves were likely to end up there because they spoke their mind.

Alberta has always been a place where history lurches violently.

Things tend to change all at once. The sensible and the dumb, the tough-minded and the mean-minded all happen together.

Klein brought to public life some of the simple qualities Vaclav Havel had called for in *Summer Meditations.* Klein was not a central European playwright. He looked like an intelligent, well-intentioned, Alberta-born scuffler making his way through life.

He approached government with the common sense Havel talked about. In his way he presented what Havel once described in a speech as the postmodern face of politics—the ability to look past sociological categories and see and hear real, individual people.

He did not share Havel's idea of the purpose of a political leader's job—letting people hear that it makes sense to behave with common decency, to help others, and to place common interests above their own.

Havel said politicians should encourage public morality. He said politicians should help people believe they can make life more pleasant and more bearable.

I believe that. You did once, Steffens, although you strayed terribly in the end and thought the Stalinists were on the right track. Maybe that was because you were getting old and could not go see Russia first-hand. One of your most caustic critics said it was just like you because you were always looking for a leader. If she was right, you might even have looked at Alberta and admired a far more benign figure like Klein.

And maybe Klein was not always like Jay Gatsby or Thomas Leadbeater Turvey at all.

Sometimes maybe he was more like you—a restless searcher for a better world, one who sometimes went down a path where travellers had to close their eyes to meanness or worse.

But earlier on, you wrote about the Golden Rule and admired the handful of mayors who ran their cities by that ideal. One of them was Sam Jones of Toledo. He even went by the nickname Golden Rule Jones. He made his city more pleasant and more bearable. He applied the same ideas in his oil-pump factory. Such things were possible in your day. They still are. Our politicians have not talked much about them.

Meanness was in the air during the early Klein years. The meanness reflected an international economy empty of any feeling at all—an entity as void of sympathy as a sky which refuses to release rain.

Alberta was not unique in this. Many places have suffered meanness and fear and anger. These forces pressed on Alberta at a time when people were also pursuing more straightforward reforms. Together they helped make up a kind of revolution.

For a long time I wondered if anyone was noticing. Alberta really had gone silent.

Then other voices began to speak. They belonged to people who remembered the past.

One belonged to Gary Kelly. He used his Kaplan Prize speech to remind his audience that he was the product of a society which thirty years earlier had tried to help people out of poverty and sometimes succeeded:

> I feel for those who now face the kind of anxiety that helped kill my mother, and that pursued my sister and me through university. We're angry that the opportunity formerly made available to people like us by public funding and student loans is now, by government policy, being closed to people who are now in the situation we once were. . . .
>
> The relentless erosion of the public sphere, by federal and provincial government policy, leaves less and less space that isn't directly subject to private interest, less and less space where all Canadians can meet to determine our common interests and aspirations. It's an erosion that, I believe, conditioned the nation's most recent failure at constitutional conciliation. . . .
>
> Contrary to what we are presently being told by our political and institutional leaders, who should know better, our only option is not accommodating ourselves as best we can to an intractable reality, economic or otherwise.

Others were unknown and remembered farther back. Tom Taylor of Calmar, a retired education professor, wrote letters to newspapers in prose of vintage splendour. He kept reviving his ideas with keen attention to the world around him. He wrote once:

> [G]lobalized corporations deny responsibility of what happens to people as a result of their actions; this, they contend, is the business of governments. By forfeiting sovereignty in economic affairs, however, governments are denying accountability for people.
>
> The red carpet for welcoming globalized corporations consists of a financial climate approved by global bankers plus developed 'infrastructure.' Costs of acquiring and maintaining this welcome

mat fall heavily upon populations with diminishing ability to support them.

And others remembered even farther back and their words mixed realism with a kind of humour and hope I never heard from Klein's supporters.

Elenor Smith of Edmonton remembered the end of the Great Depression vividly. In some ways she was still recovering from it. She wrote to me and said she remembered growing up in an atmosphere where it did not feel as if a government was promoting social antagonism:

> The down and outers used to come to the door asking for jobs—for food. My mother would always set them to work cutting the grass and pulling weeds. Then she would busy herself in the kitchen cooking potatoes, eggs and bacon, toast and tea. When the poor guy was done, she would carry the plate to the back porch and he would sit on the steps to eat. This was at Kew Beach in Toronto—we lived across the road from the park.

She remembered her father lost his business, moved the family to Kelowna and developed a fatal kidney disease.

> Since 'relief' was a social taboo—unthinkable—no decent person would apply, my mother hired herself out as a charwoman in Victoria. At age 13, I stayed home to care for my baby brother. My 12-year-old brother found work on a farm. Bill, age 16, had to give up agricultural college in Kelowna and became employed as an instrument man on a survey crew. We supported our parents until Dad died at age 43. The tragedy was, Bill and I had been exceptional students, skipping grades and always at the head of the class. Our actual educational potential has never been realized. . . .
>
> If you know of any good books, please send me a card. Age 64, I'm still working on my BA! Perhaps I should take some political science courses. I'm majoring in psychology and have a minor in anthropology.

And farther back yet. Harry Anderson of Edmonton said his wife had remembered the flu epidemic of 1918, when corpses were piled in an unheated prairie school until the spring chinook came along to thaw the ground. "I was one up on her. As an infant, I had sat on Buffalo Bill's lap (said my father) as he put ideas in my head that I would, sure as shootin', be as great a scout as he was. . . ."

Anderson said he still had slivers in his backside from the catwalks of boxcars in the 1930s, and two damaged shoulders. He had gone back to his old family farm in southern Alberta two years earlier after his wife died.

But things ain't like they was. When I couldn't find the exact spot where my old pal Mutt and I had refreshed ourselves after our strenuous day of gopher snaring, I felt sure Alberta was indeed headed down the old dirt chute. Everywhere I saw greed in its many different manifestations. What earthly good did it do them to drain that little gem of tadpoles, muskrats, dragonflies, snipes and snails; to reroute the flow of the artesian, and maybe to lose it entirely, for the sake of another sack of wheat? What they had done, really, was to wipe out an entire family history, as though we had never been there.

He had seen a lot over many years, since the days when the United Farmers of Alberta had built up communities around the province. Some of it he had not wanted to see—Depression-era politicians splitting ball teams and school rooms and whole communities. Nor did he want to see a lot of what was going on around him now. He said:

But for all that, these things did not consign human decency to the grave. Not by a long shot! Aberhart and his wonky friends came all the way from Jurassic Park to put decency on hold only. In spite of him the quiet Alberta revolution of the 1920s still persists and will endure and will live to pick up steam. They can bury the corpse, but they cannot bury its ideas.

No, they cannot. There is always a memory of something better. That is why people who want to change the world without counting human costs always fear words, history—the means of keeping the memory of human decency alive.

Postscript

Lincoln Steffens exposed much corruption and exploitation associated with the indulgent corporation laws of New Jersey. He got much of his information from James B. Dill, the author of those laws. Years later, Dill explained to Steffens why he, of all people, inspired and abetted some of Steffens' muckraking. Steffens recorded the explanation in his autobiography:

"Why, Dr. Innocent," he said, "I was advertising my wares and the business of my State. When you and the other reporters and critics wrote as charges against us what financiers could and actually did do in New Jersey, when you listed, with examples, what the trust makers were doing under our laws, you were advertising our business—free. For financiers are dubs, as you know yourself now; don't you? They have to be told, and they have to be told plain so that they get it, and so, as I say, while I gave you the facts to roast us with, what you wrote as 'bad' struck business men all over the United States as good, and they poured in upon us to our profit to do business with us to their profit. The only drawback was that when Delaware and New York and other 'bad' political sovereigns saw what Jersey was doing and how we made money and friends out of our trust policy they copied us, and they went further than we did, or, to be exact, they tried to."

Bibliographical Notes

They say you always insisted on having evidence, Steffens, so here are some of the sources and documents behind this work.

It was based largely on personal observation, much of which was reported in my columns in the *Edmonton Journal*. The columns at the start of Chapters 2 through 12 were published in the *Journal* on the dates indicated; typos have been corrected and a word or phrase has occasionally been added to explain context, or deleted to improve readability; the December 12, 1992, column was shortened considerably to remove extraneous material.

Comments from voters I did not speak to, or from letters to the editor, were taken from the *Journal* and the *Calgary Herald*.

The *Herald*'s files served as a primary source of information about Ralph Klein's career before 1989.

Government documents referred to—including annual budget speeches and associated documents, the 1993 report of the financial review commission, the report of the tax reform commission, the reports on NovAtel and Principal Group—are all public.

General inspiration was drawn from Frank Davey, *Reading "KIM" Right* (Talonbooks, 1993). Two of director Terry Gilliam's films, *Brazil* and *The Adventures of Baron Munchausen*, set out better than most books the sense of both dread and possibility at the end of an historical era.

When this book was more than 90 percent complete I read B. W. Powe, *The Solitary Outlaw* (Lester and Orpen Dennys, 1987) and the April-June 1994 edition of *The Political Quarterly*. When the book was finished I read David Remnick, *Lenin's Tomb* (Vintage Books, 1994). None of these three works influenced my own writing but they echoed some of the same ideas so strongly that I became convinced a new understanding is forming of what is happening in the world around us. However, about three years earlier, I had read and admired a story Remnick wrote for the *Washington Post* on Mikhail Gorbachev's crucial role in restoring the integrity of language in Russian political discussion.

Most of the information about your life seems to come ultimately from yourself. I consulted Lincoln Steffens, *The Autobiography of Lincoln Steffens* (Harcourt Brace and Company, 1931), Justin Kaplan, *Lincoln Steffens* (Simon and Schuster, 1974), Ella Winter and Granville Hicks, eds., *The Letters of Lincoln Steffens* (Harcourt Brace and Company, 1938).

Chapter 1: Information attributed here and in Chapter 5 to Lynn Klein was kindly offered in a telephone conversation and a fax transmission from Mr. Klein in September 1994. Among sources on Alberta history and politics are Howard Palmer's *Alberta, A New History* (Hurtig, 1990); R. Douglas Francis and Howard Palmer, eds., *The Prairie West* (Pica Pica Press, 1992); Allan Tupper and Roger Gibbins, eds., *Government and Politics in Alberta* (University of Alberta Press, 1992). There is a wide literature on Reagan-era developments in the U.S. One of the most recent books and most suggestive of comparisons with Alberta is Sidney Plotkin and William E. Scheuerman's *Private Interest, Public Spending* (Black Rose Books, 1994). On Harold Innis, see particularly Harold Innis, *Essays in Canadian Economic History* (University of Toronto Press, 1979, originally published 1956) and Gordon Laxer, ed., *Perspectives on Canadian Economic Development* (Oxford University Press, 1991). Innis has been criticized from various points of view but many of his interpretations of Canadian economic history still ring true. An important description of the larger political-economic framework for Alberta in the late 1980s can be found in Larry Pratt and Ian Urquhart's *The Last Great Forest* (NeWest Press, 1994). The boom and bust nature of Alberta is cited in many histories but receives a thorough analysis in Robert Mansell and Michael Percy, *Strength in Adversity* (Western Centre for Economic Research and C. D. Howe Institute: University of Alberta Press, 1990). For government regulation and intervention in the Alberta oil industry see David Breen, *Alberta's Petroleum Industry and the Conservation Board* (University of Alberta Press, 1993); and, Mary Clark Sheppard, ed., *Oil Sands Scientist, The Letters of Karl A. Clark 1920-1949* (University of Alberta Press, 1989). There are many sources on the world petroleum economy but I like John Blair, *The Control of Oil* (Vintage Books, 1978).

Chapter 2: The events described here were covered in minute detail by daily newspapers. See also Vaclav Havel, *Summer Meditations* (Alfred A. Knopf Canada, 1992).

Chapter 3: The failures of NovAtel and Principal Group were described vividly and in detail in the respective reports by Auditor General Donald Salmon and court-appointed inspector William Code. Both are filed in the Alberta Legislature Library.

Chapter 4: Madsen Pirie, *Blueprint for a Revolution* (National Citizens Coalition, 1994) makes quick, instructive reading. For paradigm shifts, see Thomas Kuhn, *The Structure of Scientific Revolutions* (University of Chicago Press, 1962).

Chapter 5: The information on Elaine McCoy's management innovations comes from a telephone interview in May 1994. Information on changes to oil and gas royalties can be found in an Alberta Energy Department news release of October 13, 1992, and accompanying background information titled *Changes to the Oil and Natural Gas Royalty System, Technical Detail and Financial Impact.*

The comments on the relative value of royalty reductions and the dollar exchange rate are based on a study commissioned by the oil and gas industry and available in the Alberta Legislature Library: PowerWest Financial Consultants, *Canadian Upstream Oil and Gas Profitability*, September 1991.

Chapter 8: Information about ISM is available from the company and from published news reports. On conflicting ethics, see Jane Jacobs, *Systems of Survival* (Random House, 1992). The largely forgotten 1948 plebiscite on public ownership of power companies is described briefly in Frank and John Dolphin, *Country Power* (Plains Publishing, 1993). *The Last Great Forest*, cited above, is also relevant.

Chapter 9: On Ross Perot, see *Wall Street Journal*, June 17, 1992. Two relevant sources among the many on fascism are Robert Brady, *The Spirit and Structure of German Fascism* (Citadel Press, 1971, original edition 1937), a pioneering report written before and thus unaffected by the experiences of the Second World War; and Bertram Gross, *Friendly Fascism* (Black Rose Books, 1985), which persuasively argues that fascism is a hardy political life form not eradicated in 1945 and capable of adapting to new environments. For some of the most pointed comments on the Aberhart and Lougheed regimes see David R. Elliott and Iris Miller, *Bible Bill* (Reidmore Books, 1987) and Peter Puxley, "The Psychological Appeals of Separatism" in Larry Pratt and Garth Stevenson, eds., *Western Separatism* (Hurtig, 1981). The phrase "opaque and mysterious oligarchy" comes from *Private Interest, Public Spending*, noted at Chapter 1. For Klein's early business associates, see, "They Have the Mayor's Ear," p. B1, *Calgary Herald*, April 5, 1982.

Chapter 10: Some newspaper readers thought the provincial government paid my way to Asia. Actually, the *Edmonton Journal* paid all expenses. Provincial officials did smooth out some arrangements, particularly for travel inside China. This chapter stems from personal observation but a number of sources are relevant. They include Jane Jacobs, *Cities and the Wealth of Nations* (Random House, 1984); Robert Reich, *The Work of Nations* (A. A. Knopf, 1994); Richard Barnet and John Cavanagh, *Global Dreams* (Simon and Schuster, 1994); H. Mitchell Waldrop, *Complexity* (Simon and Schuster, 1992).

Chapter 11: Evidence of the economic effect of Reagan-era policies in the U.S. is set out in Frederick Strobel's *Upward Dreams, Downward Mobility* (Rowman and Littlefield Publishers, 1993) and in Kevin Phillips, *The Politics of Rich and Poor* (HarperPerennial, 1991). For additional information on comparisons between Canadian and American taxes see David Perry's article, "What Price Canadian? Taxation and Debt Compared" in David Thomas, ed., *Canada and the United States: Differences That Count* (Broadview Press, 1993). Also useful is Roger Smith, *Personal Wealth Taxation* (Canadian Tax Paper No. 97, Canadian Tax Foundation, 1993). Alberta budget speeches always include a graph comparing Alberta's taxes with those of other provinces. There are significant comments about taxation and about the attitude of farm-based political groups to taxation in Gordon Laxer, *Open For Business* (Oxford University Press, 1989). One brief summary of current school politics in North America is Charles Mahtesian, "The Precarious Politics of Privatizing Schools," *Governing*, June 1994. The statistics on possible welfare fraud come from the 1992-93 annual report of the provincial auditor general.

Chapter 12: Bill Bennett's experiments in British Columbia are well described in Allen Garr, *Tough Guy* (Key Porter, 1985). On management issues, see Jeffrey Jones, "After the Layoffs," *Oilweek*, February 15, 1993; "Companies Don't Consider Price Paid for Job-Cutting, Economists Say," *Calgary Herald*, March 12, 1993; Susan Yellin, "Pain of Job Cuts Lingers," *Calgary Herald*, April 14, 1993; Samuel Fromartz, "Many Downsizings Acts of Desperation," *Calgary Herald*, September 9, 1993; Gordon Jaremko, "Plant Closure Kills 179 Jobs," *Calgary Herald*, September 16, 1993. Steve West's comments are recorded in Alberta Hansard. Excerpts from letters to editors were taken from: "Albertans Still Better Off," p. A7, *Edmonton Journal*, June 19,

1994; "Manning, Klein, the Right Team," letters page, *Calgary Herald*, March 14, 1994; "Government Crying Wolf," p. A7, *Edmonton Journal*, March 8, 1994. Information on job losses for men and women in the Alberta Union of Provincial Employees came from an unpublished paper by Gurston Dacks and Joyce Green at the University of Alberta.

Chapter 13: The Alberta and Great Waterways Railway scandal is described in a number of historical sources. A particularly full treatment is found in L. G. Thomas, *The Liberal Party in Alberta* (University of Toronto Press, 1959). If you were reading carefully and your memory was good you may have noticed direct references to the final pages of F. Scott Fitzgerald, *The Great Gatsby* (Penguin Books, 1950, originally published 1926). See also Earle Birney, *Turvey* (McClelland and Stewart Limited 1963, original edition 1949). Tom Taylor's letter to the editor was published in the *Leduc Representative*, April 22, 1994. Elenor Smith and Harry Anderson kindly gave permission to quote from letters they wrote me early in 1994.